Harvard Business Review

Manager's Handbook

Harvard Business Review

Manager's Handbook

The 17 Skills Leaders Need To Stand Out

Harvard Business Review Press

Boston, Massachusetts

Copyright 2017 Harvard Business School Publishing Corporation
All rights reserved
Printed in the United States of America

10 9 8 7 6 5 4 3 2

The material in this book has been adapted and revised from works listed in the Sources section and from *Harvard Business Essentials Manager's Toolkit: The 13 Skills Managers Need to Succeed* (Boston: Harvard Business School Publishing, 2004), subject advisor Christopher Bartlett.

No part of this publication may be reproduced, stored in or introduced into a retrieval system, or transmitted, in any form, or by any means (electronic, mechanical, photocopying, recording, or otherwise), without the prior permission of the publisher. Requests for permission should be directed to permissions@hbsp.harvard.edu, or mailed to Permissions, Harvard Business School Publishing, 60 Harvard Way, Boston, Massachusetts 02163.

The web addresses referenced in this book were live and correct at the time of the book's publication but may be subject to change.

Library of Congress Cataloging-in-Publication Data
Names: Harvard Business Review Press.
Title: The Harvard Business Review manager's handbook : the 17 skills leaders need to stand out.
Description: Boston, Massachusetts : Harvard Business Review Press, [2017]
Identifiers: LCCN 2016030997| ISBN 9781633691247 (pbk. : alk. paper) | ISBN 9781633692114 (hardcover : alk. paper)
Subjects: LCSH: Management—Handbooks, manuals, etc.
Classification: LCC HD38.15 .H375 2017 | DDC 658.4/092—dc23 LC record available at https://lccn.loc.gov/2016030997

Hardcover ISBN: 9781633692114
Paperback ISBN: 9781633691247
eIBSN: 9781633691254

The paper used in this publication meets the requirements of the American National Standard for Permanence of Paper for Publications and Documents in Libraries and Archives Z39.48-1992

Contents

Introduction 1

PART ONE

Develop a Leader Mindset

1. The Transition to Leadership 7
Understanding your role as a manager 7
The difference between management and leadership ... 9
Demystifying leadership 10
Handling the emotional challenges of the transition ... 13

2. Building Trust and Credibility 23
Establishing your character 25
Demonstrating your competence 27
Cultivating authentic leadership 29
Ethics and integrity 32

3. Emotional Intelligence 37
What is emotional intelligence? 39
The power of self-awareness 39
Emotional steadiness and self-control 43
Managing an employee's emotions 45
Building social awareness on your team 48

4. **Positioning Yourself for Success**   **55**

Redefining success   55

Understanding your organization's strategy   57

Planning for strategic alignment   60

PART TWO

Managing Yourself

5. **Becoming a Person of Influence**   **67**

Positional versus personal power   68

Managing up   71

Partnering with your peers   74

Silo busting and effectiveness   76

Promoting your ideas to others   78

6. **Communicating Effectively**   **85**

Finding your voice as a leader   85

Mastering the written word   87

Persuasive presentations   92

Conducting effective meetings   96

7. **Personal Productivity**   **103**

Time management essentials   104

Finding focus   107

Stress management   111

Work-life balance   115

8. **Self-Development**   **121**

Career purpose   122

Look for opportunities within your organization   124

Feedback from your boss and your team   130

PART THREE

Managing Individuals

9. **Delegating with Confidence**   **139**
   Benefits of delegation   140
   Developing a delegation plan   141
   Sharing your delegation plan with your employee   145
   Provide support   149
   Avoid reverse delegation   151

10. **Giving Effective Feedback**   **155**
    Giving feedback in real time   156
    Giving difficult feedback   158
    Coaching and developing employees   162
    Performance reviews   167

11. **Developing Talent**   **175**
    Employee development as a priority   176
    Creating career strategies with your staff   177
    Developing high-potential talent   183
    Stretch assignments   185

PART FOUR

Managing Teams

12. **Leading Teams**   **193**
    Team culture and dynamics   194
    Managing cross-cultural teams   201
    Managing virtual teams   203
    Productive conflict resolution   208

13. **Fostering Creativity**   **217**
    Plan a creative session   217
    Tools for generating ideas   220

Making sure all perspectives are heard   224
Dealing with negativity   227

14. **Hiring—and Keeping—the Best**   **233**
Crafting a role   233
Recruiting world-class talent   237
Retaining employees   244
Motivation and engagement   248

PART FIVE

Managing the Business

15. **Strategy: A Primer**   **255**
Your role in strategy   256
What is strategy?   256
Developing your strategy   259
Leading change and transitions   263

16. **Mastering Financial Tools**   **275**
The basics of financial performance   276
Understanding financial statements   277
Budgeting   290

17. **Developing a Business Case**   **297**
Stakeholder perspectives   298
Clarifying the need and value   300
Cost/benefit analysis   302
Risk identification and mitigation   305
Writing your business case   307
Getting buy-in for your plan   308

Epilogue   **313**

Sources   *315*
Index   *329*

Introduction

You've likely become a manager because you were successful as an individual contributor. You did good work and got it done on time, and developed technical and professional skills that allowed you to excel. Now you've been asked to play a larger role.

As a manager, you'll measure success differently—through the achievements of your team rather than your individual accomplishments. This calls for a different skill set. When you become a manager, your technical expertise remains important but no longer defines your responsibilities. Your job is to get results through the creativity, expertise, and energy of others. For example, your sales skills may have gotten you promoted to the rank of district sales manager, but your success as a manager will depend on other capabilities: your ability to gain influence in your organization, to manage the emotional culture of your team, to hire and retain good people, to motivate and develop the potential of each member of your team, to think strategically, to make good decisions, to inspire and enable creativity and innovation, and so much more.

Whether you're new to management or a seasoned veteran, the *HBR Manager's Handbook* will help you learn the essential skills that all effective managers must master. This book is for you if you're ambitious and want to become more efficient, more effective, more inspiring. You're already a manager, but perhaps you want to be a leader, too—someone who brings out the best in your employees and drives change within your company. The *HBR Manager's Handbook* will show you how.

What you'll learn in the *HBR Manager's Handbook*

To become an effective manager and a strong leader, you need to solve practical problems every day. You need to vet processes, draft budgets, and delegate tasks. The work is also deeply personal. Whether you're coaching an employee or negotiating with your boss, the role calls upon your empathy, resilience, and a sense of purpose. To succeed, you must complement the development of your practical skills with inward reflection and an investment in your personal growth.

The *HBR Manager's Handbook* helps you on both of these fronts with handy tips, step-by-step instructions, and concise explanations of the ideas that matter most to both your day-to-day success and your ongoing development. Drawn from the expertise of *Harvard Business Review* authors, this book shares best practices and foundational concepts from classic articles as well as emerging ideas and research. You'll read stories from real managers and learn how to apply their insights to your own work with hands-on assessments and templates. Each chapter concludes with a summary of key points and action items that allow you to put the ideas in the chapter directly into practice, quickly.

The book is organized into five parts that begin by addressing your new role and the skills and mindset that you need to develop in order to be an effective leader. The book then moves through managing individuals and then managing your team as a whole. Finally, the last part covers the hard skills that help you manage the business. Each chapter addresses one of seventeen essential skills.

In part one, "Develop a Leader Mindset," you'll learn about the basic building blocks of good management and leadership. Chapter 1, "The Transition to Leadership," walks you through the shift in your day-to-day responsibilities as well as the bigger-picture changes that come with shifting from an individual contributor role to management. In chapter 2, "Building Trust and Credibility," you'll learn why trust is so vital to your success and how to establish credibility with your team from day one. These relationships will depend in no small part on your ability to recognize and manage your emotions and those of others, a skill addressed in chapter 3, "Emotional Intelligence." Chapter 4, "Positioning Yourself for Success," prepares you to engage with your company's strategic mission and understand how it affects your own performance. These four chapters are fundamental to your work as a manager, and your engagement with these ideas will continue throughout your leadership journey.

The next four sections of the book reflect four areas of your work life in which you need to excel to manage effectively. In part two, "Managing Yourself," you'll continue to work on skills essential to your own performance as a rising leader in an organization. In chapter 5, "Becoming a Person of Influence," you'll learn about the deliberate ways you can position yourself to gain trust and sway in the organization. Chapter 6, "Communicating Effectively," addresses how to keep your audience's attention and make your point effectively, whether in writing or in person. In chapter 7, "Personal Productivity," you'll learn how to make the most of your time and keep chaos (and stress) at bay. And in chapter 8, "Self-Development," you'll take a longer view of your own professional purpose and how to take charge of your path forward.

Part three, "Managing Individuals," moves on to one of your major responsibilities as a manager: to elicit the best performance from each of your direct reports. Chapter 9, "Delegating with Confidence," deals with delegating work and holding people accountable for their assignments. Giving feedback is a critical strategy for accountability, and chapter 10, "Giving Effective Feedback," describes best practices for performance reviews, coaching, and informal, real-time feedback. In chapter 11, "Developing Talent," you'll weave these interactions into a more formal strategy to help the individual grow.

Part four, "Managing Teams," moves beyond your one-on-one relationships with your employees and looks instead at how to organize and support the work they do together. In chapter 12, "Leading Teams," you'll learn how to foster a cohesive and productive group culture. Chapter 13, "Fostering Creativity," shows how to lead productive idea-generating sessions with your team and how to build a creative environment that helps those new ideas flourish. And chapter 14, "Hiring—and Keeping—the Best," explains how to build your team by hiring the right people and keeping them engaged with their work.

In the final section of this book, we turn to "Managing the Business." Here you'll dive into the hard skills you need to measure and boost your team's performance within the organization, starting with strategic planning, execution, and thinking in chapter 15, "Strategy: A Primer." Chapter 16, "Mastering Financial Tools," offers an overview of basic financial concepts, with a deep dive into the three key financial statements that can help you gauge your organization's overall health and help you make key decisions. In chapter 17, "Developing a Business Case," you'll pull together both hard *and* soft skills to effectively pitch a new idea within your company.

Finally, the "Sources" section lists the many sources from which the information in each chapter is drawn. If you want to learn more about a particular topic, start with these resources—books, articles, and videos, many of which are available on HBR.org.

PART ONE

Develop a Leader Mindset

1.

The Transition to Leadership

When you become a manager, it isn't just your title and responsibilities that change. Your idea of work and your identity evolve, too. As an individual contributor, you focused on your contribution to your team. As a leader, you have to navigate a complex new landscape of authority to help *others* do their best, too.

This journey is one of the most significant you'll experience in your professional life, an exciting opportunity that comes with challenges, too. Management represents a major departure from what you've done in the past, and what made you successful so far won't necessarily help you advance now. To stand out from the pack, you must understand the nature of your new role as a manager *and* a leader, and prepare yourself for the changes and stress that can accompany this period of intense growth.

Understanding your role as a manager

At its most basic level, your role as a manager is to set direction for your team and coordinate resources to meet your organization's goals. Your boss and your direct reports all have different expectations about what aspects of this work are most important. Your supervisor may emphasize planning and resource management, supporting corporate goals, managing risk, and accepting final accountability for your unit. Your employees likely have a different view: they look to you to organize and direct the group's strategic goals, support them as they accomplish tasks, solve problems, and answer questions decisively, and facilitate their long-term growth.

As for your own expectations, you've spent years watching other managers and being managed by them. Along the way, you probably picked up plenty of ideas about how to do this *right* (and certain ideas about what *wrong* looks like, too). But as an individual contributor, you only saw a small part of your boss's life. How she thought about her role and the way she interacted with peers, supervisors, and contacts outside the company weren't entirely visible to you. So as you navigate these experiences for yourself, you may need to overcome two common misperceptions.

People versus tasks

When you were an individual contributor, success meant completing specific assignments: making a sales call, for example, or designing a prototype. You may naturally assume that you'll continue to use these same skills as a new manager. But now your job is to help your direct reports do these activities on their own. You coach the salesperson who makes the call or secure resources for the designer who's working on the prototype. Your purpose has shifted from *doing tasks* to *developing and directing people*.

This shift may feel counterintuitive. You once had the best sales record on the team, and now you're watching a less experienced person struggle with your old accounts. Resist the urge to show the person how *you* used to do it; your own mastery isn't the point. Instead, you must help others thrive and develop their own competencies, redefining your own success to include that of the people on your team.

Personal influence versus positional authority

New managers also often expect that their title will make it easier for them to implement their ideas and are surprised to find that the opposite is true.

Managers have formal authority to make decisions, allocate resources, and direct employees—in theory. In actuality, though, people won't do something just because you tell them to, and they certainly won't do it well. Although you can use your positional authority to force compliance, your team members won't commit fully or deliver their best work under these conditions. You also won't benefit from the value of their perspective.

Assuming a position of power means you must become *more* responsive to the needs of your direct reports and the demands of your organization. You can't simply announce a new professional development plan to your team; you also need to persuade them to take it seriously. You can't just decide on a budget for your division; you also need to convince the executive team to allocate the funds.

By contrast, when you exercise influence, your people act because they find you personally persuasive—your character, your competence, your words or actions. You're not making them do something. They're choosing to do it because you are leading them effectively. That willingness makes all the difference. It means they're more likely to put forth their best effort, and that you're more likely to achieve higher levels of team performance.

To get to this point, you must meet your direct reports where they are and engage their preexisting motivations. Down the line, your actions will create a deep well of trust that will allow you to influence your employees' behaviors, attitudes, and values. This is where your real power lies: not in your job description but inside relationships, in the reciprocal interactions of ordinary office dynamics and politics. We'll talk about this more in chapter 2, "Building Trust and Credibility," and chapter 5, "Becoming a Person of Influence."

The difference between management and leadership

We've already used the terms "leader" and "manager," but what's the difference? This topic has been the subject of much debate since Harvard Business School (HBS) professor Abraham Zaleznik published a *Harvard Business Review* article in 1977 titled "Managers and Leaders: Are They

Different?" The piece caused an uproar in business schools. It argued that the theoreticians of scientific management, with their organizational diagrams and time-and-motion studies, were missing half the picture—the half filled with inspiration, vision, and messy human nature. This, Zaleznik argued, was truly what leadership was about.

As HBS professor John Kotter later argued, *management* is about responding to complexity. To get a job done, managers must focus on control and predictability, and they must organize processes that will produce orderly outcomes. Planning, budgeting, and staffing are all management activities. When you draw up task assignments, for example, or discuss optimizing a production line, you're wearing the manager hat.

Leadership, by contrast, explains Kotter, is about producing and responding to change. Leaders see opportunities in the instabilities that their managerial alter egos want to tame, and they emphasize ideas over process. Setting direction, aligning people, and providing motivation are all leadership activities. When you coach a star employee or decide to halt your production optimization process because it's just not working, that's leadership.

Kotter argues that management and leadership are complementary modes of being and need not be in conflict. The most successful managers in today's challenging business environment leverage both management and leadership competencies selectively to benefit the organization. In this book, we'll use the words somewhat interchangeably, preferring "manager" for technical and administrative topics and "leader" for issues that touch on vision, strategy, and motivation.

While your company determines when and how you transition to management, opportunities for leadership can present themselves at any time in your career. That's because leadership doesn't always require formal authority, but rather an array of intellectual and interpersonal skills.

Demystifying leadership

Although management and leadership are deeply intertwined in practice, we have long put the *idea* of leadership on a higher plane. We often view it as requiring a set of innate traits: intelligence, self-confidence, vision, eloquence, and a mystical blend of courage, charisma, and decisiveness. Those individuals with all of these traits were deemed "born leaders." But as science has revealed the plasticity of the human brain, we no longer think about these qualities as inborn or fixed. Instead we see leadership as a constellation of skills that can be learned and capacities that can be nurtured over time. In other words: just because you weren't senior class president doesn't mean you'll never be a leader.

This also means you'll integrate leadership abilities into your personality differently from your peers, depending on your underlying disposition. If you are more of an introvert, for example, you may be more eloquent in writing than in spontaneous conversation. But many of the markers we used to take as shorthand for "good leader" are irrelevant or incorrect. For example:

- Leaders don't just work in the C-suite. Leaders are everywhere, and at every level.

- No one "looks" like a leader. Your gender, race, age, height, and the like are utterly immaterial.

- Extroverts aren't more effective leaders than introverts.

- Leaders aren't always hyperconfident in their judgment. You can change your mind and experience uncertainty.

- Leaders are as likely to be listening as talking.

Right now you already have some of the characteristics of a strong leader. Instead of burdening yourself with the question "Am I a leader?" push yourself to identify these abilities and capitalize on them. Using the list in the box "Common leadership traits," assess which of your leadership traits are most valuable in your organization's culture. Then think about your own self-image as a leader and how you want others to see you. This will help you identify what strengths to leverage and where you have an opportunity to improve in your new role and over the course of your career.

Common leadership traits

INTELLECTUAL

- **Informed.** Are you knowledgeable and well informed about your industry, your business, and your priorities?

- **Future-focused.** Do you organize short-term tasks according to long-term priorities?

- **Decisive.** Do you make decisions even though all the facts are not available? Can you make difficult trade-offs?

- **Comfortable with ambiguity.** Can you operate in uncertain environments with few dependable guideposts? Do you adapt well to change?

SOCIO-EMOTIONAL

- **Self-aware.** Do you pay attention to how your behavior affects others?

- **Engaged.** Do you empathize with other people's needs, concerns, and goals?

- **Steady.** Do you maintain a positive, focused perspective and continue to lead during turmoil and confusion?

- **Trustworthy.** Are your actions consistent with your values? Do you keep promises?

ORGANIZATIONAL

- **Collaborative.** Do you work well and frequently with your boss, your peers, and your team members to deliver outstanding collective results?

- **Influential.** Do you listen closely, find common ground, and express yourself clearly to persuade and drive influence outcomes in the organization?

- **Politically astute.** Do you understand your organization's power structure? Do you grasp how key players think? Do you know where to turn for support and resources?

- **Stimulating.** Do you challenge the status quo? Do you convince others to set high standards and stretch goals?

Your title makes you a manager, but whether you become a leader as well is up to you. Leadership "is something you need to work at versus a state of being or a destination," former HBS professor Robert Steven Kaplan explains; developing these traits is an ongoing practice.

Handling the emotional challenges of the transition

As you begin your work as a manager, you'll experience a mix of emotions, including intense feelings of excitement, pride, anxiety, and loneliness. At times, it may feel like emotional whiplash. Let's look at two examples:

- A new branch manager described the feeling to HBS professor Linda Hill "Do you know how hard it is to be the boss when you are so out of control? It's the feeling you get when you have a child . . . [A]ll of a sudden you're a mother or a father and you're supposed to know everything there is to know about taking care of a kid." That kind of stark shift can be tough to handle.

- Management consultant Carol Walker describes a former client— "smart, thoughtful, forward thinking, resourceful"—who admitted he was completely overwhelmed after six months in a new managerial position. "He had started to doubt his own abilities," Walker writes. "He looked like a deer in the headlights."

This kind of performance anxiety can be particularly unsettling if you're coming off a string of successes as an individual contributor. Self-doubt crops up in new situations, and old coping mechanisms may no longer apply.

But these feelings are perfectly normal, and they will resolve naturally over time as your skills and confidence grow. In the meantime, handle the situation in the moment by identifying the emotion and its source, and in the longer term, by taking care of your health and work-life balance.

Step 1: Label your emotions

First, label what you're feeling. Just the act of naming the emotion—"I'm feeling anxiety right now"—can help you moderate your response. Here are some common examples:

- **Performance anxiety.** "I'm afraid I can't do this job."

- **Regret.** "Why did I even take this job to begin with?"

- **Frustration.** "I keep making mistakes" or "Things keep going wrong."

- **Humility.** "I'm not as ready for this job as I thought."

- **Loss.** "I miss the identity, camaraderie, and sense of competence I had in my old job."

- **Confusion.** "I'm not sure where I fit in here anymore."

Step 2: Find the source and a solution

Once you understand *what* you're feeling, consider *where* it's coming from. What are the causes of your stress? Your answer can help you identify new ways to cope with or mitigate the problem. There are four common sources of stress for new and developing managers: role strain, problem-solving fatigue, isolation, and imposter syndrome. Each has its own symptoms—and concrete solutions (see the box "Four sources of stress").

Take care of yourself

All of these coping mechanisms are strategies you can use to deal with emotional stresses as they arise. Ideally, though, you wouldn't have to wait for a crisis to act. What preventative measures can you take to keep yourself on an even keel during the transition? We'll talk more about work-life

Four sources of stress

ROLE STRAIN

You face conflict, ambiguity, and overload in your position.

Symptoms

- You have too much work and too little time, information, and re-sources, like the rookie manager in the example in the box "Voices: Struggling to find time for important work."

- You have conflicting responsibilities, like increasing revenues and reducing costs.

- You answer to too many people: direct reports, peers, supervisors, and customers pull you in multiple directions.

Solutions

- Create quiet, regular periods during your day for uninterrupted work. Pick tasks on which you can make good headway and protect this time from interruption.

- Acknowledge your deficiencies. You can't be an expert on every-thing, so find people you can depend on to do the things you can't.

- Embrace imperfection. You can't meet every demand that's made of you. Use your best judgment, negotiate priorities as needed, and be adaptive in the aftermath.

PROBLEM-SOLVING FATIGUE

You feel pressure to solve difficult problems for other people.

Symptoms

- You feel overwhelmed by the problems your direct reports bring to you.

- You're dismayed that employees aren't meeting the standards to which you held yourself as an individual contributor.

(continued)

- You manage problem employees who provoke your anger, fear, anxiety, and frustration.

Solutions

- Draw boundaries around what kinds of problems you'll take on.

- Coach direct reports on how to solve more problems on their own. For example, ask your employee to email you a summary of possible solutions to their problem and a recommendation for how to proceed.

- Resist the urge to classify everyone who comes to you with concerns as a problem employee. Develop a physical cue to ground yourself in difficult interactions.

ISOLATION

You mourn the loss of your old work life and are acclimating to a new social distance in the office.

Symptoms

- You don't have a clear group whose values and norms you identify with, like the lonely manager in "Voices: Looking for a confidant."

- You must make unpopular decisions, and people are reacting with mistrust and resentment.

- You no longer have casual social contact with your former peers now that they're your subordinates.

Solutions

- Seek support and companionship from other people in your organization, especially past coworkers who don't report to you. For example, set up lunch with a colleague, maybe another manager who was promoted at the same time as you.

- Develop new routines for making social contact with your team. Check in with a different person each morning as you settle in for the day, or host a regular midweek afternoon coffee break for the whole office.

IMPOSTER SYNDROME

You feel chronically inadequate and struggle to conceal the fact from others.

Symptoms

- You're afraid to make or acknowledge mistakes because you think that showing weakness will diminish your power.

- You worry that you aren't a good role model because everyone can see how stressed you are.

- You fear that your direct reports' failures reflect on you.

- You feel uncomfortable with the amount of power you have over other people's lives.

Solutions

- Show some vulnerability. Share openly what you know, but also where you need more information. Seek out assistance from those who can help. Provide assistance in return.

- Admit your mistakes. Honesty isn't a weakness: it makes you more approachable and credible.

- Focus on behaviors. Instead of fixating on anxious feelings, formulate specific actions that give you a sense of control over a stressful situation. For example, plan what you'll say next time you're feeling overwhelmed, so that no matter how flustered or annoyed you are, you can gracefully own your actions or exit a situation and recoup.

VOICES

Struggling to find time for important work

I recently worked with a young manager who had become so accustomed to responding to a steady flow of problems that he was reluctant to block off any time to work on the strategic initiatives we had identified. When I probed, he revealed that he felt a critical part of his role was to wait for crises to arise. "What if I schedule this time and something urgent comes up and I disappoint someone?" he asked. When I pointed out that he could always postpone his strategy sessions if a true emergency arose, he seemed relieved.

Source: Carol A. Walker, "Saving Your Rookie Managers from Themselves," *Harvard Business Review*, April 2002.

balance for the long term in chapter 7, "Personal Productivity," but it's particularly important to focus on prevention as you take on the stress of a new role:

- **Don't neglect your personal life.** Cutting yourself off from a support network triggers a nasty feedback loop of emotional stress and poor performance. Friends and family can listen to what you're going through and reconnect you with the parts of your life—and yourself—that make you feel good.

- **Protect your downtime.** Stress takes a mental and physical toll: your brain needs a break, and so does your body. Give yourself a day, or even a half day, off occasionally and spend the time doing whatever activities you find most rejuvenating.

- **Take care of your health.** Don't skip meals, and carve out time for an exercise regime. Most importantly, try to get enough sleep.

VOICES

Looking for a confidant

I used to be fascinated by the insights of an acquaintance who acted as sounding board/father confessor to some of the top names in British industry. As director of a corporate intelligence firm, he became privy to the fears and concerns of CEOs and senior directors, usually men over the age of 55. And although he was very discreet, he said that one thing united these powerful men, regardless of their industry or background: loneliness at the top.

I was always curious about how he managed to get these executives to open up about these feelings of loneliness. His answer was novel: more often than not, he said, the main photograph on their desk didn't show their wife or their children, but their pet dog: "The only one they could really tell everything."

Source: Gill Corkindale, "How Engaged a Leader Are You?," HBR.org, March 17, 2008.

Chronic sleep deprivation impairs your thinking and puts you at higher risk for a host of medical problems, from heart attacks to depression.

- **Keep your job in perspective.** When work feels as if it's spinning out of control, recenter yourself by asking, "What's most important to me? What really counts in life?" Nothing is worth your sanity, your physical health, or your family and friends. Compromising those parts of your life won't solve your problems; it will only make you more vulnerable to a major collapse.

All new managers struggle to cope with the feelings that accompany their new responsibilities, and the truth is that this struggle never really goes away. Even experienced managers wrestle with problems like role strain and imposter syndrome, especially when events at work or at home put them under extra stress. So it's important to learn to recognize these strains and be kind to yourself as you develop your own strategies for managing them.

The first six to twelve months of your new role will be a whirlwind of new experiences. As you grow rapidly as a manager and a leader, you'll find yourself doing things you'd never thought you'd do. Some will be mundane, like helping an employee find a better desk away from the air-conditioning vent; and some others will be exhilarating or terrifying in their enormity, such as pitching a new direction for R&D, supporting a coworker through a health crisis, or going all in with your team to keep your warehouse operating during a bad storm. You'll only get to make this transition, with all its highs and lows, once in your life, but the journey of leadership will last for your whole career.

Recap

- Your role as a manager is to set direction for your team and coordinate resources to meet your organization's goals. Your employees and your boss may have different expectations for what you should accomplish as a manager.

- The nature of your work changes when you go from an individual contributor to a manager, from *doing tasks* to *developing and directing people.*

- As you adapt to this new way of working, don't rely too heavily on your positional authority to compel action from your direct reports. Instead, focus on developing personal influence.

- Management and leadership are different, but complementary, practices. As you grow into this role, you'll strive to be both a manager and a leader in your organization.

■ Leadership is a learnable skill set, and there's no single template for it, though there are common skills you can learn. Developing your leadership abilities can be a lifelong journey, but you can exhibit leadership at any point in your career.

Action items

☐ Understand where you are on your leadership path by exploring the questions in "Common Leadership Traits."

☐ Reflect on the emotions you are experiencing in your managerial role. What might be their source? Use the list of potential solutions to identify ways to manage your response.

☐ Consider your routines for exercise, family mealtimes, and sleep. If you don't have healthy habits in place, begin experimenting with better ways to take care of yourself. If you do, reinforce your intention to keep doing them as you step into your new role.

2.

Building Trust and Credibility

One of your first tasks as a manager and leader is to gain the trust of your team. But your employees won't grant that trust automatically. As a manager, you have a profound effect on how they do their work and live their professional lives. As you take charge, they will have questions such as: Will you be able to represent their work well to people outside the unit? Is it safe to speak up when they disagree with you? How will you react when they tell you they've made a mistake? What values will you act on when faced with a difficult decision? Will you be an ally and an advocate?

Gaining trust can be a particularly delicate task when you have been promoted to manage your former peers. You need to establish authority and credibility without alienating those who used to have the same title as you—or who may even have been vying for the same job—and whose allegiance you now need. See the box "Tips: How to manage your former peers."

Harvard Business School professor Linda Hill and executive coach Kent Lineback define trust as a combination of two components: *character* and *competence*. Character is about how your intentions align with your actions,

TIPS

How to manage your former peers

If you've been promoted over your former coworkers, you have a fine line to walk. Here's how to get off on the right foot.

- **Make people aware of the transition.** Ideally the team will learn about your promotion from someone else—the outgoing boss or another supervisor. Make sure there's a plan in place for getting the word out, and if you end up making the announcement yourself, be modest with the wording.

- **Don't introduce any major changes right away.** No matter how good your plan is, hold off for a bit. Aggressive change will look like a rejection of your predecessor, and you don't know how their supporters will feel about that. Don't damage these relationships right off the bat.

- **Meet with your team members one-on-one.** Don't let people form assumptions about what your new relationship with them will be like; *show* them. Spend time with each person, individually and in small groups, sharing your vision and asking for feedback. "What can I do to support your success?" is a great lead-in.

- **Distance yourself.** If you continue to socialize with people the way you used to, you'll blur the lines that define your new role and open yourself to the accusation that you're playing favorites.

- **Make peace with your rivals.** If you competed for this job with peers, acknowledge to yourself that they've suffered a loss. Don't go overboard—it will look like you're gloating—but pull them aside to say that you value their contributions. If you can, take a specific action to back up your words, like assigning them an important task.

Source: Amy Gallo, "How to Manage Your Former Peers," HBR.org, December 2012.

while competence refers to the technical, operational, and political knowledge you bring to the job. Your employees quickly form opinions of your character and competence based on both what you say and what you do, and they'll continue to refine these opinions as they get to know you better.

Establishing your character

Your *character* is about your values: Are you out only for your own gain, or the company's profit? Do you also genuinely care about the group? If you don't, Hill and Lineback warn, your people will not trust your character, no matter how able and productive you are. Demonstrate your interest in the group and its work in the following ways:

Strive for consistency.

Being consistent means that your actions align with the values you profess. For example, if you emphasize rigor and accuracy to your team, you also vet your own information carefully and invite them to question your conclusions. Keep your promises and model ethical behavior from day one, even if it means making an unpopular decision, like reassigning a well-liked employee who has a conflict of interest. By behaving consistently, you teach people that they can interpret your actions in a straightforward way, without worrying about your intentions.

Regulate your emotions.

Your employees don't need to you to be a beam of sunshine in the office, but they do need to know that you won't have a meltdown or lash out when you're under a lot of stress. Avoid extreme emotional displays like giddiness and despair, and show compassion for others when you're in a tough situation. For more about how to cultivate this quality, see "Emotional steadiness and self control" in chapter 3, "Emotional Intelligence."

Mind your manners.

Show respect for people as individuals. Be respectful by about answering emails promptly and beginning and ending meetings on time. Say hello to people in the hallways, hold the elevator door, make eye contact when you're listening, and don't multitask during meetings. Pay attention to the message you're sending with more subtle body language, too. Research by Northeastern University professor David DeSteno shows that people are likely to perceive you as untrustworthy when you clasp your hands, touch your face, cross your arms, or lean away from a conversation.

Ask questions.

You can get a lot of mileage out of a question. It solicits information, but it also *communicates* information—about who you are, what you care about, and how you regard the person you're talking to. Good questions demonstrate your own knowledge and values, and by listening attentively, you show people that you're interested in who they are and what they can do. This tactic is especially useful when you're new to a team and you don't want to come off as arrogant or close-minded.

Invite feedback.

Show that you care about your impact on others by asking people for feedback and then doing something with it. The point here isn't just to become a better manager, but to demonstrate self-awareness. Everyone has blind spots, so show that you're willing to take responsibility for yours.

Give others a chance to shine.

Prove to your employees that you genuinely welcome their input by actually using their knowledge in early decision making and problem solving. Recognize individual contributions, not just within your office but to the rest of the company, too. Show that you want their efforts to benefit *them* directly, and that they can trust you to steward their good work without trying to take advantage of it. By soliciting—and crediting—help from your team, you send the message that you don't just see them as drones or instruments to your own triumph.

Note that these strategies don't have anything to do with being likable. If your sense of humor doesn't connect with that of one of your employees, that's OK. What matters is their perception of your integrity, that you mean well by them and by the company, and that you can deliver on your promises.

Demonstrating your competence

As your employees evaluate your character, they're also taking stock of your competence. On their minds are questions such as:

- Do you understand the work your unit performs? Do you know how this work gets done in your organization?

- Do you know how to get the resources and visibility your team members need to be successful?

- Are you an effective coach and developer of talent in the organization?

Your employees will find the answers to these questions in your everyday behavior as well. Here's how you can cultivate their faith in your competence:

Plan quick wins when you start a new role.

Ultimately, people are going to judge you by your results. So produce some good ones—fast. In his classic work on the "first ninety days" of any new management role, leadership transitions expert Michael Watkins recommends picking three or four simple, well-defined problems that matter to your team or your boss and solving them in a way that's consistent with company culture. Don't overreach: failing at five tasks looks worse than succeeding at four.

Confront tough issues and knock down roadblocks.

Your employees want to know whether you have the operational and political know-how to create favorable conditions for their work in the organization at large. Identify a few of the obstacles that are holding your team back: Can you get a famously difficult executive to sign off on a resource request? Can you persuade other business unit heads to untangle a project plan that's gone to seed? Succeed with these outsiders, and your team will know you can get things done.

Research your ideas.

To build a credible position, talk with people inside and outside your organization. Review articles and research reports. Then talk about it with your team—in meetings, in the elevator, over email. As a manager, you're open to the criticism that you don't know what's *really* going on or that you don't care about the experience of the front liners. Counter this suspicion by spending a morning shadowing your delivery crew, for example, or sitting in with your engineers as they work through a bug. Show that you want to see what they see and make your desire to both learn and share information visible.

Explain your decisions and actions.

Be explicit about the motivations and values that drive you and lay out your decision-making process. Don't worry about overjustifying your actions; instead, focus on communicating your expertise and sense of the larger organizational context. These conversations are especially helpful when you're new to a group and looking for opportunities to introduce yourself to everyone. But keep your explanations tightly focused on the issue at hand, so that you don't wander into an irrelevant discourse on every single one of your credentials.

Be honest about what you do and don't know.

It never pays to fake knowledge. If it turns out you're wrong, at best you'll just look silly, and at worst, you'll cause a serious problem for the rest of the group. Ask for clarification when you need it and listen more than you talk. Don't make a big show of your expertise, either. You'll look insecure and invite unhealthy competition from your subordinates. You demonstrate confidence by engaging others openly to expand your knowledge.

Arrange for backup.

Your team might not trust you yet, so whom *do* they trust? Find the people whose opinions matter in your field and show that they support you. Cite sources like an industry journal, get an endorsement from a guru inside your own company, or hire an independent specialist. Their credibility will augment your own and show that you're willing to commit real resources to success. Their presence will be especially powerful if their expertise is in something you acknowledge isn't your strength.

Ask others to test your idea's merit.

You probably know what it's like to work for someone who falls in love with their own ideas and won't entertain criticism, or who pushes their ideas too far, too fast. Show that you welcome new input and want to test your ideas thoroughly.

Making a deliberate effort to gain others' trust may feel awkward at first, or even manipulative. But remember, the goal isn't to convince people that you're somebody you're not; instead, you're trying to show them who you really are. And that's worth some time and thought, as you'll see.

Cultivating authentic leadership

"People trust you when you are genuine and authentic, not a replica of someone else," writes Bill George, former chairman and CEO of Medtronic and a professor at Harvard Business School. George and his coauthors popularized this concept as "authentic leadership," arguing that the most effective leaders make their work a deeply personal endeavor. They act from passion and according to their values, and they bring about change by building open, meaningful relationships with people in their organization, who grow to trust them deeply. That trust comes from recognizing a real person behind the mask of power, someone who wears their motives and values and goals in the open for all to see. This authenticity is an important component of showing strong character.

Authentic leaders develop their individual styles through trial and error. To explore and develop your own authentic leadership:

Learn from your life story.

Discovering your own origin story will supply purpose and inspiration in your future. Your values and goals come from somewhere. Connecting your present self with past experiences will deepen your understanding of why you see the world the way you do and why you care about the things that matter to you. Examine your history and learn to articulate your story and share it freely.

Understand your extrinsic and intrinsic motivations.

Extrinsic motivations are the external outcomes you seek: recognition, status, wealth, and so on. Intrinsic motivations are rewards internal to the self: personal growth, for example, or the satisfaction of helping others. All leaders will acknowledge that extrinsic factors play a big role in their thinking, but it's important to understand how your work interacts with your internal sense of meaning, too. Once you identify these motivations, you can look for opportunities to nurture them.

Foster self-awareness.

It can be painful to accept feedback from colleagues and be transparent about your own shortcomings in turn. You have to open yourself to the judgments of others—people you supervise, collaborate and compete with, and want to impress. If you don't know how other people see you, any negative information, however minor, is devastating. The more clearly you understand the impression you make on others, the better you'll be at processing criticism. (You'll learn more about the power of self-awareness in chapter 3, "Emotional Intelligence.")

Complete the prompts in the box "Developing yourself as an authentic leader" to begin thinking about how you can be more authentic in your management and leadership.

While authentic leadership is a worthy goal, a simplistic understanding of the concept can lead you astray. If we adhere too strongly to what we are already comfortable doing or being, we lose the opportunity to grow in new ways, according to INSEAD professor Herminia Ibarra.

As your professional life unfolds and you confront new experiences, Ibarra explains, you need to retain a flexible sense of self. Imagine you've

Developing yourself as an authentic leader

Authentic leadership pushes you to reflect on your identity and your purpose in life. Here are some questions to guide you through this exercise.

1. **Which people and experiences in your early life had the greatest impact on you?** What impact did they have?

2. **How do you cultivate self-awareness daily?** What are the moments when you say to yourself, *this is the real me*?

3. **What are your most deeply held values?** Where did they come from? Have your values changed significantly since your childhood? How do your values inform your actions?

4. **What motivates you, extrinsically and intrinsically?** How do you balance these motivations in your life?

5. **What kind of support network do you have?** How does your team ground you as a leader? How should you diversify your team to broaden your perspective?

6. **Is your life integrated?** Are you able to be the same person in all aspects of your life—personal, work, family, and community? If not, what's holding you back?

7. **What does being authentic mean in your life?** Are you more effective as a leader when you behave authentically? Have you ever paid a price for your authenticity, and was it worth it?

Source: Adapted from Bill George, Peter Sims, Andrew N. McLean, and Diana Mayer, "Discovering Your Authentic Leadership," *Harvard Business Review*, February 2007.

worked your way up in an organization that values the chain of command. What happens when you start a new job at an organization with a more collaborative, discursive decision-making culture? Do you stay true to your "authentic" self and keep deploying a command-and-control style of leadership? Or do you push yourself to try to succeed within the new firm's culture, even if it feels fake at first?

To become a leader, you must, to some extent, shape and create a *new* identity for yourself. Give yourself permission to experiment with novel ways of working and of managing, even if they feel uncomfortable. You're not pretending to be a different person: rather, your new experiences are genuinely transforming you. What originally feels uncomfortable may end up becoming a significant moment in your personal growth.

But while you must remain open to change, you don't necessarily need to open up to everyone else about it. Avoid being too candid about the insecurity you may feel as you face new management problems or try out new leadership styles. If you're too rigid about personal transparency ("Folks, I've never owned a P&L before and I have no idea what I'm doing!"), you'll undermine your own development. Allow yourself to project self-assurance even when you don't feel like a natural. Trying on that sense of confidence may be the first step toward making it real.

Ethics and integrity

Finally, as discussed earlier, demonstrating ethical behavior is also important to establishing your team's trust in your character. It's also an important part of your role as a manager. Business ethics is a set of norms about what right behavior looks like in the workplace and how you should navigate the many conflicts that may arise between the interests of stakeholders like customers, workers, management, investors, the general public, and so on. It extends into every part of your work, intersecting with your legal responsibilities (to comply with all laws and regulations) and your fiscal responsibilities (to create wealth for the company and profits for the shareholder, for example).

In the past, consideration of ethics was the province of a company's human resources department, general counsel's office, and senior management. That's no longer the case: it's now a primary duty of frontline managers. In many business schools, ethics is taught as one of the core responsibilities of all managers. It's an obligation you hold to your company and its shareholders, but also toward the people you manage. At the simplest level, your ethical position determines whether they feel safe in your organization—from harassment and assault by customers or colleagues, for example. And even minor ethical failures can do serious damage to office morale. If your people don't trust you to set the right tone, they can't contribute freely. Instead, they'll hold back their best work out of fear and self-protection.

What does it mean to be responsible for the ethics of your unit? First, you must *set an example* of moral values and standards of conduct:

- **Assume responsibility for the tough calls.** Don't ask someone else to take the fall when ethical obligations conflict or when they dictate an unpopular action. For example, if you need to let a popular employee go, take responsibility for the decision yourself.

- **Examine your own decisions for bias—publicly.** Model the questions you want others to ask. Laura Nash, who's considered business ethics from the perspective of both a consultant and an academic at Harvard Business School, suggests asking questions such as, "How would you define the problem if you stood on the other side of the fence? Whom could your decision or action injure? Are you confident that your position will be as valid over a long period of time as it seems now? Could you disclose without qualm your decision or action to your boss, your CEO, the board of directors, your family, society as a whole?"

- **Demonstrate genuine concern for *all* your company's constituencies.** Your economic duties to shareholders and investors don't erase the ethical responsibilities you have to customers, employees, suppliers, and the broader community. For example, if you supervise someone who brings in a lot of business but also sexually harasses the people they work with—even people outside your team—don't sweep their behavior under the rug.

Second, you must *ensure ethical behavior* among your team. That means scrutinizing individual decisions and actions, but also promoting an ethical culture at large. The two things are linked: in such a culture, people are proactive about testing their decisions against shared moral standards. They don't hide conflicts or ignore them until the conflict has become more material. Ethical thinking is a habit they take pride in.

The key to this culture is to encourage transparency around ethical issues. If you don't bring dilemmas out into the open, your employees develop distorted private beliefs about how everyone else is behaving. Maybe they think that no one else is struggling with these problems, and that ethical problems are actually ethical lapses that they should be ashamed of and conceal. Or maybe they think that *everyone* resolves ethical challenges in the same way: by breaking the rules when it's convenient.

You can counter this thinking by making it safe for people to tell you difficult truths. Your direct reports know things you don't. Tell them explicitly that you want to hear bad news and then reward those who come forward by listening without judgment and thanking them for speaking up. Then keep their information in confidence or acknowledge them publicly, as circumstances demand.

Your company likely has ethics guidelines that detail the code of behavior required of employees, and your company's general counsel can likely help with any potential legal implications. These codified standards are helpful, but what makes ethics so difficult is that not everyone has the same rules; our ethical compasses have been conditioned by our upbringing, our education, and the behavior we observe around us. You ultimately need to have your own compass for ethical issues. The fact that someone in your company tells you something is ethical doesn't make it so; even the fact that something is legal doesn't make it ethical. If your instincts tell you an ethical issue may be surfacing, consult with your boss or someone else in a leadership role as appropriate, to discuss your concerns and request guidance.

Trust is the single most powerful tool you have to get work done. It's not a game you play with your employees, saying and doing the things you think they'll like. Instead, the actions you take to earn their trust genuinely transform you into the leader they need. Being mindful of your character, your competency, and your ethical standards is essential to your ability to earn credibility as a leader.

Recap

- One of your first tasks as a manager and leader is to gain the trust of your team.

- You gain trust by consistently demonstrating character and competence.

- To demonstrate character, show that you value the team by giving team members a voice, recognizing them for their achievements, regulating your emotions toward them, and showing respect.

- To demonstrate competence, achieve quick wins but also underscore the credibility of your plans and ideas by citing your research and reasoning, and also by being frank about what you don't know.

- Authenticity helps make you trustworthy to the team that you lead. But beware of using authenticity as an excuse not to try new leadership approaches, even if they don't feel comfortable at first.

- Demonstrating ethical behavior is important to establishing your team's trust in your character, in addition to being a vital part of your role as a manager.

Action items

- ☐ As you come into a new managerial role, identify three to four simple, well-defined problems that you can tackle as quick wins.

❏ For your next team meeting, prepare a list of questions you can ask specific attendees. For example: "Dinesh, you've been the creative lead on this project for the past year. What have you and the rest of the team learned in that time that's changed the way you approach the design process?" Use this type of questioning to involve team members in decisions or acknowledge their contributions.

❏ When you make your next big decision, clearly communicate how you've come to your conclusion—what research you've done, what factors support your choice, and so on.

❏ Use the box "Developing yourself as an authentic leader" to reflect on your background and experiences to better understand your own unique style of leadership.

❏ Make ethics a regular consideration in your decision-making process on your own and with your team. Pose questions like, "What ethical issues are at play here?" or "Who benefits from option A? What conflicts of interest do we have to consider there?"

❏ Practice owning your biases publicly, and invite other team members to do the same: "Cards on the table, I have a friend at vendor B, and I really respect her. That may speak well of the company, but it might be coloring my judgment, too."

3.

Emotional Intelligence

Since the idea of emotional intelligence (measured as "emotional intelligence quotient" or EQ) was introduced in the 1990s, it's become essential to how we think about successful leaders. John Mayer, one of the psychologists who coined the term, defines it this way:

> [E]motional intelligence is the ability to accurately perceive your own and others' emotions; to understand the signals that emotions send about relationships; and to manage your own and others' emotions.

This skill may be "soft" compared to, say, delegating or budgeting, but that doesn't mean it's unimportant. Research by Daniel Goleman, the author and psychologist who introduced emotional intelligence to management thinking, has shown that it is a more powerful determinant of good leadership than technical competence, IQ, or vision. EQ is now a criterion in hiring and promotion processes, performance evaluations, and professional development courses.

CASE STUDY

How to build emotional intelligence

Juan was a marketing executive for the Latin American division of a major integrated energy company. He was charged with growing the company in his home country of Venezuela as well as in the entire region, a job that would require him to be a coach and a visionary and to have an encouraging, optimistic outlook.

Yet 360-degree feedback revealed that Juan was seen as intimidating and internally focused. Many of his direct reports saw him as a grouch—impossible to please at his worst, and emotionally draining at his best.

Identifying this gap allowed Juan to craft a plan with manageable steps toward improvement. He knew he needed to hone his powers of empathy if he wanted to develop a coaching style, so he committed to various activities that would let him practice that skill. For instance, Juan decided to get to know each of his subordinates better; if he understood more about who they were, he thought, he'd be more able to help them reach their goals. He made plans with each employee to meet outside work, where they might be more comfortable revealing their feelings.

Juan also looked for areas outside his job to forge his missing links—for example, coaching his daughter's soccer team and volunteering at a local crisis center. Both activities helped him to experiment with how well he understood others and to try out new behaviors.

Juan was trying to overcome ingrained behaviors; his approach to work had taken hold over time, without his realizing it. Bringing them into awareness was a crucial step toward changing them. As he paid more attention, the situations that arose—while listening to a colleague, coaching soccer, or talking on the phone to someone who was distraught—all became cues that stimulated him to break old habits and try new responses.

Source: Adapted from Daniel Goleman, Richard Boyatzis, and Annie McKee, "Primal Leadership: The Hidden Driver of Great Performance," *Harvard Business Review*, December 2001.

While it's easy to dismiss emotions as something that doesn't belong in the workplace, managers and leaders benefit greatly when they are aware of their own emotions and those of the people around them and are able to demonstrate emotions with intention instead of reacting in ways that aren't thoughtful or productive. Goleman and his collaborators describe one such transformation in the case study described in the box "Case study: How to build emotional intelligence."

In this chapter, you'll learn how to nurture your EQ, especially the components of awareness and self-regulation. And you'll discover how to help your employees manage their emotions both individually and as a team.

What is emotional intelligence?

Goleman describes emotional intelligence as a combination of five skills and traits that we start forming early in life and that ultimately form a core part of our personalities. By understanding each element described in the box "Emotional intelligence: five components," you can learn how to handle challenging or emotionally charged situations in the workplace with greater ease and better outcomes.

EQ isn't something you can measure objectively, but you can get a sense of your own perceptions of your strengths and weaknesses on each of these measures. (See the box "Questionnaire: Understand your perceptions of your own emotional intelligence" at the end of this chapter.) The more intentional you are in your understanding of and attentiveness to your EQ, the more emotionally steady you'll be in the workplace.

We'll look at a few of the components of emotional intelligence more closely in the rest of this chapter, focusing on two in particular: self-awareness and self-regulation.

The power of self-awareness

Self-awareness means being observant and honest about your actions, feelings, and behaviors and how they affect those around you. To achieve this kind of self-knowledge, you don't need to be overly critical, but you do need

Emotional intelligence: five components

SELF-AWARENESS

Definition

The ability to recognize and understand your own moods, emotions, and drives, as well as their effect on others.

Hallmarks

- Self-confidence
- Realistic self-assessment
- Self-deprecating sense of humor

SELF-REGULATION

Definition

The ability to control or redirect your disruptive impulses and moods. The propensity to suspend judgment—to think before acting.

Hallmarks

- Trustworthiness and integrity
- Comfort with ambiguity
- Openness to change

MOTIVATION

Definition

A passion for work for reasons that go beyond money or status. A tendency to pursue goals with energy and persistence.

Hallmarks

- Strong drive to achieve
- Optimism, even in the face of failure
- Organizational commitment

EMPATHY

Definition

The ability to understand the emotional makeup of other people. Skill in treating people according to their emotional reactions.

Hallmarks

- Expertise in building and retaining talent
- Cross-cultural sensitivity
- Service to clients and customers

SOCIAL SKILL

Definition

Proficiency in managing relationships and building networks. An ability to find common ground and build rapport.

Hallmarks

- Effectiveness in leading change
- Persuasiveness
- Expertise in building and leading teams

Source: Daniel Goleman, "What Makes a Leader," *Harvard Business Review*, January 2004.

to be realistic. Cultivating self-awareness is hard, because we often mask what's toughest for us to handle with emotions that feel safer.

To develop awareness around your behavior, identify patterns in the way you act on your feelings. When you feel angry, do you lash out or do you withdraw? When a task intimidates you, do you hang back or take over? Audit yourself briefly at the end of each day, for example, during your commute: What positive and negative emotions did you have today? When during the day did you feel effective, and what behaviors felt off? What do you think was driving your emotions and actions today?

You can ask yourself these questions on the spot, too—for example, after you lose your cool with an employee or when you ace an important task. Don't just focus on your problems; your successes have just as much to teach you.

Feedback from coaches, trusted colleagues, and even from your employees can help you gain perspective on what's going on, according to Goleman. How do they experience your moods and behaviors? A close friend or family member may be able to help you here as well, so consider reaching out: "I've been feeling really energized at work lately, and I'm not sure where the boost is coming from. Can you help me figure it out?"

Ideally, the reactions you observe in yourself will be *adaptive*, meaning that they will resolve the fundamental emotional problem you're facing. For example, you recognize that you're routinely impatient with one of your team members, so you adapt your approach to working with him to eliminate the frustration. But we all engage in some actions that are *maladaptive* and only make the situation worse. Classic maladaptive responses include:

- Procrastination

- Denial

- Brooding

- Jealousy

- Self-sabotage

- Aggressiveness

- Defensiveness

- Passive aggressiveness

The concept of pattern is important here. Everyone procrastinates sometimes. But as individuals, we tend to gravitate toward particular behaviors or thought progressions, our "go-to" reactions. If you regularly shut down during conflict, denial might be an important emotional pattern for you. Or if conflict usually causes you to cycle through the same thoughts over and over ("She's *wrong*. I can't believe she doesn't see it! She made *one* good point, but mostly she's just *wrong*"), you're probably prone to brooding.

These emotional habits affect everything from our performance on a project to the impressions we make on our peers. But the patterns you've observed aren't written in stone; they're plastic. Once you become aware of any negative effect you have on others, you can adapt and mitigate the impact.

Emotional steadiness and self-control

If you're self-aware, you know when you're angry. The next step is to use that self-knowledge to manage your emotions. This ability, which Goleman calls *self-regulation*, matters for three reasons.

First, your team reacts to your mood. A leader's mood is communicable; your emotions color the experiences of everyone working around you. Goleman and his colleagues term this mechanism *mood contagion*. If you're pessimistic and depressed, your team will be, too, even if it's not their natural disposition. If you wear your stress on your sleeve for all to see, your team members will feel more stress as well. That's because moods are transmitted at the physiological level through an open-loop system that involves hormone levels, cardiovascular functions, sleep rhythms, and immune functions. Our bodies respond involuntarily to these signals, and these distinct physical changes eventually combine in an all-encompassing emotional experience—good or bad.

Second, emotional steadiness allows you to question or slow down your decision making in high-stakes situations, so that you don't make emotionally charged or ill-conceived choices. In today's business environment, the ability to keep a level head through rapid upheavals or long periods of uncertainty will serve you well.

Finally, your self-control underwrites your integrity. You need to be able to moderate your impulses so you can say no to ethical temptations that might harm your career or your organization. Impulsive actions don't need to be illegal to compromise your leadership; if you throw a contract to a friend, sleep with an employee, or even go back on your word to your team, you risk losing your employees' respect and confidence. Stress in particular can bring out the worst in all of us in the workplace. Self-control in highly stressed situations is invaluable.

Managing your hot buttons

No matter how diligently you work to manage your emotions, you probably still have hot buttons—behaviors you're particularly sensitive to in other people or things you're personally touchy about. Maybe you loathe being interrupted, especially by a certain self-important colleague. Or perhaps you feel embarrassed about your public-speaking skills and poorly handle challenges to your ideas when you're giving presentations.

When you find yourself confronted by a hot button, you often can't contain the negative feelings it sparks. Perhaps you snap at the colleague who interrupted you, lose your ability to articulate your thoughts, or start to tear up in the middle of your presentation.

Business strategist and executive coach Lisa Lai suggests a three-part strategy for keeping calm in testy situations:

- **Acknowledge what's happening.** Put your self-awareness into action. Hot buttons always have a history. Maybe you react so poorly to being interrupted now because it was a major problem at your last job or in a personal relationship. Don't let those associations control you: recognize the history that's being triggered, but make a conscious decision not to project that past onto this situation. You don't know how this moment is going to unfold.

- **Abstract yourself from the story.** What's happening feels personal; that's why it has the power to rile you. But what if it weren't? What if being interrupted wasn't a referendum on your worth or status, or about *you* at all? You don't know why your counterpart is behaving this way, and you don't have to play out their drama. So imagine you are watching this situation happen to someone else: what would be the best thing for them to do?

- **Develop a physical cue.** Heightened emotions take you deep inside your own head, but you can use your body to help redirect your thoughts. When you feel things escalating, make a subtle gesture or movement to anchor your focus firmly in the present moment. Lai herself presses her palms on the underside of a table or against each other; you can take a few deep breaths, hold a pen or other object firmly in your hand, or pick a place to fix your gaze for a few seconds while you gather yourself.

The good news is that you can recover even if you do snap at one of these triggers. If you do something you regret, acknowledge what happened. If you yelled at or humiliated someone in your outburst, start by apologizing. Then take a leap and explain what really happened for you: "I was angry and I'm not proud of how I acted. I've tried to understand what made me lash out like that, and I think I felt disrespected when you interrupted me." It's hard to wade back into the emotions that provoked your behavior in the first place. But research shows that people respond with heightened compassion and forgiveness when you appropriately disclose your emotions.

Managing an employee's emotions

Just as good managers regulate their own emotions, they also monitor and react to the emotional states of the individuals on their teams. While you can't control how they feel or even how they choose to act, you *can* steer them in a more productive path. For example, if Pedro is pouting in a meeting about a new initiative, his disaffection may derail your team's support. But by working with Pedro to address his emotions and help him express them in a more positive way, you can defuse the tension in the meeting and better understand his point of view, perhaps learning something important in the process.

To do this, you must acknowledge an employee's emotional state, communicate that you value them as a person, and explain that you aren't willing to ignore inappropriate behavior. Then you can help them understand and solve the underlying problem. Here's how:

Step 1: Spot the emotion

Don't wait for the dam to break: watch for telltale signs, like a gap between what someone's saying and their body language—for example, if someone says they're on board with a decision but they avoid eye contact or get red in the face.

> *You seem unhappy with this choice. Help me understand what you're thinking right now.*

Step 2: Practice active listening

Engage your employee to search for the issues that are motivating their emotional response. What can you infer about the facts this person is working with, about the values driving their reactions? What word choices and body language seem extreme, what phrases or ideas do they keep returning to? Follow up by paraphrasing what you've heard and asking open-ended questions about it.

> *I can see this decision process has been frustrating for you. Help me understand. What's behind your frustration?*

Step 3: Reframe your employee's emotions

Use the information you've gathered to develop a hypothesis about what's going on, and then test it. If your employee is resisting a new training process, for example, do they not see its value, or do they believe it won't be well implemented? Make an informed guess and ask for their response. If you're right, your employee will feel heard; if you're wrong, their reaction will still teach you something useful.

I'm hearing that you think this process will be inefficient, and you don't want to waste your time. Is that right? What am I missing?

Once you've successfully completed this reframing, you can proceed with normal conflict-resolution techniques (see chapter 12, "Leading Teams").

This process may make your employee feel vulnerable, especially if it takes place in a group setting. The rest of the team may feel vulnerable, too, if they identify with their colleague's distress or if their colleague is attacking them. To get to a productive resolution, assure everyone that you're conducting this conversation in good faith.

Step 4: Defend the team norms—gently

Call out unacceptable actions, especially if other people are involved. The rest of your group needs to know that you take the rules you've all agreed on seriously, and that you have their back. But do so gently, with empathy for how the person is feeling; take into account how calling the employee out will affect him emotionally.

I know you're frustrated, but sarcasm isn't helpful in a discussion like this. Can you restate your point?

Step 5: Offer an apology or sympathy if it's appropriate

Sometimes what's going on with an employee is . . . you. Perhaps you did something inappropriate; maybe you unconsciously hit one of his hot buttons, or you might just be intimidating. When you acknowledge your own influence on the employee's emotional landscape, you signal that you're on his side and you want to help him resolve whatever's at the heart of his problem.

I'm sorry I was dismissive when you first raised these concerns.
I'm sorry that you're going through that in your personal life.
I definitely don't want this issue to add to your stress right now.

These strategies will help your employees maintain their equilibrium in the moment and develop their emotional intelligence over time. You're helping them become stronger contributors to the group—and to your organization.

Building social awareness on your team

Raising your individual employees' EQ will improve group dynamics, but you can also develop the emotional culture of your team as a whole by establishing a set of common expectations for how you'll interact every day, guidelines around how you'll all handle stress and overcome challenges, and rules about how decisions are made, according to Vanessa Urch Druskat and Steven B. Wolff, who, as researchers at Case Western Reserve University and Marist College, developed the theory of group emotional intelligence. These norms will help manage the group's mood, especially under pressure. A positive mood will, in turn, influence the motivation and productivity of each member of the team.

A handful of small, targeted interventions can have a big effect. Here are some suggestions:

Set ground rules—and stick to them

- Call group members on errant behavior.

- Assume that undesirable behavior takes place for a reason. Find out what that reason is. Ask questions and listen, and avoid negative attributions.

Take time away from tasks

- Gather for periodic outings outside the office to get to know one another.

- Have check-ins at the beginning of your regular meetings to ask how everyone is doing.

- Acknowledge and discuss group moods. Make time to discuss difficult issues and address the emotions that surround them.

- Express acceptance of team members' emotions.

- Support members by being flexible and offering emotional support or material help if they need it.

When things get tough

- Reinforce that the team can meet a challenge. Be optimistic. For example, say things like, "We can get through this" or "Nothing will stop us."

- Create fun ways to acknowledge and relieve stress and tension.

- Remind members of the group's important and positive mission.

- Remind the group how it solved a similar problem before.

- Focus on what you can control; focus on problem solving, not blaming.

When making decisions

- Ask whether everyone agrees with a decision.

- Ask quiet members what they think.

- Respect individuality and differences in perspectives.

- Validate members' contributions. Let others know they are valued.

- Protect members from attack. Never be derogatory or demeaning.

When you implement new rules, involve your team. Remember that you're not alone as a manager in trying to create a culture of self-awareness. Your team members are critical to the process. Consult the team as you create your ground rules, and make explicit compacts around language you will use to address conflict or break tension.

Creating cultural change isn't easy, especially around emotions. But remember, you don't have to change the way people feel and think all at once. If you can tweak the way they *behave* even a little bit, the emotional stuff will follow on its own.

———————

Developing your emotional intelligence is work that will continue throughout your leadership journey. It's a foundational skill that underpins the leader's mindset: how you manage your own motivation and build relationships that support your goals; how you help your employees get better at their jobs; how you help many diverse personalities work together toward a common goal; and how you make the right business decisions under stressful, changing conditions.

Recap

- Emotional intelligence is a more powerful determinant of strong leadership than technical competence, IQ, or vision.

- Emotional intelligence as Daniel Goleman originally defined it is a combination of self-awareness, self-regulation, motivation, empathy, and social skills.

- While you can't gauge your own emotional intelligence objectively, you can begin to get a sense for your perceived strengths and weaknesses through self-reflection and by getting feedback from trusted friends and family members.

- Your mood as a manager is literally contagious. Our bodies communicate stress, hope, and the like with others at a physiological level.

- Keep your cool in hot-button situations by acknowledging your triggers and then using thought exercises or physical cues to pull yourself out of the emotional whirlwind.

■ Spot strong emotional reactions on your team before they bubble over. Help your employees articulate their reactions in productive ways by practicing active listening and reframing what you hear in language that will help all of you move on to normal conflict-resolution techniques.

■ Promote positive emotions by defending team norms, offering an apology or sympathy when it's appropriate, and helping your employees save face after embarrassing outbursts.

Action items

☐ Chart your emotional patterns by making notes in your calendar during each day or after a particular emotional episode. Then look for correlations. How do your moods affect your productivity and your interactions with colleagues? Do certain activities tend to fan emotional states like irritation or enthusiasm? Consider whether your reactions are adaptive or maladaptive.

☐ Check in with a colleague or friend and ask for feedback on your moods and behaviors.

☐ Think back to a recent conflict on the team. What were the turning points as things went south? Where were the key gaps in understanding? If the problem has been resolved, what actions made it better? Are there one or two explicit team rules that could have prevented the whole situation? Get input from key players or witnesses.

☐ Experiment with one or two new rules to solve a recurring problem with office dynamics—for example, your team's tendency to become pessimistic or fractious when they're under pressure. Explain why you're implementing this rule and set a fixed period of time for the test. During this time, press your employees to uphold the new rule; write it on the wall during meetings, include it at the bottom of emails, and uphold it carefully with your own actions. Then check back in with the group: Do they think it worked? How did it affect the group's dynamic?

QUESTIONNAIRE

Understand your perceptions of your own emotional intelligence

Great leaders move us—they inspire, motivate, and energize us. How? They do it through emotional intelligence. Dan Goleman woke us all up when he published his groundbreaking book on the topic (in 1995). Since then we've learned a lot about EI competencies, such as self-awareness and empathy, and about what people can do to develop them.

To gain a deeper understanding of your own emotional intelligence, respond to the statements in this questionnaire as honestly as possible, checking one of the columns from "Always" to "Never."

To calculate your score, as you finish each section count the checkmarks in each column and record the number in the "Total per column" line. Multiply your total score for each column by the number in the row below it, and record it in the row below that. Add this row together to get your total score for how you perceive yourself along each of the dimensions of EI.

Reflecting on your strengths and where you can improve is important, but don't stop there. Other people's perspectives matter too. After reviewing your scores, ask one or two trusted friends to evaluate you using the same statements, to learn whether your own insights match what others see in you.

Source: Annie McKee, "Quiz Yourself: Do You Lead with Emotional Intelligence?" HBR.org Assessment, June 5, 2015. Questions adapted from the Hay Group's "Emotional and Social Competency Inventory" and Richard Boyatzis's article "Competencies in the 21st Century" (*Journal of Management Development*, 27:1 [2008], 5–12).

EMOTIONAL SELF-AWARENESS

		ALWAYS	MOST OF THE TIME	FREQUENTLY	SOMETIMES	RARELY	NEVER
1	I can describe my emotions in the moment I experience them.						
2	I can describe my feelings in detail, beyond just "happy," "sad," "angry," and so on.						
3	I understand the reasons for my feelings.						
4	I understand how stress affects my mood and behavior.						
5	I understand my leadership strengths and weaknesses.						
	Total per column						
	Points per answer	x 5	x 4	x 3	x 2	x 1	x 0
	Multiply the two rows above						
	TOTAL SELF-AWARENESS SCORE *(sum of the row above)*						

POSITIVE OUTLOOK

		ALWAYS	MOST OF THE TIME	FREQUENTLY	SOMETIMES	RARELY	NEVER
6	I'm optimistic in the face of challenging circumstances.						
7	I focus on opportunities rather than obstacles.						
8	I see people as good and well-intentioned.						
9	I look forward to the future.						
10	I feel hopeful.						
	Total per column						
	Points per answer	x 5	x 4	x 3	x 2	x 1	x 0
	Multiply the two rows above						
	TOTAL POSITIVE OUTLOOK SCORE *(sum of the row above)*						

EMOTIONAL SELF-CONTROL

		ALWAYS	MOST OF THE TIME	FREQUENTLY	SOMETIMES	RARELY	NEVER
11	I manage stress well.						
12	I'm calm in the face of pressure or emotional turmoil.						
13	I control my impulses.						
14	I use strong emotions, such as anger, fear, and joy, appropriately and for the good of others.						
15	I'm patient.						
	Total per column						
	Points per answer	x 5	x 4	x 3	x 2	x 1	x 0
	Multiply the two rows above						
	TOTAL EMOTIONAL SELF-CONTROL SCORE *(sum of the row above)*						

HOW WOULD YOU DESCRIBE YOURSELF?

	ALWAYS	MOST OF THE TIME	FREQUENTLY	SOMETIMES	RARELY	NEVER
ADAPTABILITY						
16 I'm flexible when situations change unexpectedly.						
17 I'm adept at managing multiple, conflicting demands.						
18 I can easily adjust goals when circumstances change.						
19 I can shift my priorities quickly.						
20 I adapt easily when a situation is uncertain or ever-changing.						
Total per column						
Points per answer	x 5	x 4	x 3	x 2	x 1	x 0
Multiply the two rows above						
TOTAL ADAPTABILITY SCORE (sum of the row above)						
EMPATHY						
21 I strive to understand people's underlying feelings.						
22 My curiosity about others drives me to listen attentively to them.						
23 I try to understand why people behave the way they do.						
24 I readily understand others' viewpoints even when they are different from my own.						
25 I understand how other people's experiences affect their feelings, thoughts, and behavior.						
Total per column						
Points per answer	x 5	x 4	x 3	x 2	x 1	x 0
Multiply the two rows above						
TOTAL EMPATHY SCORE (sum of the row above)						

4.

Positioning Yourself for Success

In the previous two chapters, we've looked at the emotional and interpersonal skills you'll have to draw on to genuinely motivate your employees. But leadership is about more than having followers; you need somewhere to *go*. What does success look like for you—and for your team? How will you define that ultimate objective? As a manager, you need to think critically about your relationship to your organization's overall strategy and the opportunities you and your team stand to take advantage of.

In this chapter, we'll talk about shifting your mindset to think differently about success in your new role. You'll also learn about how to connect your own objectives and your team's goals with the organization's strategy, and how to identify and mitigate the risks that may stand in your way.

Redefining success

As you transition from individual contributor to manager, you'll view problems and measure success in new ways. Your personal performance is no longer the be-all and end-all: your primary responsibility now is getting things done through others. From this perspective, success is built on:

- Clearly defining expectations for your team members

- Meeting your team's targets and objectives

- Furthering the company's objectives through your group's achievements

- Honing your direct reports' skills and managing their tasks effectively

In other words, you succeed only when your group succeeds. Over time, you'll learn to find your team's accomplishments as satisfying as your own used to be. But it may take some time to achieve this sense of satisfaction, because you're further removed from the actual work than you were. As a result, your relationship to the outcome may feel distant, ambiguous, or even unrecognized. Coaching an employee may take months or even years to truly pay off. No one outside your team may ever see your amazing technique for running meetings. And when it comes to your unit's accomplishments, you'll rarely get the same instant gratification you got in the past with a successful outcome that was clearly your doing.

How can you still feel gratification under these changed conditions? Many managers learn to enjoy:

- Seeing and helping other people succeed and thrive in the workplace

- Discovering that they can be effective coaches who bring out the best in others

- Seeing themselves adapt to their new identity and master new responsibilities

- Developing compelling strategies and plans to achieve business targets

- Celebrating the success of your team when they meet their commitments

Understanding your organization's strategy

As part of managing your team, you need to understand how you fit into the bigger picture. Your organization has an overarching plan for developing its competitive advantage, likely served by a series of cascading goals for business units and individuals. In chapter 15, "Strategy: A Primer," you'll learn more about how such strategies are created, but for now it's only important to consider the expectations for your performance. As a manager, you work through your employees to support the company's overall plan; your own strategies and goals must align with the priorities set from above. So as you make your own plans, clarify *what* you're supposed to be delivering and *how* you're supposed to do it.

Step 1: Gather information about your strategic objectives

In addition to reviewing any strategy documentation that your team, division, or organization may have, begin with a "listening tour"—a series of conversations with key figures in your organization that will help you clarify its strategic objectives. It's obviously important to interview your boss, but you also want to understand the perspectives of other leaders in your group or organization.

But don't just look up for answers. Consider coworkers below or lateral to you. You also want to hear from people with insight who may not have positional power to act on their ideas, but they will have a good read on what's really going on. Who's been at the company for a long time? Who's worked closely with the current leadership? Who recently transferred from a company that went through a similar change process? For example, a peer in R&D might have niche knowledge about how technology in your field is likely to evolve, while someone in market research may have the most up-to-date information about how your customer base is evolving. Use the sample language in the box "Defining strategic objectives" as a template for these conversations.

As you conduct these conversations, press for clarity and specificity. "I hear you saying that innovation is a priority for my team. Where would you like to see us focus?" If open-ended questions aren't getting you answers,

Defining strategic objectives

YOUR ORGANIZATION

- "What are the company's major strategic objectives right now?"

- "What are the major needs/challenges/opportunities we're facing over the next six months? Year? In the long term?"

- "I'm hearing that ___ is our primary priority right now, and that long term we're preparing for ____. Am I reading the landscape right? What am I missing?"

YOUR TEAM

- "How do you see my team fitting into this picture?"

- "What are your top priorities for my group? What are the big needs/challenges/opportunities you'd like to see us tackle in the next six months? Year? In the long term?"

- "I'd like to see my team do _____ and _____. What are your thoughts?"

YOU

- "What role would you like to see me play in carrying out this strategy?"

- "What are the major needs/challenges/opportunities you'd like to see me take on in the next six months? Year? In the long term?"

- "I think I'd be most useful doing ___ and ___. What are your thoughts?"

- (With your boss or key peers) "What are *your* major objectives right now within the organization? How can I support them?"

offer limited choices: "I think there's a lot of opportunity to innovate with the way we conduct client relations and with our inventory technology. Where would you like us to focus?"

Reflecting on your conversations, note the gaps and contradictions in what you're hearing. Do different people emphasize different strategic goals? Is your supervisor tasking you with projects that don't match the priorities she's defined? If you can, press to figure out where these inconsistencies are coming from: "How do you see this special assignment supporting the overall direction you've sketched for my department?"

Step 2: Analyze risk in your strategic objectives

Once you've identified the goals and opportunities in front of you, also review all the information you've gathered and ask where the biggest risks are:

- What are the major sources of uncertainty in your team's future?

- What *external* risks can you identify? Think about categories like funding; competition and conflict with other units in the company; the status of your patrons or protectors within the company; and potential reorganization.

- What *internal* risks can you identify? Think about upcoming personnel changes, team dynamics, and office politics.

Filter everything you're learning through a more personal question, as well: What will it take for *you* to be successful in your role? This isn't vanity on your part. Now that you're a leader, your bosses expect you to be a strategic thinker, and that means learning to evaluate the risks and opportunities that you personally must navigate. Ask yourself these questions:

- What are the major sources of uncertainty in your own future?

- What *professional* risks to your success can you identify? Think about categories like your professional goals; your experience, training, and accreditation; your network, especially within your company; and work logistics (for example, a difficult commute).

- What *personal* risks to your success can you identify? Think about your health, your family, your finances, and your personality and disposition.

Once you understand the major risks to your success, analyze them from a few different angles. First, which of these risks are most likely to have an impact on your success in a very direct way? What do you absolutely need to plan for? For example, if you know that your workload makes it hard to meet important deadlines—say, submitting legal filings to a court—you must find a strategy for dealing with this problem.

Second, which risks are impossible or impractical to counter? What *can't* you plan for? For example, you may not know if your company or division may be sold in the coming year, but if you haven't seen any indications of it, it may not be worth planning for. You can compensate for this risk by solving a related problem—say, planning for delays or creating new ways to strengthen your personal relationships with that team.

Third, which are easy to plan for? Are there high-value actions that would be easy for you to take? For example, if your inexperience with a particular coding language compromises your ability to lead a new product rollout, find out if your company will pay for you to take a course in the language or bring an expert in from outside the company.

Finally, who else in your organization do these risks touch? Who can be a strategic ally? For example, if your team needs expanded IT support to meet its performance targets, look for another unit in the company who's also underserved to help you press for more resources.

Planning for strategic alignment

After all your research and reflection, it's time to make a plan for what you will do to be successful in this landscape. The goals you set should emerge from what you've learned about the overall strategy of your company and your own position. The real power comes from aligning your goals with the highest purpose of the organization; ideally, every person you supervise will understand their individual goal, the goal of the unit, and how the unit's activities contribute to the organization's strategic objective. Draw on these questions to frame your goals:

- What metrics do you or your team need to meet to help the company succeed?

- What do you or your team need to provide to customers or customer-facing groups in your organization to achieve the company's vision?

- Which functional groups do you or your team work most closely with and how can you ensure alignment around shared priorities?

- What processes do you or your team need to excel at for the company to satisfy your customers and shareholders?

- What will you or your team need to learn and how will you or your team need to improve for the company to meet its goals?

As you start to make concrete plans, remember that you're tethered by your budget, staff, and schedule boundaries. If those parameters aren't clear to you now, start figuring them out. Which are absolutely immovable? Which are elastic? The better you understand your constraints, the more creative you can be within them.

Your answers to these questions constitute a list of action items. You've just defined the metrics you need to meet, the services you need to provide, the processes you need to excel at, and the improvements you need to make to be successful.

Becoming comfortable with your new managerial identity involves some profound shifts in your beliefs, attitudes, and possibly even your values. As you begin to shift to a leader's mindset, you may discover—like many new managers—that aspects of the job you worried about or dreaded are actually fulfilling in ways you never expected. Whether you're earning the trust of a former peer or deftly handling an employee's emotional outburst, you'll develop competencies that are rewarding in and of themselves, in addition to making you stronger as a manager.

Recap

- As you transition from individual contributor to manager, you'll view problems and measure success in new ways.

- You also need to understand how you and your team fit into the bigger picture of your organization and its objectives.

- By analyzing the risks that may threaten your achievement of these objectives, you can better position yourself for success.

- Define concrete plans about how you will achieve your objectives by considering the metrics you'll use, the groups you'll work with, and the processes and capabilities your team needs.

Action items

- ❑ Using the questions from the "Defining strategic objectives" box, gather information by talking to your boss, colleagues, and other people whose influence or experience makes their perspective useful.

- ❑ Analyze the risks associated with your strategic objectives and consider how you might deal with each issue.

- ❑ Identify allies in your organization who are also affected and could help you going forward.

- ❑ Use the list of questions in the section "Planning for strategic alignment" to establish your own strategic goals that align your team's work with the organization's overall strategy.

❑ Practice recognizing—and savoring—success in your new role. Establish a ritual at the end of each week when you recall your achievements (and the achievements of your team) from the past five days. If it's all a blur, prompt your memory by looking at your calendar or doing a mental review of each day.

PART TWO

Managing Yourself

5.

Becoming a Person of Influence

Do your colleagues listen when you suggest a new idea? Do they seek out your opinion? Does your boss respect your recommendations and take you seriously when you argue for a new approach? Do people in other areas of the business know you and respond well to your work with them? In other words, are you a person of influence in your organization?

In chapter 2, "Building Trust and Credibility," we discussed the importance of establishing your employees' confidence in you as their manager. That foundation is essential to be seen as a strong leader, one that others want to follow. The next step is to use that trust to execute your vision and drive business success in the organization at large.

Influence, as we'll use the term, represents your ability to persuade others and have a positive impact on your organization's decisions, plans, and results. Success in your role as a leader means trying new approaches and strategies. To do this, you need to convince others in your company to follow—and to endorse—your ideas. You also need to be able to advocate effectively for your team, in order to both keep their trust and also enhance the work that they can do for the good of the organization.

You might think that purposefully pursuing influence is distasteful, and surely you don't want to be seen as scheming and manipulating people to always get your way. But influence really isn't about getting "your" way. It's about helping to create positive and productive outcomes for your organization, with and through others.

To do this, first you need to understand the basis of your power; then you can wield it to better work with peers, collaborate across silos in your organization, influence your boss, and promote your ideas.

Positional versus personal power

Influence is a combination of two kinds of power. Your role as a manager automatically gives you *positional power* in your organization—power that comes from your job description and title, like the ability to hire and fire people or approve a budget. In earlier generations, corporate cultures put a greater emphasis on a manager's positional power, and there was an expectation that if you told direct reports to do something, they'd do it without question. But as hierarchies are giving way to flatter organizations and looser networks of collaboration, you can't rely on just your job title to get things done. As a manager, you need to work *through* other people—your direct reports, who can execute your vision; your peers, who can support it laterally; and your management team, who can make or break it from above. Getting their buy-in requires a different approach.

To exercise influence up and down the chain of command, you need to also draw effectively on your *personal power* by cultivating social capital. Relationships, reputation, reciprocity, institutional knowledge, and informal know-how—social capital represents all of the trust, value, and goodwill you've created in your organization. For example, when you increase the organization's profits or help your team secure good year-end bonuses, you create economic value for your higher-ups and direct reports alike. Down the line, when you want their buy-in for a new initiative, they'll be more likely to accept your plan and throw their weight behind your leadership. Your past success has both generated goodwill and earned respect.

If you maintain a strong network of connections in the organization and you support initiatives that are important to others, you will be seen as a valuable ally. You can gain social capital over time by cultivating a few key habits, according to leadership coach Lisa Lai:

Take action and solve problems.

Find and solve real problems for the organization, and for your direct reports, peers, and supervisors. Identify opportunities to become better, smarter, and faster. Suggest specific changes that could be positive for employees, customers, or partners.

Signs that you need to work on this behavior include:

- You tend to ignore problems until they either go away or become the norm.

- You think more about coping mechanisms than solutions.

- You struggle with turning complaints into to-do lists.

Be a team player.

Embrace change and try to deliver the best possible results, even if the decision isn't one you'd choose. Work hard when no one's watching.

Signs that you need to work on this behavior include:

- When someone suggests a new way of doing things, your predominant reaction is fear or annoyance.

- You don't feel ownership of an outcome when you've objected to the process that produced it.

Have informed opinions.

Develop a deep, comprehensive understanding of your business and of your company's power structure. Listen as much as you talk. Provide constructive input when you have an opinion.

Warning signs that you're struggling with this behavior include:

- You don't contribute in the moment because you're not sure what you think.

- You beat yourself up afterward for being quiet, or you blame others for talking over you.

- You change your mind frequently.

Help other people succeed.

Support your boss and acknowledge their authority. Support and respect your peers, even when you disagree. Offer opportunities to other people. Avoid bad-mouthing the company, leadership, and customers.

Warning signs that you're struggling with this behavior include:

- You withhold information and opportunities from others in the organization.

- You prioritize making yourself look good over promoting the successes of your colleagues.

- You're indifferent to other people's career trajectories because you don't think they affect you very much.

Respect others.

Treat your coworkers with respect. Be direct and honest, and take direction easily. Learn to work well with others, including people you don't really like. Manage conflict productively, without undue negativity.

Warning signs that you're struggling with this behavior include:

- You have a history of enemies and rivals in the office.

- You tend to hold grudges.

- You disrespect or disregard people's professional abilities if you don't like them.

Demonstrate integrity.

Share what you can with others without breaking confidences. Avoid barking or biting unless you have to, and use positional power only when it matters. Don't let others bully you, and stand up for what you believe is right.

Warning signs that you have work to do in this area include:

- You share other people's personal information even when you know you shouldn't.

- You lose your temper and make threats to people under your authority.

- You let other people talk you into doing things you don't want to do.

These strategies help you strengthen your relationships and build your social capital, all to the benefit of your ability to influence others.

Managing up

Whether you're asking for a raise, securing more resources for your team, or developing a new strategy for your group, you need to garner influence with your managers in particular. They are a key figure in your professional life, with the ability to open opportunities, connect you and your team with useful resources and relationships, offer you advice, and advocate for you and your team in higher levels of the organization. If you can't influence them, you'll be frustrated at best and professionally sidelined at worst.

When you exercise this influence, you're reversing the traditional power flow in the relationship. That's "managing up"—that is, making a conscious effort to affect the perceptions, opinions, and decisions of your managers. To do this effectively, you need to understand your managers' motivations and their hot buttons, set commonly understood expectations for your performance, and adapt yourself to their way of working.

Put yourself in your boss's shoes

Think about what professional life looks like from your manager's perspective. What are their performance targets, and what professional trajectory are they on? What other motivations play into their decisions? What are the major pain points in their job right now?

Some of these questions you can ask about directly, but others you're going to have to figure out by observation. Pay attention to what stresses them out, what pushes them into overdrive, what tasks they're most likely to micromanage.

Understanding what your boss is incentivized to accomplish can help you make sure your ideas are generally aligned with their needs. And you'll be able to position your ideas in a way that highlights the value to your boss as well as the organization.

Discuss expectations

To become a person of influence with your manager, you need to know what they expect from you and how you will work together, and what you can do to make sure those interactions work smoothly. You may have gathered some information on the listening tour you conducted when you entered the job (see chapter 4, "Positioning Yourself for Success"). But if you haven't discussed strategic outlook and expectations with your boss, now is a good time. Ask questions like:

- "What are your major objectives right now within the organization? How can I support them?"

- "How do you prefer to communicate with the people you manage? How would you like me to share information or updates with you? What's a good way for me to bring questions or problems to you when they arise?"

- "In the past, when you've worked really well with a direct report, what do you think made that relationship so successful? What behaviors or habits are really important to you in the people you manage?"

Thinking about your boss's other relationships is also helpful. Understand who their allies (and rivals) are. Watch their interactions with others. What kinds of people do they get along with best? What work habits annoy them the most? What is the best way to earn and maintain their trust over time? Knowledge is most definitely power in this situation, so be honest with yourself about how they're likely to perceive you. The more you understand, the better you can align with them.

Gathering this information will help you meet their expectations for your performance more successfully. But you may also need to manage their expectations if they're unreasonable or if they actively interfere with your ability to deliver results. If you need to challenge their demands, prepare for a conversation by thinking through:

- What specific expectations do you want to negotiate? How can you link the changes you care about (for example, moving a deadline) with something else *they* will value highly (for example, expanding the scope of the work or meeting a higher-quality measure)?

- How will you link your proposal to your supervisor's goals and show that you put those goals first? To communicate your honesty and sincerity here, use the trust-building strategies that you already know they respond to best, like asking for feedback about how your proposal could better serve their needs.

Adapt yourself to your boss's work style

You'll be better positioned to influence your boss on the important points when you make your daily interactions as frictionless as possible. Tailor your work style to theirs: do they prefer short or long conversations? Do they like to get in early on the decision-making process or review a final recommendation? What kind of evidence do they find compelling? How much time and attention are they prepared to provide on a given day? What particular expertise or skills do they rely on you for? What idiosyncratic preferences do they have about how office life should proceed—for example, how to run a meeting, write an email, or arrange a workspace? Be proactive in making whatever accommodations you can.

In order to partner with and influence your managers, you need to understand and adapt to them in a way that makes your working relationship positive and productive. And doing so will also increase your influence in the wider organization.

Partnering with your peers

To get your job done, you depend upon many people over whom you have no authority. These relationships are exemplars of the principle outlined earlier—that influence is founded in your personal power rather than organizational hierarchy. Collaborating with those who work outside your chain of command is vital to your success, requiring you to actively achieve trust, credibility, and alignment.

Making this more difficult, in many cases your colleagues' priorities will be fundamentally different from yours. Your goals may not be aligned and, in some cases, they will be diametrically opposed: you want to create a new product that could threaten the success of one of their best sellers, for example.

Here's how you can become a person of influence with your peers throughout the organization:

Foster a network inside your organization

Many managers shy away from formally cultivating a network because it smacks of politicking and self-promotion. But, as Harvard Business School professor Linda Hill and coauthor Kent Lineback write in their book *Being the Boss*, "If you don't engage the organization and exercise influence effectively, if you hold yourself above the political push-and-pull, you will limit your effectiveness as a manager."

These robust professional ties support collaboration in a few ways. First, they let you obtain and provide information more easily; you can get a better understanding of what else is going on in your department or ask for feedback on a new idea. A network can also help you better connect your group to the rest of your organization by trading resources or sharing expertise. And they also allow you to form coalitions around shared goals.

To create this kind of network, seek out people with whom you have a rapport and who are genuinely invested in your development. Cultivate ongoing partnerships in which you have a reliable stream of give-and-take. These are stable relationships with a lot of overlap and history that won't wilt under the first favor asked.

By creating these connections before you need them, you will be in a much better position to influence positive outcomes with and through others in your network. If you believe you can't afford to invest the time to build your network, consider this: you can't afford *not* to invest the time.

Make your enemies your allies

Do any of these people sound familiar? The rival who got passed over when you were promoted. The insecure colleague who needs to be right about *everything*. The coworker who openly disdains your personal style. Your first thought might be to avoid these people and the conflict they represent. Whether someone just rubs you the wrong way, or whether you have genuinely competing and divergent interests, it's possible to defuse the negativity and reorient the relationship around shared goals and interests. Initiate a one-on-one meeting—maybe afternoon coffee or lunch at their favorite spot—and follow these steps.

1. **Redirect.** Help your colleague channel their negative emotions away from you by focusing on what you *do* have in common. For example: "It sounds like we've had similar experiences getting used to this new role. I really admire how you handled the transition." With some people, you can be honest about the source of tension and recast the problem between you in a favorable light: "I know it might seem like we're supposed to be rivals, but I think it's great that we have the same skill set and totally different perspectives. You're the only person here I can talk to about X topic and trust I'll get an honest, smart response."

2. **Reciprocate.** Give before you ask. Show them you're willing to give up something of value that's also concrete and immediately actionable. If you make a promise of future support, find a tangible action you can take *now* to make good on that commitment. This reinforces that you want to establish an ongoing relationship rather than just ask for a favor.

3. **Reason.** Make a clear, plausible suggestion of how you think you two could work together to support each others' and the organization's success. What are your expectations for a relationship, and why do they make sense for your colleague, too? End by presenting them with a decision point: Will they commit to this pact now? Consider putting an end date on your offer so that your coworker understands that this new relationship, with its attendant benefits, is something they need to be committed to. An easy way to do this is to say that if you don't hear back from them in a certain number of days, you'll assume they aren't interested. This will create a sense of urgency or importance associated with the discussion, without demand or pressure.

Bringing your allies on board, never mind your enemies, requires energy and tact. But it's worth it; after all, you're not doing this just to make friends and amass power (although both may happen as a result). The influence you develop in your relationships with peers will make all the difference as you work to extend your leadership outside your unit, to shape the way your entire organization works together. The most successful and upwardly mobile leaders have strong, collaborative, respectful relationships with their peers.

Silo busting and effectiveness

Working effectively with colleagues in *other* units is also critical: it can help you get the resources and buy-in you need to do your job, deliver better results, and influence your organization's overall direction. It can also make your organization as a whole more effective—if you collaborate on a new product, rather than duplicating efforts, for example, or if you take on an initiative to standardize a process across the company. This is where your efforts to build trust and credibility really begin to pay off for you as a leader.

Managing these collaborations can be challenging, however, especially if you work in a company with units or systems that operate in isolation from one another. Your peers don't necessarily know you, so you haven't had the opportunity to earn their trust. What's more, their business cultures, priorities, goals, and incentives probably differ from yours. To align your efforts:

Identify key players.

If you're tasked with collaborating with people in a different unit, take some time to understand them and who *their* stakeholders are. How are they perceived in the organization? Who else has relevant positional power? Who has personal power with or over the people you're ultimately trying to persuade? What are the personality issues in play? Who is likely to undermine your efforts if they feel you're encroaching on their unit's territory? Don't be afraid of including the latter group in your conversations; they'll cause you more trouble off the team than on it. Be willing to acknowledge other people of influence in the organization and join forces.

Understand their incentives.

Make sure the motivations of this team are aligned with the change you're trying to make. Learn about the performance goals of team members from other groups and look for areas where there are likely to be conflicts with the initiative you are proposing. Consider how you will mitigate them. Are there other incentives you can invoke? Material help or information for one of their projects? Intangibles like status, respect, or pride? Visibility and involvement in strategic initiatives can have a persuasive effect.

Carve out time to collaborate.

Formalize your initiative by creating a team with a defined membership and mission: "I'm inviting all the engineering and HR managers together so we can talk about a problem we're all facing—how to improve diversity in our workforce." If you're collaborating with people outside your chain of command, keep the meetings casual and under the radar or look for an ally higher up who will sanction your work. In either case, let people know that you value their input and look forward to collaborating with them on the initiative.

Adopt a negotiator's mindset.

The individuals on your cross-unit team may not share the same goals, but you surely have some common ground. Focus on interests rather than positions: What's most important to your opponents? Don't get hung up on what you *can't* do for them; think creatively about what you *can* do that they might value. What value do they bring to the table? What good ideas do they have that you never considered?

Avoid using positional power in these situations unless absolutely necessary. Personal power can be much more influential in terms of securing interest and collaboration from others.

Promoting your ideas to others

We've talked about how to garner and leverage personal power to become a person of influence in your organization. As with the mechanics of influence, which depend on understanding your audience's point of view, the same principles of persuasion apply when you want to argue for a specific idea, plan, or business case.

The first step: determine whether an appeal to your audience's *hearts* or their *minds* will be more effective. "Heart" here means their emotional center, the hopes, fears, and memories that shape their attitudes. An appeal to people's minds, on the other hand, speaks directly to their reasoning power. While hearts and minds are both important targets for persuasion, it's better to use one or the other to frame your initial discussion. You'll be most persuasive if you tailor your case as narrowly as you can to your audience by making a calculation about whether logic or emotion is going to be most effective.

Focus on two questions. First, *how personal is the issue at hand to your audience?* If you're broaching a topic that's tied up in their identity or their vested interests, you should be prepared for a strong emotional response that even they might not understand. You'll need to work through, or at least disarm, this reaction to bring them around to your point of view, so come ready to address their hearts. On the other hand, if they don't have much at stake in the decision or if they're good at keeping their egos in check, they'll likely respond well to straight reasoning.

Second, *where are you in the decision-making process?* If you're at an active decision point and you're trying to win votes, lean hard on logic. If you're trying to solicit interest early on or get buy-in after the fact, emotions are a better target.

As you make your assessment, avoid sweeping generalizations about gender or function. Don't follow persistent biases; for example, that women are more emotional than men, or that finance people only respond to cold, hard facts.

For some more specific scenarios, see exhibit 5-1.

Once you know whether you're targeting your audience's hearts or minds, you can tailor your argument accordingly.

EXHIBIT 5-1

Winning employees' hearts or minds

Win hearts when . . .	Win minds when . . .
• You're introducing a new idea and trying to pique interest.	• You're talking to people who won't feel personally implicated by what you have to say.
• You want to raise the bar on performance or commitment.	• You're presenting a correction to the facts underlying a decision.
• You're leading a team that is struggling with discord or conflict.	• You need to address a highly complex or technical set of problems.
• You're presenting something that's disruptive to the listener's sense of self.	• You want to help an overwhelmed team stop overanalyzing and see a situation clearly.
• You're talking to people who are in a heightened emotional state.	• You're trying to change direction on something previously decided.
• You need to gain support for a decision that's already been made.	

Winning hearts

To draw out your audience's emotional response in service of your argument:

Make it personal.

Your argument needs a "hook"—an opening idea that goes right to the heart of what your listeners care about. What's in it for them? What frustrations will your proposal remove, what excitements will it draw on? Address people directly, and when you talk about the overall benefits for the organization, tailor your pitch to the things that matter most to them. For example: "I know we're all worried about job security as our company looks for a buyer. The initiative I'm proposing will make our whole unit more valuable to the organization—and to any buyer."

Speak explicitly to a big emotion.

Fear, anger, betrayal, pride, ambition, joy—these feelings come from an intensely personal place. If your listeners are resisting change because they're afraid of trying something new, validate that emotion and then disarm it: "Changing how we do this will be scary, because we'll all have to learn something new and risk failure. But we're all in the same boat here: we can learn together and support each other while we make mistakes."

Tell a story.

Stories bring your ideas alive. They grab your audience's attention with riveting plots and characters that individual listeners can relate to, evoking powerful emotions. They also simplify complex ideas. Think about Aesop's fable "The Boy Who Cried Wolf." The moral of that story is a fairly subtle idea about the costs of lying, not that it's bad or that it doesn't work, but that it harms us down the line when others learn to disbelieve even our truths. But everyone who hears that story intuitively and emotionally knows what it means. Good stories stay in our minds because they force us to draw out the meaning for ourselves.

Use metaphors and analogies.

Metaphors represent overarching worldviews that shape people's everyday perceptions and actions, such as "Business is war." Analogies are comparisons that include the words "like" or "as": "Finishing this project was like climbing a mountain in a snowstorm." You can use both of these rhetorical tools to give people a new, vivid way of thinking about a familiar idea. A good metaphor or analogy strikes like lightning, illuminating your point of view without overexplaining or belaboring your point.

Winning minds

If you've chosen a strategy that focuses on the logic of the argument, try these tactics:

Present compelling evidence.

Variety is impressive, but you want to focus on the kinds of proof that your audience is most likely to care about. Listeners who care about expert endorsements will like *testimonials*, while *statistics* will work on audiences who work with numbers or who want to quantify the big picture. *Data visuals* can be very powerful with wide audiences—slides, flip charts, video clips, or product samples.

Ask striking questions.

Questions stimulate your listeners' attention and invite them to contribute—in a controlled way—to the point you're making. *Disturbing questions* focus their attention on their most pressing problems ("How many sales did we lose to last week's software malfunction?"), while *leading questions* influence how your listeners interpret facts and what they remember ("Don't you think our competitors would do X if given the chance?"). And *rhetorical questions* press the listener to accept a proposition that you've formulated ("Are you willing to risk that we'll look so unprofessional again?").

Deciding whether to tap into hearts or minds is easy when you're present-ing your idea to an individual or a small, like-minded group. The bigger challenge comes when you're trying to persuade a group with diverse per-spectives. Then your best bet is to briefly discuss the problem you're trying to solve and how your solution helps the business, your employees, or your customers. Next, cater messaging to different perspectives in the room. For example, appeal to both minds—"If you're wondering why this problem is compelling, let me share the data with you"—and hearts—"And for those of you who are wondering what this means for our employees, let me tell you a story about how it affects Fatma in marketing." You've appealed to hearts.

Whatever approach you take, the more thoughtful you are at the be-ginning of this process, the more effective you'll be.

―――――――

Much of your ability to influence others is driven by your understand-ing of their different perspectives and your willingness to reach out to them. Whether you are presenting a proposal to the board of directors, trying to convince your boss to take you seriously, or working with peers in your group or across the organization, think about how your actions will make other people feel, and assess what problems you can solve for them. This approach to becoming a person of influence in your orga-nization can result in relationships that are positive, productive, and permanent.

Recap

- Influence is a combination of two kinds of power, *positional* (having to do with your title) and *personal* (having to do with your social capital).

- You need to manage up because your boss is a key figure in your professional life. They can open opportunities and advocate for you, but without their support, you will be frustrated.

- To become a person of influence with your peers around the organization, foster a network that can help you obtain information, share expertise, and form coalitions.

- Working with colleagues across silos can be particularly challenging because their cultures and priorities may be different from yours.

- To promote a specific idea to others, consider their point of view.

Action items

Foster your cultural capital by:

- ❏ Solving a small problem for someone else. Follow up on a specific issue that is plaguing a direct report on a daily basis. Take a task off your boss's plate.

- ❏ Learning something new about your company. Ask a peer to explain a new technical point. Talk to someone who's been at your organization longer than you about how your unit has evolved.

- ❏ Offering someone an opportunity. Ask a team member or peer to kick off a team meeting or ask a subject-matter expert to educate your team.

- ❏ Providing support to a peer. Explore how you can support an initiative that matters to one of your peers and fosters business success. Find a way to help.

- ❏ Invest time in outreach to build and extend your network of peers. Request small amounts of time with peers you have an opportunity to learn from, share information with, or partner with to achieve business outcomes. Use a specific opportunity as your reason for reaching out and making the connection.

In situations in which you need to manage up:

- ❏ Put yourself in your boss's shoes. Consider the goals and pressures that motivate their professional lives and how you can help them succeed.

❏ Clarify their expectations. Through conversation and observation, figure out what kind of working relationship they want with *you*. Negotiate problematic expectations by showing how the changes you seek will benefit *them*.

❏ Adapt yourself to their work styles. Make your daily interactions as smooth as possible by accommodating habits like their communication style or decision-making process.

In situations in which you need to persuade, evaluate in advance of a discussion whether you'll be most successful appealing to your audience's emotional center or their rational side:

❏ To win hearts, make your argument personal and have it speak to the emotion of the situation. Tell a story and employ metaphors and analogies.

❏ To win minds, present compelling evidence and push your audience to engage with it by posing incisive questions. Appeal to the logic that supports your case.

6.

Communicating Effectively

To succeed as a manager in today's frenetic business environment, you need to be able to capture and keep people's attention. Whether you're speaking informally with your team, presenting to a group of your colleagues, writing an email or report, or leading a meeting, your ideas are constantly competing for your listeners' and readers' focus. One moment they're following your analysis of third-quarter financials and the next they're thinking about an email they have to respond to, or their child's head cold.

When we're on the receiving end of communications, we crave compelling, concrete, simple doses of information with an authentic voice. Creating this kind of communication requires careful planning and preparation, whether for writing or speaking, in a memo, presentation, or meeting.

Finding your voice as a leader

We're accustomed to thinking that great communicators have a special kind of charisma, a way of holding themselves or of writing that makes them sound authoritative. John Antonakis, Marika Fenley, and Sue Liechti, researchers at the University of Lausanne, studied charisma in dozens of business leaders and found several physical and rhetorical tactics that were universally effective—so effective that in one study, they resulted in a 60 percent improvement in how observers rated leaders' competence.

But charisma isn't a magic trait that some people have and some people don't. Becoming a masterful communicator is possible for anyone who learns the set of behaviors these researchers identified:

- **Animated voice.** Monotone voices sound apathetic, so vary the volume of your voice when you speak. Use your voice to express emotion and pace yourself. Use pauses to create drama and convey a sense of control over your environment.

- **Facial expressions.** Make eye contact, and let listeners see as well as hear your passion. You don't want *every* emotional reaction to be transparent (for example, it's rarely a good idea to show anger), but smiles and frowns, concern and amusement, all communicate your humanity.

- **Gestures.** Your body language can emphasize a point. For example, clasp your hands to illustrate "working together," "integration," or "solidarity." Or let your palms fall open to demonstrate "opening doors," "transparency," and so on. You can experiment with your own vocabulary of gestures by practicing your presentations in front of a mirror.

- **Expressions of moral conviction or shared sentiment.** Affirming shared beliefs and experiences can be highly motivating, as sociologists have long known. When you reflect back to your group members their own values or ideas, you activate these primal feelings of solidarity and excitement. Build around points of connection.

- **Contrasts.** These are easy to learn and use: some variation of "Not this—but that," or "On the one hand—on the other hand." The form generates drama naturally and is pleasing to our brains, which like dualities.

- **Three-part lists.** Three is, indeed, the magic number: it shows a pattern, gives an impression of completeness, and is easy to remember. Use this technique when you're at the dramatic high point of a comment, especially a call to action.

But for these techniques to work, you also need to integrate them into your natural presentation. A robotic sequence of gestures and three-part lists will fall flat unless they're infused with your own verbal style and physical habits, not to mention your own values and experiences. Especially when you present to an audience that already knows you—your team, for example—remember that the figure you strike "on stage" needs to gel with the leader they know from the break room. To bring your self-presentation into closer alignment, ask yourself:

- In what situations do you feel most comfortable communicating? How can you adapt the tactics you use in that setting more broadly to other settings?

- What authentic parts of yourself are you struggling to express at work right now? For example, maybe you *feel* passionate and assertive about your work, but you don't come across that way in meetings. How could one of these tactics help you convey that part of yourself more clearly?

Practice using the tactics outlined here until you find what feels most comfortable to you and allows you to feel natural and most compelling in front of others.

As a new leader, you may not feel that you've found your authentic voice just yet. But as you work on understanding what matters to you as a leader and how you want to present yourself in the presence of others, you'll start to develop your own voice to communicate and influence others.

Mastering the written word

Many people you work with may know you almost entirely through your writing, from emails, reports, proposals, and presentations to texts, IMs, and social media posts. Yet, with this form of communication, you have limited tools to capture and keep others' attention: you can't lean forward or gesture to emphasize a point. That's why good writing isn't just about grammar and usage, but structure, clarity, and voice. You don't need to be a professional writer to achieve this effect; instead, take the following steps as you compose and refine your words.

Step 1: Prepare

Before you begin writing, you need to know what you're trying to say. Are you arguing for a particular idea or point of view? Are you providing background context for a discussion? Are you documenting an internal process? In the *HBR Guide to Better Business Writing*, writing and usage expert Bryan A. Garner recommends writing out your three main points as full sentences, spelling out your logic as clearly as you can. That way, when you begin to write, you already know the ideas you want to convey and the supporting points you'll make.

Begin thinking about your audience as well at this early stage in the process. What do they already know about your topic, and what questions will they have? Is your audience internal or external? Will they be opposed to or aligned with your ideas? Will they want just the headlines, a detailed outline, or both? Pick an organizing principle that will make your idea as accessible as possible to your reader. (See exhibit 6-1.)

Once you've chosen an organizing principle, create an outline that places your ideas and supporting points in order. This may feel like overkill for, say, a simple email. But the more you practice this process, the more you'll realize that even the shortest written communication benefits from preparation and a structured approach.

Step 2: Write your first draft

You don't need to start writing at the beginning of your outline. Begin writing the section or material you feel most comfortable with, keeping your outline in front of you. When you've finished that, choose the next item you're comfortable writing, and so on. Stop periodically to compare your draft to your plan. Many writers save the introductory material until the

EXHIBIT 6-1

Organizing methods for writing

If you're writing:	Consider using this organizing method:	By:
Feasibility studies, research results, and planning reports	Compare and contrast	Evaluating the advantages and disadvantages of two possibilities
Any type of internal document intended for particularly busy readers	Order of importance	Putting the most critical information at the beginning of your document
A document that traces a series of events	Chronological	Listing events in the order in which they occurred
Instructions or user manuals	Process and procedure	Describing who does what and when
Trip reports, descriptions of machinery, and research reports	Spatial arrangement	Describing one aspect of your topic at a time
Work orders, training materials, and customer service letters	Specific to general, or general to specific	Starting with a specific or general concept your readers are already familiar with and then moving to a specific or general concept that's new to them
Technical reports, annual reports, and financial analyses	Analytical	Formulating a hypothesis and testing it through questioning

Source: Adapted from "Writing Skills" in *Harvard ManageMentor*. Boston: Harvard Business School Publishing, 2016. Electronic.

end; it's often easier to compose an engaging and effective opening paragraph once you know what your conclusions are.

Garner suggests writing your first draft as quickly as possible. "Your sentences will be shorter than they otherwise would be," he says. "Your idioms will be more natural, and your draft should start taking shape before you know it. If there's a painful part of writing, it's doing the first draft. When you shorten the duration, it's not as painful."

Step 3: Edit your draft

Once the draft is complete, set it aside for as long as you can. Getting some distance will help you spot places where you've overplotted your argument, gone off-message, or let your voice falter.

When you dive back in, review your draft to see whether you've set forth your ideas in a logical, focused, and clear manner. Have you stated your main message clearly? Have you articulated any action items clearly? Is the information accurate? Barbara Wallraff, a longtime editor and columnist for the *Atlantic*, suggests that when you reread, you should ask yourself, "How do I feel about what this says? How do I feel about the writer?"

In addition to the content of your draft, review your writing style. This is the time to polish what you've written. Aim for unfussy language that's easy to read:

- **Keep your sentences short.** Your point will get lost in too many complex clauses, so break them into separate statements. And avoid loading up the text with unnecessary words.

- **Watch for language that's overly formal.** Readers will lose the thread of your argument, or simply lose their will to understand it, if your writing is stilted.

TIPS

How to write an email

When writing an email message, keep it professional and brief.

- **Pick a standard font in black.** Anything else is hard to read and raises questions about your professionalism.
- **Capitalize and punctuate properly.** No lowercase "i's" or missing question marks. Says business writing expert Bryan A. Garner, "It takes less time to write a clear message the first time around than it does to follow up to explain what you meant to say."
- **Include a short, descriptive subject line.** It will help your email stand out in a cluttered inbox, especially if it's a call to action ("Prepare for Friday's meeting").

- **Use the simpler word.** "Transmogrify" is not a better way of saying "change." Contrary to popular belief, complex word choices don't make you appear smarter.

- **Avoid repetition.** "I'm *excited* about this *exciting* opportunity" looks sloppy. The best way to catch these issues is to set aside your writing for a few moments and come back to it.

- **Create strong patterns.** If you present A, B, and C ideas at the beginning of the document, don't refer to them as C, A, and B later on. Also, make your lists parallel; if the first three bullet points are complete sentences, be sure the fourth one is too.

- **Proofread for grammar and usage errors.** *Affect* versus *effect*, subject-verb agreement—don't get caught making these common but embarrassing mistakes. Keep a reference bookmarked on your computer (for example, Mignon Fogarty's "A Quick Guide to Avoiding Common Writing Errors," on HBR.org).

- **Get to the point quickly.** Put key information—what you're asking, a deadline—up front. Don't waste words buttering up the recipient: "May I ask a favor?" is more effective than a paragraph of praise and apologies.

- **Break up big blocks of text.** People won't read long paragraphs, so trim the fat and press return. If you can, keep the length of your emails to a single screen of reading.

- **Reread and revise before you send.** Give yourself the opportunity to fix typos and tighten your wording. The more important or extensive your recipient list, the more time you should spend on this step.

Source: Adapted from Gretchen Gavett, "The Essential Guide to Crafting a Work Email," HBR.org, July 24, 2015.

Emails are a particularly tricky form to master, although we write them all the time; for special tips, see the box "How to write an email." Once you're happy with your draft, consider sharing it with colleagues as well. As a proxy for your intended audience, they can give you feedback on what is working and what isn't.

Persuasive presentations

Presentations are a hybrid form of communication, a combination of oral speech, text, and images. They've become one of the standard ways professionals share information with groups and, increasingly, with individuals as well. While this format may seem less dense than a written report, it's more challenging to put together. Visuals compete with words for the viewer's attention, and the emphasis on images means presenters often give short shrift to basics like structure and audience.

To create a powerful presentation, you need to distinguish the slide deck itself from your presentation as a whole. Too often we elevate the deck itself as the main event, but your voice should never play second fiddle to a screen. So what *is* the right way to combine these forms?

Step 1: Decide whether you'll use slides

Slides can be a powerful ally in your ability to communicate with an audience. They can also undermine your presentation by giving people something besides you to focus on, so use them selectively. In smaller, informal settings, it's better to use a whiteboard or handouts than a big glowing screen. When you do use slides, create them *after* you've prepared your key messages.

Step 2: Plot it out

Fundamentally, presentations are a kind of storytelling, says Nancy Duarte, who works with speakers at TED talks to improve the quality of their presentations. Duarte argues that an effective presentation, like a good story, has a beginning, a middle, and an end. Within that structure, it juxtaposes the status quo—"life as the audience knows it"—and then disturbs that status quo by introducing provocative new ideas: "Right now customers use our service mostly to get updates about their weather. But what if we could provide them with other locally specific information on demand?" Use an opening like this to set up a conflict that the rest of the presentation will work to resolve.

The middle of your presentation can be used to elaborate the problem and your proposed solution by going back and forth between the way things are now and the way they could be. In the scenario Duarte started, she imagines the presenter continuing:

> *Our backend is set up right now to provide meteorological data,* but *the infrastructure we've created could incorporate other datasets that are similarly organized, like traffic.* However, *our engineering team does not have experience building out this kind of capacity.* But *we're prepared to bring on experts who have worked on projects like this in the past.*

Toggling between your current reality and a better, alternative future creates excitement and tension. (See exhibit 6-2.)

EXHIBIT 6-2

Persuasive story pattern

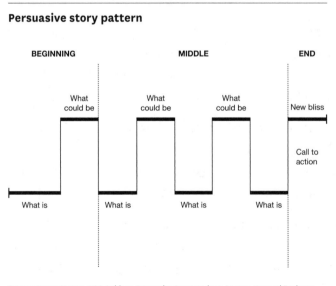

Source: Nancy Duarte, *HBR Guide to Persuasive Presentations*. Boston: Harvard Business Review Press, 2012.

Make a hard sell at the end of your presentation. Don't finish with a long to-do list: "next steps" followed by a dozen bullet points is not exactly inspiring. Either summarize key points for a compelling appeal to the minds of your audience or, instead, speak directly to their hearts:

> *After the problems with our last major expansion effort, I know we're all afraid of failing again. But if the past few years have taught us anything, it's resilience. We've worked so hard to get back in the game; finally, I think we have a project that takes advantage of everything we've learned.*

Step 3: Prepare your visuals

Once you've outlined the overall narrative, it's time to make your slide deck. Think "less is more." People should be able to understand a slide in three seconds, which means you need to streamline the content aggressively. Here are Duarte's proven rules for a great deck:

- **Slideshow ≠ talk.** Don't subject your audience to a read-along; nothing is more likely to lose their attention. Don't lay out your entire argument on a slide. If you choose to use presentation notes or a teleprompter, conceal them from the audience's view.

- **One idea per slide.** People can only process a single stream of information at once. Choose text or visuals that reinforce key points (for example, an icon that illustrates a key metaphor) or that will help the audience remember your takeaways (for example, a buzzword).

- **Storyboard on sticky notes.** Their small size will force you to simplify your content, and it's easy to play around with the order. Create a full outline this way before you open up PowerPoint and start fiddling around with slide formats.

- **Fresh visuals.** Brainstorm visual concepts, a *lot* of them. It's better to pick a slightly weird metaphor or image than something tired and forgettable. For tips on displaying data, see the box "How to make data pop."

- **KISS (Keep it simple, stupid).** Pick readable, simple fonts in a large size. An occasional pop of bright color can add visual interest and conceptual emphasis, but don't let the aesthetics get in the way of legibility.

Step 4: Perform like a pro

After you've planned a well-structured presentation, get ready for the actual event:

- **Rehearse.** Don't memorize your talk word for word; it will sound stiff and boring. But know the material well enough that the environment, technology, and audience won't throw you off your game.

- **Have a plan for interacting with your audience.** When will you take comments? How will you respond if someone interrupts you or questions you aggressively? If someone asks you something you don't have an answer for?

TIPS

How to make data pop

How can you communicate the *meaning* of your data quickly?

- **Include the minimum you need to make your point.** You don't need to overwhelm the viewer with numbers; too much information is distracting and even off-putting.

- **Show the eye where to go.** Help people see what's most important by highlighting key information with bright colors and big labels.

- **Leave plenty of white space.** It will make your data look cleaner and give viewers' eyes a neutral place to rest while they're sorting out the structure of your chart.

- **Stick to the schedule.** One of the biggest ways you can show respect for your audience is by starting and ending on time. If you've allotted time for questions or other kinds of participation, honor that commitment.

Presentations are a performance with a live audience. You'll have to think on your feet and adapt the material you prepared to your listeners.

Conducting effective meetings

Whereas presentations and the written word are mostly unidirectional—I talk, you listen—meetings are participatory. You're managing not only your own communications, but everyone else's, too. By taking a little time to prepare and follow up, you'll keep the room engaged, stave off any brewing conflicts, ensure that all voices are heard, and keep the session on track and effective.

Step 1: Prepare before the meeting

Step back and ask yourself what you want the meeting you're planning to accomplish. Do you need stakeholders to make a decision? Are you sharing information with a group? Will your team brainstorm new ideas? Once you have a clear objective in mind, create an agenda. Consider what activities need to happen during the meeting to accomplish your purpose, and how these events should logically flow. Then assign a leader and a length of time for each item.

You may also decide to ask someone else to officially facilitate the meeting. This person will guide the conversation and take care of pre- and post-logistics, like sharing agendas, call-in numbers, or notes. Additional meeting roles may include a scribe, who records key ideas, disagreements, and decisions; a timekeeper, who makes sure the meeting sticks to its agenda; and experts you can call on for an opinion.

When you plan your attendee list, include key decision makers, experts, and stakeholders. Run your list by key attendees to make sure you're not missing anyone important or including anyone extraneous. The number of attendees should depend on the meeting's purpose: a general rule of thumb is to invite fewer people if you're meeting to make a decision and more if you're brainstorming or sharing updates.

Finally, you (or your facilitator) will need to prepare the logistics. Make sure the room is set up, including projector hookups and teleconferencing technology. Distribute materials ahead of time, including the agenda and any necessary background readings.

As a busy manager, you'll be tempted to skip some of this preparation for your standing or routine meetings. If you want people to be excited about your meetings, do the work up front to make them productive and meaningful.

Step 2: Conduct the meeting

Start on time and begin by explaining the group's goals and introducing each person's role—for example, the facilitator or timekeeper. Then establish some ground rules for how you'll conduct the conversation—whether you expect people to put away their phones and laptops, how those participating virtually should jump into the conversation, who is the decision maker, and so forth.

As the meeting progresses, keep everyone engaged by highlighting agenda transitions, summarizing progress, and underscoring major decisions or announcements. Empower the timekeeper to signal when you're going over or to interrupt a speaker, if necessary, to keep moving forward.

Efficiency in a meeting should never come at the cost of full participation, however. Ask the whole group, "Have we forgotten anything?" "Does anyone have a different point of view?" Be prepared to shut down people who talk too much and draw out the silent types. Keep an eye out for body language that indicates someone wants to contribute—leaning forward, quick indrawn breaths, eye contact. If someone hasn't spoken at all during the meeting, elicit his thoughts. And give virtual participants verbal cues (for more tips on this, see the box "Tips: How to run a virtual meeting").

When you're ready to close, repeat the key points of the conversation, including decisions, next steps, and personnel assignments, and check for

TIPS

How to run a virtual meeting

Virtual meetings present special challenges. Will the virtual participants be able to follow what's going on? How will you keep people's attention when you're not in the same room? Keith Ferrazzi, a leadership consultant and researcher, lays out these best practices for creating a strong sense of group identity without slowing down the meeting:

- **Use video if possible.** When we can see each other's faces, we feel more connected with one another and more engaged with the topic of the meeting. By watching facial expressions, you'll also be able to perceive vital information about your team's emotional responses and buy-in. At a minimum, consider using photos in materials distributed so everyone has a visual reference for those remote to the location.

- **Have the team provide updates in advance.** Instead of having everyone provide a status update during the meeting (like "a bunch of fifth-graders reading to each other around the table," says Ferrazzi), ask participants to send out a half-page report ahead of time on key agenda items. Make it clear that everyone is expected to prepare for the meeting by reviewing these messages, as well as the rest of the agenda. People should come prepared to have a truly informed discussion.

- **Kill the mute button.** In theory, using the mute button is good etiquette because it prevents disruptions for the rest of the group. In fact, it's a license to multitask, even to leave the room mid-meeting. It's rude, and it can put a serious dent in the meeting's liveliness and productivity. You can also limit multitasking by calling on participants directly to contribute or by rotating the roles of timekeeper or scribe.

Source: Keith Ferrazzi, "How to Run a Great Virtual Meeting," HBR.org, March 27, 2015.

understanding. Then end with motivational message: "Great discussion today, thanks so much. We got a lot done!"

Step 3: Follow up afterward

Send a follow-up note the next day, summarizing what the team accomplished and holding members accountable for future progress. Stick to high-level details:

- Decisions or outcomes you want people to remember

- Who is responsible for next steps, including you

- Due dates attached to those action items

Send the note to all attendees and anyone else who needs to know what happened.

If any members seemed dissatisfied during the discussion, follow up with them individually, preferably in person so you can discuss their concerns face-to-face. You might learn something important that never came up in the meeting itself, or you might hear useful feedback about your own leadership, and you'll gain buy-in for the group's work down the road.

From memos to meetings, effective communication that engages your audience's attention will help to to persuade someone to your way of thinking. In the long term, though, the benefits are much greater. The more effectively you communicate, the more influential you become.

Recap

- Finding your voice as a leader involves learning a set of rhetorical tactics and behaviors and incorporating them into your authentic way of speaking.

- All types of written communications benefit from taking a moment to prepare and review, so you're presenting your thoughts in the most compelling and professional light.

- When creating a presentation, consider the slide deck and the meat of your presentation separately.

- For a meeting to be effective, you need to prepare the agenda and invitation list carefully, and elicit all participants' viewpoints during the meeting itself.

Action items

To find your voice as a leader:

- ❏ Pick one rhetorical tool and try it out in a conversation. Contrasts, three-part lists, and expressions of moral conviction or shared sentiment will seem more natural in day-to-day interactions, whereas metaphors, similes, and analogies should be reserved for larger, more formal discussions.

- ❏ Choose emotionally heightened conversations to try new tactics. Practice your new skills when you're debriefing a direct report in your office, for example, not just making small talk in the parking lot. Serious interactions will give you better fodder, and you'll have more time to pause and gather your thoughts before you speak.

- ❏ Observe yourself speak. Make a video of yourself as part of your practice; it's much more realistic than just watching yourself in a mirror. Choose something informal like a status update or a more elaborate script you wrote for a past presentation. Review the video to observe your facial expressions and gestures: How animated are you? Work on one specific behavior—for example, smiling—and practice it in all your interactions for the rest of the day.

When you need to write something:

- ❏ Prepare by knowing what you *really* want to say (write three sentences), understanding who your audience is, and deciding on an organizing method.

- ❏ Write your first draft quickly. Don't necessarily start at the beginning.

☐ When you edit, review the content, polish your style, and check your grammar and usage. Aim for simplicity instead of trying to sound impressive.

When planning a presentation:

☐ Plot your presentation out in narrative form before you even open your computer. Tell a story with a beginning, middle, and end.

☐ Decide whether you'll be using slides.

☐ Prepare your visuals. Storyboard your presentation with sticky notes, and limit yourself to one idea per slide.

☐ Perform like a pro by practicing ahead of time. During the presentation itself, stick to your schedule.

When running a meeting:

☐ Prepare for the meeting by defining your purpose, creating an agenda, inviting attendees, assigning roles, and prepping logistics.

☐ During the meeting, establish your ground rules for group interactions, keep things moving, and make sure all voices are heard. Close the meeting on time by summarizing your accomplishments and next steps.

☐ Follow up afterward by sending a note to all attendees. Seek out critics to discuss (and disarm) their opposition.

7.

Personal Productivity

You did a great job juggling all your many tasks as an individual contributor; that's probably one of the things your organization saw when it chose to promote you. But many new managers are surprised by how much more they're responsible for now: not just more work, but more *kinds* of work, all seemingly top priority. You need to think strategically and plan for the future, while optimizing execution every day. You can feel as if these responsibilities are pulling you in a hundred different directions at once: "Did you see my email?" "I need you to take this over." "Could you help with this?" "What's your plan for the next fiscal year?" "When are you going to be home for dinner?"

To orchestrate your time and your energy so you can meet all these demands, you must manage your *personal productivity*. That phrase covers everything from corralling your calendar to understanding tricks to make you more productive and help you relax. In this chapter, you'll learn how to prioritize calls for your attention, stay focused, and keep stress—and work—from controlling your life.

Time management essentials

Your time is valuable. Time management is a deliberate practice that helps ensure you're using all the time available to you in the best way possible. You may not feel able to justify the effort it takes. But the payoff is worth it. It will allow you to see patterns and begin making adjustments so you can get the *right* work done at the right time and become more effective.

Step 1: Understand how you spend your time now

A schedule is like a budget, says Elizabeth Grace Saunders, a time management coach: you can't manage your assets unless you understand your current spending habits. Start by logging your activities for at least a day or two, preferably for an entire week. Use a time-tracking or calendar app or a simple spreadsheet, noting your activities in half-hour increments, as well as any major interruptions. Keep track of unplanned activities like fielding phone calls in the middle of a meeting or dipping into administrative work when you're supposedly preparing a presentation.

Step 2: Look for patterns

When you've completed your log, collect the activities into five to ten categories and tally the minutes you've spent on each. Consider categories like answering emails, planning, dealing with crises, project work, managing people, administrative work, relaxing time, personal chores done at work, and professional development.

Now analyze the data you've collected. How are you distributing your time across all these activities? How much time do you spend on planning, compared with crises and fires? How much time do you spend on your own project work, versus managing your team members? As you look at your tallies, what surprises you?

Now step back and ask yourself the most important question of all: *Does my time usage match my highest priorities?* What's the payoff associated with each activity? Which activities are tied to your core responsibilities and which aren't so relevant? Which investments have the highest impact for you, personally and professionally? For example, assess whether you are spending more time on a side project than you should, not enough time planning for the future, and whether you are taking enough breaks in your day to stay productive. Are there activities you've been doing that really should be performed by someone else—or not at all? Look for items that you might hand off to a colleague or a direct report.

Step 3: Make a goal-driven master plan

Look at your list of activity categories and allocate time to each based on your goals and priorities. You'll have to make smart trade-offs here, and it might take some iteration to get right. The first time through, ask yourself: "In an ideal world, how much time would I spend on these activities?" These numbers may not add up to forty or even sixty hours each week. So the second time, ask yourself, "What's the minimum amount of time I can afford to spend on these activities?" Minimize the amount of time you are spending on low-priority items; this can free up time for more important work.

In a well-balanced schedule, however, your highest-priority items may end up occupying only a small fraction of your time, and that's OK. Your mission here is only to find *enough* time in your schedule to meet these goals, and if that's a mere five or ten hours a week, that's fine.

Step 4: Execute your plan: time boxing

Now it's time to allocate the time you've assigned to each item into a schedule. Using a technique called *time boxing*, you'll break your schedule into short blocks and then slot a category into each block, breaking it up into tasks. (See exhibit 7-1.)

Start by reviewing the week ahead: What deadlines, meetings, and tasks are coming up? What longer-term commitments do you need to work on in this time frame? Then prioritize that task list. Put deadline-sensitive items up top ("Prepare for presentation on Wednesday"), followed by goal-oriented actions ("Research strategic plan"). You'll schedule both of these around your recurring obligations ("Weekly staff meeting"). Note the categories that these tasks fall into.

EXHIBIT 7-1

Time-boxing tool

Schedule for Monday and Tuesday mornings

Time	Monday	Tuesday
8:00 a.m.	Planning Task: Prepare for budget presentation on Wednesday Actual time spent:	Planning Task: Research SP Actual time spent:
9:00 a.m.	Planning Task: Research strategic plan (SP) Actual time spent:	Project work Task: Follow up on new leads Actual time spent:
10:00 a.m.	Managing others Task: Plan to delegate invoicing to Ivan Task: Review résumés for administrative assistant position Actual time spent:	Managing others Task: Meet with Ivan about invoicing Actual time spent: Personal tasks Task: Call Mom for her birthday Actual time spent:
11:00 a.m.	Communication Task: Respond to emails Task: Call Asana back Actual time spent:	Team meetings Task: Weekly staff meeting Actual time spent:

Source: Harvard Business Review, *Managing Time* (20-Minute Manager Series). Boston: Harvard Business Review Press, 2014.

Next, allocate a specific block of time to each category. Within each box, list the tasks you'll accomplish. As you go, calculate the amount of time you are spending on each category so you match your allocations in step 3.

Put the time boxes into your actual calendar, wherever you keep track of your appointments, so you treat your boxes with the same respect as you would a meeting with your boss.

As you begin, it's much better to overestimate how much time each task will take than to underestimate. But for this technique to work, you need to be able to make accurate time estimates, so keep track of how your schedules work out. You can use these experiences to make a better plan next time.

Finding focus

Even with a perfectly calibrated schedule, disciplining your attention can be difficult. You have a big task to work on, and you know when you have to work on it, but you just got five emails while doing your *last* task. Or you have a problem from yesterday that you still haven't solved, or a deadline for another project looming tomorrow. A news story you're antsy to check up on. A sheaf of papers that's not aligned *quite so* with the corner of your desk.

Finding your focus is about learning how to tune out all this mental noise so you can concentrate on the work at hand. That concentration can be powerful. Psychologists call it "flow"—when you're so completely engaged in what you're doing that you lose track of time. Mihaly Csikszentmihalyi, who pioneered research on flow, describes the concept this way:

> *Imagine that you are skiing down a slope and your full attention is focused on the movements of your body, the position of the skis, the air whistling past your face, and the snow-shrouded trees running by. There is no room in your awareness for conflicts or contradictions; you know that a distracting thought or emotion might get you buried face down in the snow. The run is so perfect that you want it to last forever.*

Flow boosts both performance and motivation. You do your best work in this state, and you feel good about yourself, too. But to achieve it, you need to eliminate the behaviors and environmental cues that send your brain off-task.

Forestall interruptions

Interruptions often take you away from the task at hand for much longer than you had planned. Diving back in is hard: according to research at the University of California–Irvine, getting back on track after being interrupted can take more than twenty minutes.

Plan ahead for these obstacles and temptations. When you need to focus, close your door or put up a "do not disturb" sign. Turn off notifications on your phone and computer, at least for email and chat applications. Consider disabling your Wi-Fi entirely, or use a service to block certain websites for a given amount of time. Experiment with different tactics, and don't be afraid to tell your colleagues about your efforts: "I'm going to be working on the budget presentation early this afternoon, so I'll be off email

---

TIPS

How to protect your time from other people

Your direct reports come to you for help or a decision; your peers want your support for their own goals; and from time to time, your boss wants a favor, too. Being smart about how you respond to these requests will let you make the most of your time and still support your colleagues appropriately.

- **Know when to say no.** When someone asks for a favor or offers an opportunity, ask yourself: Is this work valuable to my organization? Is it important to my professional goals? Is it important to me personally? Am I the *only* person who could do this task? If I say no, will I damage the relationship? If none of these questions elicit a strong yes, then that's a good sign you shouldn't do it.

- **Learn how to say no.** If you've decided that it isn't something you can do, politely decline, delegate, or suggest a replacement. Some scripts for these awkward conversations:

  - "Thanks for thinking of me. Unfortunately my plate is full at the moment, and I have to say no. I'll look forward to seeing how your project turns out."

until after three." If you *are* interrupted, know how to refuse a request or end a conversation if you need to get back to work (see the box "Tips: How to protect your time from other people").

Organize your space

If your environment is disordered, you'll spend precious minutes looking for materials you need to get work done. You'll also be more vulnerable to distraction, as other objects or obligations catch your eye. Here's what you can do to make your office conducive to focus:

- "I can't take this on right now, but I'd like to offer the opportunity to Omar. He's been looking for a chance to take on more leadership in our team, and I think he'd handle this really well."

- For your boss: "I'm not certain I can take this on successfully with my current set of priorities. I could use your guidance on what's most important to you."

- **Exit conversations.** Sometimes all people want from you is your attention and even that's too much. But escaping from an enthusiastic conversationalist can be uncomfortable, so try these scripts:

  - "Do you want to continue this conversation over lunch tomorrow? Right now I have to get back to work."

  - "Can you send me an email about your question, so I can follow up later? Right now I need to finish this task."

  - "Sorry, someone's waiting for this work so I need to get it done now. Can I swing by your desk in an hour?"

  - "I hate to cut you off, but . . ." "Sorry to be rude, but . . ."

Eliminate the clutter.

If your workspace is really a mess, set aside a block of time to clean it up. What papers can you file? Pass on to someone else? Throw away? Once you've completed the initial purge, get in the habit of tidying up your desk when you're transitioning between tasks.

Keep what you need within reach.

Put objects you use every day on your desk—a particular notebook, a pad of sticky notes, your headphones. Store everything else in a drawer, out of sight. This might feel odd at first, but it helps significantly with focus.

Make yourself comfortable.

Do you get a crick in your neck when you look at your computer monitor for too long? Does your desk chair give you a backache? Adjust the height and positioning of these objects, and make sure the rest of your space is aesthetically pleasing to you, too. Harsh light or busy sightlines can be as distracting as a loud noise when your brain is restless.

Organize your email

An update from your employee. A question from a client. An invitation from your boss. You'll have to respond to these messages at some point, but when you expose yourself to a stream of notifications, you undermine your ability to meet the priorities you've already established for yourself. Email can become an excuse to procrastinate when you fall out of flow on a project, and it doesn't serve you well to allow email to hinder you from completing important work. Here's what you can do to keep the mayhem in check:

Clean up your inbox.

The guilt or stress you feel over unanswered messages can be as intrusive as a new notification, so just as you set time aside to clean your physical space, also make time to clean your virtual space. Sort your emails by sender and delete the backlog of messages you don't need, as well as the ones you've already responded to. Then create three folders in which to file all the emails that are still in your inbox: follow-up, hold, and archive. Messages that require a thoughtful response go into the *follow-up* folder, while notes about future events, like an invitation, go into *hold*. *Archive* everything that requires no further action, but that you still want to keep a record of. Going forward, use this system to sort new emails as they arrive.

Start over.

If you don't have time to go through all your old messages, don't. Put them all in a separate archive folder and start fresh with a new inbox. This strategy might seem ruthless—you totally *were* going to get to all those messages someday!—but if you honestly can't sort through fourteen thousand unread messages, declaring "email bankruptcy" allows you to move on and focus on your future productivity. But save this move for emergencies only; don't develop a reputation as someone who is nonresponsive by leveraging this option too often.

Turn off notifications.

If you really need to concentrate, turn off notifications or close your email client altogether. Set up an auto-reply for the time you're offline: "I'm stepping away from email until five to get some work done, but you can reach me by phone or text if something urgent comes up."

Stress management

Stress and lack of focus are actually two parts of a vicious cycle. You can't focus, so you don't get work done. When you don't get work done, you become too stressed to focus. And repeat.

"Stress is a physiological response to any change, whether good or bad, that alerts the adaptive fight-or-flight response of the brain and body," says Dr. Herbert Benson, founder of the Mind/Body Medical Institute and an associate professor of medicine at Harvard Medical School. Maybe a colleague caught you off guard with a difficult question during a presentation, or perhaps your boss just added another urgent assignment to your already full plate. Sometimes internal issues trigger stress, like when you worry about failing at a new and difficult assignment. The likelihood of managers experiencing stress in the workplace is very high in today's fast-paced and complex organizations.

There is *some* good stress, of course. Stress is a natural, even useful reaction that can motivate you and help you focus under pressure. Business culture often seizes on this; how often have you been asked, as motivation in the face of a big challenge, if you are tough enough, smart enough, committed enough to succeed.

The best managers know how to balance the benefit of stress, while protecting from the negative impact of stress. According to psychiatrist and attention deficit disorder expert Edward Hallowell, too much stress actively sabotages your ability to perform: "When you are confronted with the sixth decision after the fifth interruption in the midst of a search for the ninth missing piece of information on the day that the third deal has collapsed and the twelfth impossible request has blipped unbidden across your computer screen, your brain begins to panic, reacting just as if that sixth decision were a blood-thirsty, man-eating tiger." The result: bad stress. The signs can include uncontrollable anxiety, disorganization, and even anger, disengagement, physical exhaustion, and illness, all of which lead to poor performance, not to mention a lower quality of life.

These reactions are a matter of neurochemistry, not moral fitness. The frontal lobes of your brain, where nuanced cognition like decision making, planning, and learning happen, start sending distress signals to the deep regions of the brain that govern your survival instincts. And those regions respond with a range of powerful, primitive signals: fear, alarm, withdrawal.

All this means that your ability to evaluate information and solve problems crashes just as the rest of your mind and body lock into crisis mode. "In survival mode," says Hallowell, "the manager makes impulsive judgments, angrily rushing to bring closure to whatever matter is at hand."

To better manage your reactions, establish routines that will regulate your general stress levels and adopt practices to relieve high tensions in the moment. The more effectively you monitor yourself, the more you'll be able to help your team members manage their stress, too.

Routines to regulate stress

Your daily life contains many sources of stress, even before you factor in a big deadline or sick child. By adopting healthy habits like these, you can protect your personal reserves from that everyday wear and tear:

Promote positive emotions.

Foster a trusting, respectful culture among your team members where you can derive comfort from your colleagues even in crisis. Spend time on emotionally rewarding relationships at work, even if they're not strategic, and express appreciation regularly. Make a habit of toggling between the task you're working on now and the big picture, so you can take pleasure in the progress you've made and touch base with what's really motivating you. When you start to feel overwhelmed, breathe deeply and cut yourself some slack. Develop a ritual for regularly thinking about meaning, perhaps each day as you get ready to leave. The more consciously you connect your work to a larger sense of purpose—whether that's changing the world or securing your own financial stability—the better you'll be able to weather each day's ups and downs.

Take care of your brain and body.

Being attentive to your physical well-being will lower your stress at work and improve your ability to lead. The value of sleep cannot be overstated. Stay rested by setting an early bedtime. Diet is important, too. Eat healthy foods at intervals that make you feel your best. Limit alcohol intake. Finally, exercise releases a host of stress-fighting chemicals, and you don't need to be a marathon runner to reap the benefits. Walking up and down a flight of stairs or down a hallway a few times a day will do the trick.

Reduce the stress of everyday decision making.

You have a limited amount of mental energy, so don't spend it on low-impact decisions like, "What should I have for breakfast this morning?" or "When should I go through my voice mails?" Put these choices on autopilot by limiting your options (granola or a Danish) or establishing a routine (checking your voice mail at ten each morning). Social psychologist Heidi Halvorson suggests you give yourself extra support around difficult decisions by constructing "if-then" propositions in advance: "*If* I find out our budget isn't being increased, *then* I will go for a walk around the block to stay calm and relaxed."

In-the-moment interventions

Establishing patterns, good habits, and routines should help you stay calm as you go about your normal daily life. But when something specific causes your stress levels to rise, take a short break to disrupt that tiger-fighting survival response:

Do something else.

People do better with difficult tasks when they're fresh off something simpler, like an easy rote task. You could talk with a friend, solve a fun puzzle, or even write a short description of something you know well, like your house. You're giving your brain some breathing room to reset its circuits.

Step away.

If you have an emotional response while interacting with others, excuse yourself from the meeting you're in or graciously end the phone call. It's better to take a moment to govern your reaction than have an uncontrolled emotional response. Don't be embarrassed to let others know what you're doing: "I need a moment to process all this, so I can bring a clear mind back to the table. Let's take a ten-minute break."

Try desk yoga.

If you need some physical relief from the tension but you can't leave your desk, try a few office-friendly stretches. You can slowly roll your shoulders, alternating left and right, or use your hand to gently press your ear to your shoulder. Flex your clasped hands behind you to stretch your chest, or twist your torso at the waist, keeping your feet flat on the floor. Breathe deeply and let your muscles relax into each pose for ten to fifteen breaths.

Work-life balance

For many professionals, the daily tug of war between work and time with family, friends, community, and self is in itself a source of stress. Where does work end for you? When you close your computer for the day? When you physically leave the office? When you enter your home? Greet your family? Fall asleep? Does it *ever* end?

Work-life balance is how you organize the relationship between your professional and personal lives. It includes the habits you rely on to protect and renew your energy, the boundaries you set around family and leisure time, and the strategies you use to negotiate conflicts between the two.

Here are the best practices for finding synergy where you can and drawing lines where you can't:

Avoid burnout

In addition to your other routines to regulate stress, take breaks during the workday to refresh your energy, like checking in with someone you love or going for a walk around the block. Avoid surfing the internet as a break strategy, as it tends to deplete your motivation; focus instead of replenishing it. Even staring out your window is better.

In the evenings, build in time when you can truly recharge. Instead of sitting on your sofa watching television, do something that actively engages your brain in a pleasurable way, like cooking a meal or visiting with a friend. After a certain time each night, put your digital devices away in a drawer or a closet and maintain a strict "no email" rule. In addition to whatever family time you set aside, be sure you also get some "me" time.

Protect your weekend

Weekends are your time for regular rest, recovery, and human connection. Even if you can't promise yourself a clear forty-eight hours, do set some boundaries around when you'll read and answer emails or work on important projects.

The best way to uphold these boundaries, of course, is to be strategic with your time during the week. Negotiate deadlines that you can't reasonably meet in a five-day workweek, and frontload your schedule so you're not tackling all the important tasks at the end of the week. Finally, give yourself a compelling reason *not* to work by committing to personal plans for the weekend. If other people are counting on you to show up at a concert or go to a soccer game, you'll be more motivated to tie up loose ends before you leave on Friday.

Own your relationships

Sometimes work *will* take over everything else. Whether your business lost an important client or you're going through a seasonal busy period, you can manage the impact on your most important relationships and negotiate reasonable expectations in advance. The people closest to you—like your spouse and family—may struggle with your work-life balance as much as you do. Your best bet: talk about it.

Start the conversation by providing context about why your work is so intense right now and explain the purpose of all this effort: "By putting in all this time now, I'm helping my team prepare the best presentation we can make to potential investors. When we can bring another investor onboard, the company's finances will stabilize and my job will stop being so crisis driven."

Then ask about what this shift in your work means for them: "Can you tell me how you think this will make things harder for you?" If you disagree, ask for more information: "Can you give an example to help me understand?" Don't minimize or debate their point of view. Exercise compassion and express genuine remorse for the hurt they're feeling. And be specific; if you can't give loved ones your full attention and presence during this time, you can at least show them you understand and care about what they're feeling.

Talk to them, too, about how you might minimize the impact: "How can I make this better for us, our family, our relationship?" Also ask how you could handle things better in the future. Bring up difficult situations you think might develop: "School is ending soon, which means new sched-ules for our kids and more child care overall. What are your thoughts about what I can do when that changes?"

This conversation has two purposes for you. First, you want to reaffirm your connection with the person you care about and to be transparent about what makes this situation so hard. But you're also looking for fixes that would mitigate the negative effects your work is having on the relationship. Stew-art Friedman, a professor at the Wharton School, suggests that you might be holding yourself to higher, or at least different, standards than your loved ones do. Maybe your daughter doesn't care if you miss dinner, as long as you can still drive her to school in the morning. Or maybe your parent doesn't mind if you miss some family dinners, as long as you continue to participate in a shared community activity. You won't know unless you ask.

Recognize that it's not a zero-sum game

Friedman argues that work-life "balance" itself is a misnomer. Work, fam-ily and friends, community, and self-development will always be in flux, and there will never be a perfect equilibrium between them. And work is a *part* of life, after all. You vent and celebrate your achievements with your family, trade war stories and seek professional advice with your friends, share your expertise and build your skills in your community. And the leadership growth you bring to each of these spheres will help you in the others, like the executive Friedman coached who gained leadership experi-ence and strengthened his relationship with his family by joining a local community board in his neighborhood.

To develop your career sustainably, you need to integrate these parts of your life without sacrificing your own happiness. Friedman argues that your professional future actually hinges on your ability to preserve a rich life outside work. Authentic leaders ground themselves in a clear under-standing of who they are and what they value, which is borne out in human experiences outside the office as well as in it.

There's something even more elemental at stake here than your job: your health and happiness. A bad work-life balance can undermine your health in a variety of ways, from hypertension and poor sleep to depression and substance abuse. The cost to your relationships will also be high. If you take a deliberate approach to balancing and combining your personal and professional duties, you can protect your health and help your family pull through times of stress *with* you.

———————

To achieve your strategic objectives in this role and feel satisfied with your life overall, you need to take charge of your personal productivity. Learning how to manage your time, focus, and stress frees you up to think about the bigger picture and get the most out of each day. Do this for yourself, your colleagues, your team members, and your loved ones, who all need you operating at your best.

Recap

- Managing your time is a deliberate practice that will help ensure you are using all the time available in the best way possible, matching up the time you have available with your goals and priorities.

- As important as finding time to do your work is finding focus in order to do it well.

- Stress is a physiological response to change, and it comes in good and bad flavors. Embrace positive stress and develop patterns to mitigate unhealthy stress.

- To minimize your stress, invest time to care for your body and your brain.

- Work-life "balance" may be a misnomer; aim for positive work-life integration.

Action items

To get a handle on your time:

- ❏ Understand how you use your time by tracking at a very detailed level for a few days.

- ❏ Look for patterns in the data you've collected about your time use: Does it match your priorities? Analyze what's creating the gaps between your expectations and reality.

- ❏ Make a goal-driven master plan mapping how much time you'd ideally spend on each work activity, differentiating your highest and lowest priorities.

- ❏ Execute your plan by allocating time proactively to your highest priorities with time boxing on your calendar.

To improve your focus:

- ❏ Clear your primary work surface. Leave out items you use all the time, and sort the rest into storage or the trash.

- ❏ Get comfortable. Adjust the height and positioning of your computer and your chair so you can work without any pain. If you don't have a comfortable chair, acquire one today.

- ❏ Clear your inbox. Sort emails if you have time or dump them all in a backup folder for later reference. Develop a consistent habit for how you'll proactively manage email moving forward.

To better manage stress and your work-life balance:

- ❏ Commit to reconnect to the meaning of your work at the start of every week. Remind yourself why you do what you do to rediscover your inspiration.

- ❏ Limit the toll of decision making by adopting consistent routines for the things you do everyday (get dressed, check in at home, and so on).

❑ When you're feeling especially stressed, give your brain and body a moment to recoup by doing a puzzle or some stretches.

❑ Build in time to relax during the workweek so you don't burn out. Protect your weekend by keeping Thursday and Friday free of major deadlines whenever possible.

❑ Look ahead to any big deadlines that might pose challenges to your personal relationships and sit down with the people involved to let them know what's coming and to brainstorm together about fixes that might alleviate some of the stress.

8.

Self-Development

For your career to be fulfilling, it's important to actively manage your own growth. Too often, people assume if they work hard, their career will unfold the way they hope. But because of the fast pace of global innovation and change, professionals must update their skills and broaden their abilities more frequently than ever before.

You are the best advocate for your own interests. Your manager juggles multiple responsibilities and priorities, and may discuss your career aspirations only at an annual performance review. Your manager will also appreciate your proactive willingness to set goals, keep your expertise current, and ask for growth opportunities. While many organizations support career growth through training and other programs, a lot of the work of self-development will depend on what *you* make happen through your own choices and actions.

For most people, the idea of a "lifetime" career is passé. Imagine, instead, your career unfolding on a lattice, not a ladder. A lattice is a broad, flexible structure that allows for multiple routes to many destinations, versus the simple "up" imperative of a ladder. This chapter will help you progress along your career lattice by discovering your interests and values, finding opportunities for growth, cultivating new skills in light of what your organization and industry will need in the future, and forging relationships within your company and industry.

Career purpose

The first step in your self-development is articulating your career *purpose*. What do you want out of your work? How should your career fit into your life overall? What do you hope to accomplish as a leader?

Clayton Christensen, a professor at Harvard Business School, says this is the single most important thing he teaches his students each year—to "keep the purpose of their lives front and center as they [decide] how to spend their time, talents, and energy." That's because without a sense of

---

QUESTIONNAIRE

Find your purpose

Think about these questions as you plan your personal and professional development.

- **What are you good at?** How can you get better at those things? What biases do you have about what's worth mastering?

- **What do you enjoy doing?** What activities or pastimes did you especially love when you were a child, before the world told you what you should or shouldn't like or do?

- **How do you work best with other people?** Do you prefer to work alone or with others? What kind of relationship is most generative for you—as a subordinate, a supervisor, a peer, or a collaborator? Do you produce better results as a decision maker or an adviser?

- **Do you perform well in the presence of ambiguity?** Or do you need a highly structured and predictable environment?

---

purpose, you won't know how to react to the challenges and opportunities that come your way.

To develop your sense of purpose, think about important questions we often sideline in our day-to-day work lives (see the box "Questionnaire: Find your purpose").

Nick Craig (president of the Authentic Leadership Institute) and Scott Snook (senior lecturer at Harvard Business School) have trained thousands of managers and executives. They recommend that once you have answered questions like these, you construct a simple, positive statement of purpose based on your responses. There is no one format or single right approach to developing your statement of purpose. Just tap into what resonates with you. It's OK if the statement you craft doesn't quite fit on the

- **What are your values?** What kind of person do you want to see in the mirror each morning? What organizational missions or cultures are compatible with your values?

- **Where do you belong?** What does all your self-knowledge tell you about where you can be successful and happy? What type of organization, doing what type of work, with what kind of people, to serve what positive outcome?

- **What should you contribute?** Think about your current work and your overall position in life. What needs do you see around you? Given your strengths, your way of performing, and your values, what unique and significant contributions can you make to fill these needs?

- **Think about two of your most challenging life experiences.** How have they shaped you?

Source: Adapted from Clayton M. Christensen, "How Will You Measure Your Life?," *Harvard Business Review*, July–August 2010; Peter F. Drucker, "Managing Oneself," *Harvard Business Review*, January 2005; and Nick Craig and Scott A. Snook, "From Purpose to Impact," *Harvard Business Review*, May 2014.

first try. As you revise, push yourself to make it more concise and direct, and ask other people for their reactions. Does it sound like *you*? Does it capture your essence?

Your statement of purpose will serve as the foundation for the self-development strategy you'll work on in the rest of this chapter. Return to it periodically, when you're making a big decision or working through a particularly stressful period. And keep it in your back pocket as you continue to consider your own growth and development. Your purpose may shift over time, so reviewing it periodically and adapting it to your current thinking is very powerful.

Look for opportunities within your organization

Once you're clear on your career purpose, begin to look for opportunities to grow toward those goals. Maybe you want to expand certain skills with your current role by taking on special projects or stretch assignments. Or you may feel that you've accomplished what you wanted to in your current role, and you're ready for the next step in your career—a permanent role or a tour of duty in which you learn about a different part of the organization.

Consider starting your search for more within your current company. First, you've invested time and effort building your reputation, earning trust, and establishing credibility there. You're also familiar with the culture. Your strongest networks also operate within your organization, which means you may have more access to opportunities in-house than in the broader industry. Your company has also likely invested a great deal to develop your talents; you have knowledge and experience it doesn't want to lose. In some cases, you'll want to consider other organizations (if your current situation is highly toxic or you want to learn how a different kind of business operates), but it usually makes sense to start close to home.

Step 1: Investigate formal development

Begin with your company's formal process for developing talent. Your supervisor is responsible for helping direct reports clarify their goals and find appropriate growth opportunities, so make an appointment with them first. Come prepared to talk about the direction in which you'd like to grow. Ask questions about the opportunities available to you. If you feel comfortable, share your statement of purpose and ask for your boss's reactions and ideas.

Other sources of information at this stage could include:

- Your company's human resources department

- Formal training programs, such as leadership training provided by your organization, technical apprenticeships, or outside degree programs that your company will underwrite

- Company job postings for current openings

- Internal networks that may support your development, either your own web of influence or connections organized through HR

- Mentoring relationships, either formally organized by HR or undertaken through your own initiative

- Temporary assignments—for example, taking on new tasks during a colleague's maternity leave or sabbatical

Step 2: Conduct internal informational interviews

Informational interviews are a good way to gather more insight about any of these options. For example, if you're wondering if you'd want to transfer to another department, you might ask HR to set up a conversation with an employee or manager there. Or, if your boss knows about and supports your ambitions, you could ask them to introduce you to someone there. Use a referral when possible; hiring managers are especially open to meeting with someone who's been recommended by an acquaintance they respect. (See also the box "Case study: When interviews yield offers.")

When you sit down with your colleague, remember that you're there to learn, not to ask for a job (at least not yet). You should be prepared to lead the conversation. Come armed with research and good questions. A good place to start is with these five questions based on work by career strategist Daniel Porot:

- "How did you get into this line of work?"

- "What do you enjoy about it?"

- "What's not so great about it?"

- "What's changing in the sector?"

- "What kinds of people do well in this industry?"

CASE STUDY

When interviews yield offers

Informational interviews within your company can help you form connections, but conversations with those outside your organization can also help give you perspective. In either case, you need to prepare before taking the time of those who are helping you.

Two years ago, Matt McConnell, who lives in Southern California, wanted to move from finance to marketing. He wasn't entirely sure of his direction, so he began using informational interviews to learn about other peoples' careers in the hopes of narrowing his focus. "I was also using the interviews to learn more about other organizations to see whether they might be places I'd want to work," he says.

His first informational interview didn't go very well, and Matt takes full responsibility. "I didn't prepare," he recalls. "He could tell, and he told me that I was wasting his time."

Matt learned an important lesson. "I've never made that mistake again. I now always overprepare," he says.

To get ready, he reads people's LinkedIn profiles, does a Google search on their careers, and checks out their company's website. He tends to ask the same questions, usually in the realm of how the person got started and how they ended up in their current role. "But I also make

Respect your interviewee's time: ask for no more than twenty minutes, and honor the time limit. Thank them afterward with a handwritten note.

Step 3: Propose a job

Sometimes interviewing for an open job posting or having an informational interview leads to a new role that's just what you want. But if it doesn't, don't give up. Instead, propose the job you *want* to do. This takes

---

notes about particular questions I want to ask so that I have something to reference if the conversation stalls," he says.

Matt also has a postmeeting routine. "I ask for a business card and immediately send a handwritten thank-you note. The thank-you is typically three lines long, and I always mention one specific thing from our meeting that resonated with me so they know I was listening and found their time valuable," he says.

"Early on in my career I worried that I didn't have anything to offer anyone in return. [But] I learned that people enjoyed sharing their experiences and offering advice, so I make sure to communicate my sincere gratitude."

Matt eventually had an informational interview with a marketing head of a quick-service restaurant group that yielded results. "After our meeting, the person called me and said her company was hiring for a role she thought I'd be perfect for," he says. "She'd given my name to the HR department, and they were planning on calling me within the next thirty minutes to do a phone interview. That phone interview led to in-person interviews and eventually a job offer at that company."

He worked at the company for a few years before moving on. He's now the marketing manager for Astrophysics, a company that designs X-ray scanners for security screenings.

Source: Rebecca Knight, "How to Get the Most Out of an Informational Interview," HBR.org, February 26, 2016.

a lot of preparation, but can be highly effective in leveraging your skills to the benefit of your organization. You can start by researching unseen opportunities within your organization. What customer or internal need is unaddressed? Where could the organization grow? Try to imagine your company as an outsider would see it and gather as much information as you can from colleagues, company meetings, shareholder conference calls, and other venues. Here are some questions that can guide your search:

- **Which departments or business areas have momentum?** A department that's growing rapidly may be eager to add someone who is already familiar with the organization's mission and culture.

- **What opportunities exist for you in a different market, location, or country?** Relatively few people are willing to relocate for their job, yet companies are hungry for workers who have experience across multiple markets.

- **What entrenched problems does your organization face?** How could you get involved in helping solve them?

As an idea for your next role takes shape, consider how you'd implement this change. Who would do your current work? What skills could you acquire to make this an easier sell to the company? Brainstorm about in-house, off-site, or virtual seminars and workshops you could attend, and figure out how participating in those programs would fit in with your current responsibilities.

When you're ready to pitch, pick the person who has the best mix of power and credibility to make your proposal a reality *and* with whom you have the best relationship. Your direct manager, mentor, or sponsor is a good target. Be clear about the benefit of your expanded or new role to the organization. Explain why you think you're best suited for the work, with detail about your competencies and your track record. Lay out how the transition would work, including a timeline for handing off your current role or subset of responsibilities and securing early wins in the new one.

Step 4: Pursue incremental opportunities

Don't be discouraged if the company doesn't immediately embrace your idea. You should be prepared to negotiate for an incremental, temporary, or transitional career move, like:

- **Growing in place.** Can you make changes to your current role and gradually add desired responsibilities or scope? If even this step meets resistance, consider starting a small project on your own. You might have better luck petitioning your company later if you can bring concrete results to the table.

- **A cross-functional team.** Can you partner with workers from different departments to bring your idea to fruition? This option helps you expand your networks and gain insight on other career paths.

- **Job rotation.** Does your company offer special assignments or rotational roles?

- **In-house internship.** Could you forge an agreement to intern under a supervisor to learn a new role?

Step 5: Look elsewhere

If you don't find an opportunity at your organization, it might be time to consider whether you need to look elsewhere. Searching for a position at a new company makes sense when:

- Your core interests don't match what your employer can offer.

- Market volatility has made your employment precarious.

- Your job is meant to be done for a short time and doesn't have a viable career path.

- Your organization isn't a good cultural fit for you and your preferences.

Use your network to research job opportunities, schedule informational interviews with leaders in the industry, and connect with decision makers. Reach out to mentors who are outside your workplace. And when you find an opportunity you want to pursue, enlist someone to introduce you (via email or a phone call) to the relevant hiring manager. In some fields, jobs posted online garner hundreds of résumés. A personal introduction and note of recommendation can distinguish you as someone an organization should interview. If you don't have a connection, put the request out to your network. See if someone you know can make an introduction to a person within the organization you are interested in.

When looking for a job outside your organization, keep these tips in mind: First, don't be disrespectful when talking about your current company. Second, don't use company time to pursue other opportunities. Use vacation or after-hours time for your research and interviews. Third, plan to provide sufficient notice to your current employer and leave as graciously as possible to avoid burning bridges.

Feedback from your boss and your team

The people who work with you directly can also play a role in your growth. They know more about how you work than anyone else, and they have unique perspectives on both your strengths and your weaknesses.

Receiving feedback can be inherently stressful, setting off your insecurity, fear, and anxiety. This information is important to hear, but its emotional impact can be overpowering. As research shows, that's because we listen more closely to negative information than to positive information, and remember it more vividly. So it's easy to become fixated on our deficiencies, while neglecting our strengths.

To learn from your immediate coworkers, you'll need to practice hearing and using criticism in positive ways. And you must also learn to spend as much time considering your strengths as your weaknesses.

Asking for and using criticism

One of the best ways to receive genuine, real-time feedback is to ask for it. Make this a part of your normal routine. At the end of a group meeting, when you're closing out a coaching session with an employee, or when you're driving back from the airport with a colleague after a business trip, ask this question: "Do you have any feedback for me about how that went, and how I could do better next time?"

Whether people—especially your employees—actually take you up on those questions will depend on how you react to even the first whiff of criticism. Does your response teach them to stay silent from now on? Or do you reward their honesty with respect, attention, and gratitude?

Criticism is easier to receive when you're aware and in control of your own emotional reactions. Executive coach and Stanford Graduate School of Business lecturer Ed Batista recommends that when you hear the words, "Don't take this personally, but . . . ," you stop and recognize three elements of the conversation:

- **Your threat response.** Your brain is following age-old neurological and physiological patterns. Acknowledge that you're being triggered and remind yourself that your *perception* of threat doesn't mean you are actually under attack.

- **The power dynamic.** We become extremely sensitive to status during these conversations, and it's tempting to project a lot of negative motivations onto the other person. Is he lording his power over you or trying to assert supremacy? Is she trying to undermine your authority? Acknowledge your fears and choose to make the generous assumption: "This feels bad for me, but I think they're trying to help."

- **Your agency.** If you're feeling ambushed or blindsided, you might freeze up. It might not seem like it, but you *do* have a choice about whether you participate. Ask yourself, "Do I need to step out right now? Or can I continue to hold this conversation?" Giving yourself the option to leave may actually settle your emotions.

One of the best ways to assimilate feedback as it's being shared with you is to listen actively and probe for more insight: "Tell me more." "I'm not sure I knew that about myself. Help me understand what you're seeing." Asking for more information takes you out of a personally defensive posture and puts you back in the inquisitive, curious mindset that is the hallmark of great leaders.

Over the long term, you can make these experiences easier by deepening your relationship with the feedback givers. When it's time to talk about more difficult topics, you'll feel safer and more curious about their input. You'll also be able to relate the negative information to the bigger picture; your sense of purpose and your plans for growth.

Know your strengths

Not all feedback needs to be negative. When you reach out to your colleagues to collect their constructive criticism, you should also engage with them on your strengths. The "Reflected Best Self" exercise, created through the University of Michigan's Center for Positive Organizations, can structure this process. Your goal here is to compose their experiences (and your own) into a unified vision of your best self to measure future decisions and actions.

Start by picking a wide range of people: family members and friends, past and present colleagues, teachers, mentors, and so on. Ask them to describe your strengths and to share specific stories about when they've witnessed those traits.

Then organize all the material you collected and search for common themes. Group examples by theme and then take a stab at explaining who you are or how you behave when you live up to those ideals. Exhibit 8-1 shows an example of one row of a table you can create listing your strengths; each row would highlight examples of a different theme.

Once you've compiled these memories and themes, turn the bullet points into prose. Use the feedback and your own observations to write

EXHIBIT 8-1

Reflected best self—sample row

Common theme	Examples given	Possible interpretation
Curiosity and perseverance	• I gave up my promising career in the military to get my MBA. • I investigated and solved a security breach through an innovative approach.	I'm at my best when I'm meeting new challenges. I take risks and persevere despite obstacles.

Source: Adapted from Laura Morgan Roberts, Gretchen Spreitzer, Jane E. Dutton, Robert E. Quinn, Emily Heaphy, and Brianna Barker, "How to Play to Your Strengths," *Harvard Business Review*, January 2005.

a two- to four-paragraph description of your best self. Try opening with these phrases:

- "When I'm at my best, I . . ."
- "I enjoy . . ."
- "Others rely on me to . . ."
- "My best work is . . ."
- "I feel most like myself when . . ."
- "I thrive when . . ."

Now reread what you've written: Where is your current role best aligned with the self-portrait you just created? Where are the biggest sources of friction? What elements of your role do you have the power to alter—the composition of your team, the way you do your work or spend your time?

Finally, design some small experiments to bring your job into better alignment with what you've learned or put yourself in the best possible position to succeed. Instead of initiating a grand overhaul that requires approval from higher-ups, try making two or three targeted adjustments at a time. For example, if you're at your best when you're collaborating with others, look for areas of overlap with your peers in other units and start a regular series of meetings about how you could better work together.

Engaging with feedback from your boss and employees will advance your thinking about the kind of leader you want to be. Building around your strengths and mitigating or improving in areas of weakness will allow you to develop into a stronger leader. It also supports your career development process over time, throughout your career.

In order to supervise others well, you must invest in your own competencies —influence, communication, personal productivity, and self-development. To connect with and advocate for your employees, you must develop personal power and an authentic voice. And to help them organize their work, you must understand how to prioritize your time and projects. These skills make you a stronger contributor in the organization, but as a manager, they also deeply affect the overall functioning of your team.

Recap

- The first step in your self-development is articulating your career *purpose*: What do you want out of your work, and what do you want to accomplish?

- Search for development opportunities by first examining the options available in your workplace.

- Feedback from those you work with can help you understand where to grow—as well as your areas of strength.

Action items

To define your career purpose:

- ❑ Complete the "Find your purpose" questionnaire at the beginning of this chapter.

❏ Reformulate the answers to your questions into a statement: "My purpose is . . ."

❏ Refine your statement, sharing it with friends, family, and colleagues to get their input.

To find opportunities within your organization:

❏ Take advantage of formal development opportunities your company offers. Talk to your boss and to the HR department to find out what's available.

❏ Conduct informational interviews with internal leaders about any functions that interest you. Use your contacts within the company to set up meetings and come prepared with good questions and great manners.

❏ If no existing opportunities catch your fancy, propose the job you *want* to do. Figure out where there's an unmet need or untapped opportunity in your company, and how your current team will survive your transition.

❏ If you can't move to a totally new role, pursue incremental opportunities in your current position, such as joining a cross-functional team.

❏ If you truly see no chances for growth in your current organization, use your network to find opportunity elsewhere. Exit as graciously as possible.

Solicit feedback from your boss and your team:

❏ Ask for feedback as often as possible—at the end of a meeting or after a presentation—from your colleagues as well as those above you in the organization.

❏ When you receive criticism, be prepared for completely natural emotional responses that may pop up. If the feedback feels bad or wrong, why? What happens if you make a more generous set of assumptions about where the other person is coming from?

- ❏ If you start to feel overwhelmed by negative feedback, excuse your-self from the conversation and don't return until you've regained your equilibrium.

- ❏ Also use the "Reflected Best Self" exercise to ask for positive feedback and use it to triangulate a picture of who you are at your best. Use that information to reverse-engineer your job: how would it work for your best self?

Managing Individuals

9.

Delegating with Confidence

Delegating is one of your most important responsibilities as a manager. Your role is to ensure the right people are doing the right work, at the right time, and in the right way. That includes what work you'll do and what each member of your team is responsible for. The most effective managers spend less time "doing" and more time planning work assignments, organizing resources, and coaching people to achieve their best possible results. While most managers never get away from "doing" altogether, the goal is to ensure that your work is high priority and high impact for the organization.

Still, it can be hard to give up control over specific tasks, especially if you like doing them and you're good at them, even if your workload is overwhelming. You may also hesitate to delegate an item that's something of a stretch assignment for your staff (won't it just be easier if you do it yourself?). And once do you make an assignment, you must maintain accountability for the work without crossing over into micromanagement. Chances are you also worry about overburdening your very busy team members.

In this chapter, you'll learn *why* it is important to delegate, how to make a delegation plan and share it with your employees, how to track progress and provide support, and how to avoid the most common managerial mistakes.

Benefits of delegation

One of the common misconceptions managers have about delegation is that delegating signals weakness—that they should be able to do everything on their own. But effective delegation can have real benefits for you, your people, and your organization.

When you delegate, you remove tasks from your to-do list that others are qualified to handle. This gives you more time to focus on activities that require your unique skills and level of authority: planning, business analysis, coordinating operations, obtaining resources, addressing personnel issues, and developing your employees. If you can give these core tasks the time they require, your performance *and* your job satisfaction will improve.

For your staff, delegation creates new opportunities for growth and boosts motivation. Imagine that you ask an employee to prepare the agenda for an upcoming meeting. The person will help set goals for the meeting, draw up a blueprint for the conversation, recruit presenters and seek advice from other stakeholders, and create and circulate relevant materials—tasks that may seem routine or bothersome to you, but will give your direct report increased visibility and new insight into how your company works.

From an organizational perspective, delegation helps you maximize your company's resources and improve productivity. The math here is simple: if you make the most of each team member's abilities, you'll maximize the group's output. Less simple are the intangible benefits you'll create in terms of group dynamics. Trust will deepen across the whole team—trust in you, for extending meaningful opportunities to grow and have influence; trust in each other, for performing well and getting results; and trust in themselves, for mastering new challenges.

Developing a delegation plan

Once you have identified a task to delegate, start by making a written delegation plan *before* you talk to your employee. It should detail everything from why the assignment is important to the deadlines involved.

Making a good plan is important. If you assign a task to someone who lacks the right skill set, for example, you're setting both of you up for failure and disappointment. Or if you fail to make accommodations for an employee's extra-heavy workload, you might push him into burnout. And without a clear, comprehensive description, you don't know that the employee will actually do the work you need done. A written delegation plan creates a record that you and your staff can refer back to as the work progresses. You can use it to hold your employee accountable, troubleshoot if the project goes awry (did you describe the work inaccurately?), and bolster your argument for the employee's promotion.

Here's how to create your delegation plan.

Step 1: Decide what to delegate

To decide what you should delegate, assess your workload and identify tasks, projects, or functions that don't require your specific set of skills and authority. Identify work that could easily be done by other staff members or outside resources with a minimum of coaching or on-the-job training.

If a task, project, or function is too important to delegate to someone else, think about sharing responsibility. You may be able to subdivide work so you handle one part and delegate the rest.

Avoid delegating if:

- You can't precisely explain what you want the other person to do. If you can't articulate what problem needs to be solved or what exactly needs to be done, it's best to wait to assign responsibility for the work until you can clarify these things.

- You'll put your own development or ability to lead in jeopardy by delegating. For example, suppose you need to develop your interpersonal skills so you can interact more effectively with your team members. Avoid delegating work that requires extensive interaction with your team, such as leading meetings or talking with employees to learn about their career goals.

- You'll undermine a project's success by delegating. For instance, let's say you have extensive experience developing marketing plans and you were hired for these skills. Your unit is launching a major new product line, and the marketing plan will prove critical to the line's success. You decide to retain responsibility for defining the strategic elements of the plan, but you delegate the tactical components.

Step 2: Why—*clarify your purpose*

Why are you delegating work? Think about the specific problems you want to solve or benefits you want to achieve. Questions to consider include:

- Why do you want to delegate *this* particular slice of work?

- How will delegating affect your own work experience? Will it lighten your workload, lower stress, or let you focus on other managerial responsibilities?

- What impact do you want this assignment to have on your employee? In what sense is this work an opportunity for the person? In what sense is it a burden?

- Are you facing a trade-off between time and project scope? If so, is it more important to meet a deadline or to create a stellar final product? How will delegating help?

Step 3: What—*define the work*

What exactly do you want your direct report to *do*? Be as specific as you can about the activities you'll hand off and the outcomes you want to see. Is the assignment a task, project, or function?

- **Tasks** are discrete activities, like writing a report or planning a meeting. They usually have a clear timeline, work process, and outcome. For example: "I'd like you to administer a customer survey. We need the results (data plus analysis) by next Friday."

- **Projects** encompass multiple tasks that fulfill a specific objective, like assessing customer needs or developing a new code of conduct. They require more time, resources, and coordination than a single task.

- **Functions** represent an ongoing activity in your unit, like staff training or interfacing with IT. Unlike tasks or projects, functions don't have a start and end date; they're a continuous responsibility. That doesn't necessarily mean they're more onerous, though. Planning an annual training session involves less work, for example, than a major project or high-profile task.

You should be able to name the overall task, project, or function you're delegating and list all the associated subtasks and deliverables. You also want to have a clear sense of what skills the work requires. Here is an example:

- **Project:** Develop a new employee code of conduct.

- **Tasks:** Review the current company code and industry standards; hold a focus group or administer a survey; meet with HR and a company lawyer; circulate a draft for input; present final recommendations.

- **Skills:** Research, planning, analytical thinking, written and oral communication, and knowledge of group scheduling and survey apps.

- **Deliverables:** A complete and final draft of the new code of conduct, around forty pages. A presentation on the proposed code to the company leadership.

This is the basic road map you'll give when you talk to your direct report about the assignment. For very experienced employees, you may not need to itemize the work in this much detail. But, in general, it's better to overspecify so you can clear up any misconceptions at the outset.

Step 4: Who—*choose someone to do the work*

Who's the right person for this assignment? There are a lot of factors to balance here, including:

- **Availability.** Who has the availability to take this on? If an employee is too busy to accept a new assignment, how can you help them free up time?

- **Skills.** Who has the cognitive, interpersonal, and technical abilities to do the job well? Who would build important new skills if you gave them this assignment?

- **Motivation.** Who would really embrace this assignment? How does the work align with employees' career strategies or personal goals? Who has relationships—with customers, vendors, with other staff—that this assignment could benefit from?

- **Assistance required.** How much help will the person need from you to be successful? Will you be able to provide that oversight?

- **The team dynamic.** Have you delegated a lot of work to this person in the past? Will this assignment look like favoritism—or like a punishment?

You should be able to explain to your employee and to your own boss why this individual is right for the job: "Luis is well-equipped for this project from a technical standpoint, and it's a great opportunity for him to gain leadership experience."

Step 5: When—*determine the timeline*

When will this work be done? Deadlines are important, but think about time constraints *throughout* the work process. Are you waiting for certain inputs to arrive or for a key collaborator to become available? If the assignment has multiple phases (planning, testing, implementation, or the like), how long will each phase take?

You should be prepared to give your employee a clear deadline and/or timeline for the work.

Step 6: How—outline the process

How will your employee do this work so that it meets your standards? You don't need to make a step-by-step plan (that can veer into micromanaging, which we'll deal with later in this chapter). But do think about factors like:

- Will your employee need to collaborate with anyone to complete this assignment?

- How much authority will the person have to make decisions and manage other people?

- What will *your* role be in this process? When will you check in with your direct report, and when should the person seek your approval for any actions?

- What's the budget for this work? What other resources will your staff need (including extra training), and how will you help secure these resources?

- How will you hold your employee accountable to the project's timeline, budget, and quality standards? What metrics will you use to measure these things?

Sharing your delegation plan with your employee

Now that you've drafted the assignment, it's time to bring your employee in to communicate your delegation plan, ask for input, clarify any questions, and agree on a clear timeline and benchmarks for the work.

Your goals here are twofold, requiring you to talk *and* listen carefully. On the one hand, you want to outline your expectations for this assignment, so that your employee clearly understands what you're asking and what success should look like. On the other hand, you want to find out whether your plan as it stands is doable, and make whatever accommodations you can to help your employee do a good job.

But each of these goals draws on different kinds of authority; that's partly what makes delegation so hard. How much are you giving direction, versus soliciting input and consent? If your employee resists the assignment, how will you handle it? Making an assignment and setting expectations is a manager's prerogative, an attribute of your positional power. But in order to make sure the work actually gets done well, you may need to take a more flexible attitude. Remember that leveraging your personal power is all about connecting with others, engaging in active dialogue, and developing the best possible outcome with and through others. By using your personal power when delegating, you're more likely to secure buy-in and encourage enthusiasm with your staff. Avoid using positional power unless absolutely necessary.

The best way to manage these competing goals is to hold the conversation in two distinct phases. Explain to your employee that in the first half, you'll explain the assignment, and then you'll have a chance to discuss and clarify the plan.

Step 1: Explain the assignment

Come prepared with your written delegation plan so that you don't misspeak or skimp on the details. You want to be as clear and precise as you can in this conversation to avoid any miscommunications about what you're asking. Prepare a copy of the assignment so your employee can review the details, take notes, and walk away with a written mandate for action.

This conversation should cover the same basic issues you looked at during your planning phase: why, what, who, when, and how. You may want to linger over details at the end of this list (deadlines, work processes), but your employee still needs a lot of detail at the front end. Think of it as setting context: What's the purpose of this assignment? How does it fit into the bigger picture for your team or for the organization? Why are you engaging them, and what are the benefits? If it's a stretch assignment, they might also worry about being up for the challenge. So emphasize any special training or coaching that you plan to make available.

Step 2: Agree on the plan

Once you've laid out your initial plan, it's time to answer questions, resolve concerns, and incorporate good suggestions from your employee, who might be eager to ask questions. If not, try some of these scripts:

- "What questions do you have about all this? What's not clear?"

- "What ideas do you have about how we could improve this assignment?"

- "Do you have any questions about the scope of your authority here, or about how you'll collaborate with others?"

- "I see us working together in X way on this assignment. Do you have any concerns about that?"

- "Is this timeline doable? What problems do you anticipate with the schedule, and what ideas do you have about how to solve them?"

- "I think this is a great opportunity for you to build X skill set. How do *you* see this assignment fitting in with your professional goals?"

- "What do you need from me in order to be successful?"

You don't have to accept every suggestion or request, or agree with every idea. But think about what you *can* offer before you say no flat out. For example:

- "I like your ingenuity, but I don't think that will work. Here's why . . ."

- "I don't think we can meet that request, but we could do X for you instead. Would that address your concern?"

For all your diplomacy, your employee might not react well to this conversation. Perhaps they feel overworked or exploited; maybe they're scared about taking on more than they can handle and failing publicly. Watch for nonverbal cues that your employee isn't particularly enthusiastic about the opportunity and gently inquire about their concerns. If they have a clearly negative response, ask questions and listen carefully to their answers. Do they have valid concerns? Are you able to address them? Are their arguments making good sense? Should you consider changing the scope of the work, adding a collaborator, or reassigning the project to someone else? If you realize you need to go back to the drawing board, end the conversation graciously: "Thanks for the honest response. You've raised some important issues, and I need to do more research/review this plan before we move forward. I'll follow up with you soon."

If you can't change the assignment or judge that no change is necessary, let your direct report know you understand their feelings. Then reiterate why this work is so important, why you trust them to do it, and what the payoff will be for them down the line. Above all, tell them that you want them to succeed and will do everything you can to help them. Consider language like:

- "I hear that you're anxious/frustrated/overwhelmed, and I'm sorry about that."

- "I *do* believe that you can do this work, and do it well. I wouldn't be asking you if I didn't have confidence in your abilities."

- "It's going to be a difficult couple weeks. But your contributions will matter a lot, because . . . "

- "I know this is an additional burden. I *also* think that it's a real opportunity for you to build your skills/develop your network/ advance your career/get recognition outside our group."

- "I want you to ace this assignment, and I will give you all the help I can."

- "Thank you for taking this on. I know you're not happy about it, and I'm grateful for the commitment and character you're showing here."

Step 3: Document your agreement

After the meeting, send an e-mail summarizing the assignment, including deliverables, deadlines, benchmarks, collaborators, quality standards, process requirements, and the date of your next check-in. If you've promised to supply any resources or help, include those details, too. If anyone else needs to know about this assignment—your boss, other staff—you can copy them on this e-mail.

Alternatively, you can ask the employee to document their understanding and send it to you. This can be a good test of their understanding.

Provide support

Your responsibilities don't end when you hand off an assignment. Indeed, your biggest challenge as a delegating manager is to ensure that your direct report doesn't fail. Their good performance matters in itself, and it also colors your reputation throughout the company and with the rest of your team. If something goes wrong, you need to help solve the problem before it's too late.

Monitoring progress (without micromanaging)

To set a rhythm for the work with your employee, hold routine progress updates. This means setting a clear timeline for the work, ideally something you did during your planning phase. For small tasks, it's enough to check in once or twice before the final deadline. For longer, more elaborate projects, consider tying these exchanges to a regular event, like a staff meeting or weekly email status update. Ask your direct report to share a few key pieces of information during each update: where they are with the schedule, what milestones they have achieved, what problems they are facing, and if they have any questions.

Use this window to review your employee's progress and to take whatever steps you need to keep things moving. And document whatever advice or directions you share with them in response to their updates.

Many well-intentioned managers take monitoring their employees' progress too far, however. Avoid hovering over your direct report, second-guessing decisions, and initiating unnecessary or prolonged discussions. Don't pepper your employee with suggestions and questions: "Have you tried this? Any update on that? Don't forget the deadline!" This behavior wastes time and communicates a lack of confidence.

Avoid this kind of micromanaging by thinking of your role here as a monitor and a coach. As a monitor, you'll check in regularly to view the project's vital signs, like benchmarks and quality standards. You'll ask questions like, "What task/phase of the project are you doing right now? Are we on schedule? Can you take me through your recent work?" As a coach, you'll debrief periodically with your employee to troubleshoot and lend your support. You'll ask questions like, "What barriers are you facing right now? How might you overcome those barriers, and what resources or help do you need to do so? What do you need from *me* going forward?" You can even role-play difficult discussions or provide active advice on how your employee can engage others effectively.

Monitoring and coaching work well when your employee has the skills and access to solve whatever problems arise with the plan. But when they lack the skills or influence to solve a problem, you may need to take direct action to remove the roadblock.

Coaching your delegate

Once you have these routines in place, you may need to only offer a few light touches to keep the work on track. When a problem arises, however, you may need to become more involved. Initiate a coaching relationship in order to:

- Help your employee assess the situation

- Encourage them to come up with their own solutions

- Confirm your confidence in their ability to make decisions

- Provide positive reinforcement for the work done so far

For step-by-step advice on how to conduct a coaching session, see the section "Coaching and developing employees" in chapter 10.

Remove roadblocks

If an issue comes up that your delegate can't handle alone—if another manager is refusing to share data, for example, or if there's a companywide systems outage—again, you might need to become more involved. Can you modify the project schedule? Offer more resources? Take on a few subtasks yourself, so the work still comes in on time?

Take this responsibility very seriously as you begin to delegate work. Your role is to eliminate roadblocks that prevent productive work by your team. This may require courage if you have to engage with your peers or boss. Don't shy away from this as one of the responsibilities that comes along with delegation.

Avoid reverse delegation

Sometimes your employees delegate to *you*, either by giving up entirely on a task you've given them or bringing so many problems and decisions back to you that you're effectively carrying the weight of the assignment. Reverse delegation is dangerous; you're not seeing the benefits you identified in your delegation plan, and it can create problem-solving fatigue (a common challenge for new managers in particular). Examine your behavior for three common mistakes that enable reverse delegation:

You fail to provide background information about the task.

You have a wider view of the company than your staff does, and if you've been at the company a long time, you might also have a longer institutional memory. So don't assume your employees know how to navigate company politics—that a certain colleague should always be consulted early on, or that another should only be shown polished work, for example. If the assignment cuts across units, give your employee a briefing on who the relevant players are and what organizational objectives are at stake. And if you're delegating an assignment that someone else has done before—leading a strategic review, for example, or planning a yearly meeting—share the previous year's materials or put them in touch with the person who had their role the last time around.

You take over the wheel as soon as something goes wrong.

At some point, every frustrated manager thinks, "It would be easier if I just did this myself." That might be true in the short term, but in the long run, your effectiveness depends on the competence and adaptability of your team members. They need to climb their own learning curve and work through their own mistakes. When you feel your panic or exasperation growing, push yourself to ask your employee questions before you take action: "What do *you* think the problem is? What options do *you* see before us? What course of action would *you* recommend we take?"

You withhold positive reinforcement.

When your neediest employee comes to you with a basic question about an assignment they were supposed to complete a month ago, you may not see much to praise in their behavior. But if you truly do believe they can do the work (and why would you make the assignment if you didn't?), you'll motivate them more successfully with encouragement than with blame. Expressing frustration and disappointment only undermines their confidence and creates an avoidant mindset: "This work makes me feel bad about myself, so I'll do literally anything *except* finish it." Some well-placed constructive feedback might be necessary. But it's equally necessary to express your appreciation of the work they've done so far and your conviction that they can finish it.

When you delegate with confidence, you craft assignments that your employees can complete successfully. By planning the handoff carefully, you set them up for success.

Recap

- Delegation lowers your stress and lets you focus on high-priority, high-impact tasks that *only* you can do. It also gives employees managerial experience and meets a deep human need for continual growth. Finally, it allows you to maximize your company's resources and improves team performance by deepening trust and boosting self-confidence.

- Making a plan is important so that you don't assign a task to a person with the wrong skill set, for example, or miscommunicate what you want them to do.

- When meeting with your direct reports, talk *and* listen; you want to hear that they understand the assignment, and what questions or concerns they may have.

- Your responsibilities don't end with the handoff. Monitor your direct report's progress in a way that corresponds with the magnitude of the project.

- Keep an eye out for reverse delegation, in which the burden of the work stays with (or returns to) you.

- There is a difference between routine check-ins and micromanaging, which wastes time and communicates a lack of confidence.

Action items

Plan your delegation:

- ☐ Determine what assignments are appropriate to delegate by analyzing your own use of time.

- ☐ Clarify the purpose of this assignment to yourself: How will this arrangement benefit you, your employee, and the company?

- ☐ Define the task, project, or function you're handing over. Itemize the subtasks and deliverables associated with the work.

❏ Choose someone for the assignment who has the time, skills, and motivation to do a good job.

❏ Specify a timeline for the work: deadlines and any other time constraints.

Schedule a meeting with your team member and:

❏ Explain what you're asking, following the "why, what, who, when, how" structure of your delegation plan.

❏ Ask for feedback. Incorporate suggestions, and address concerns where you can.

❏ Follow up after the meeting with an email that documents your agreement in as much detail as possible.

Support your team member:

❏ Monitor progress and have routine project updates for a larger-scale delegation.

❏ If your employee is stuck on a particularly difficult problem, set up a coaching session to help them come up with a solution and provide guidance.

❏ When your employees come across a problem they simply can't solve on their own, take direct action to remove the roadblock.

❏ Give your delegate encouragement during the course of the project.

10.

Giving Effective Feedback

Giving your employees feedback is critical to helping them succeed in their jobs. *Positive* feedback reinforces good work. Praise and coaching advice can create genuine bonds between you and your employees. Those moments when you tell your direct report, "You've done a great job! Congratulations," are powerful connections that build trust and respect for you as a leader.

Corrective feedback urges the recipient to change course or adjust practices that aren't working. Managers—even experienced supervisors—often dread these conversations. Nobody likes having to tell a direct report that their work is subpar, or that they need to adjust their attitude. But when handled well, these conversations produce real change in your employees' behaviors, skills, and outcomes. These interactions create value for yourself (a more productive team), for your organization (better outcomes), and for the employee (pride in their resilience and growth).

Whether you are preparing to give a performance review, looking for ways to turbocharge a star's abilities, or simply need to help a struggling employee get back on track, this chapter helps you deliver feedback in a way that your employee can hear, understand, and implement.

Giving feedback in real time

Your organization probably has several defined mechanisms for giving feedback to employees: coaching sessions, annual reviews, performance interventions, and so on. Each serves an important role. But feedback conversations aren't just a hoop to jump through when these formal appointments roll around. Instead, they should be a continuous practice in your everyday work.

The best time to give feedback, whether positive or constructive, is in the moment. Sharing your real-time reaction to an employee's performance or behavior allows you to acknowledge what you appreciate or offer workers the chance to turn their failures into successes right away. It can be stressful to issue corrective feedback, so you may be tempted to hold off until the behavior occurs again. Don't! Whether you're praising your employees or admonishing them, you will communicate most effectively about the situation when it's fresh in your minds.

Contrast these two approaches to the same situation:

> You've noticed that a bottleneck is occurring during a production phase overseen by your direct report Gerhard, who normally prides himself on his efficiency.
>
> Approach 1: Gerhard's been kind of touchy lately, and you're wary of what he'll say if you point out that he's holding up the rest of the team. Plus, you figure Gerhard usually knows what he's doing—he must have a plan, right? You decide it makes the most sense to wait a few days to see if the problem gets worse before you talk to him about it. The next week, two other employees, Britta and Daniela, request a meeting. They explain that because Gerhard missed a key deadline, the entire production schedule is in jeopardy. And the

problem may be too late to fix—you may need to ship the product to your client later than promised. Once Britta and Daniela leave, you know you need to talk to Gerhard. This conversation will be much harder than the one you would have had a few days ago.

Approach 2: *After chatting with Gerhard's teammates Britta and Daniela to understand more fully what is going on, you approach Gerhard. You acknowledge the quality of his prior work and ask what he thinks is happening now. As he describes the issue, you discover that he has mistakenly understood that a new step in the production process requires more recordkeeping than it really does. You clarify the requirements, and Gerhard is delighted to stop doing work that had been both time consuming and frustrating. Within a day, the production schedule is back on track.*

In the first scenario, delaying your feedback caused you to miss a key piece of information and put an important revenue stream in jeopardy. Your choice to avoid providing real-time feedback did both the business and Gerhard a disservice. Gerhard will still feel badly about his performance, and you still need to have a tough (now tougher) conversation with him. In the second scenario, your conversation with Gerhard quickly leads to a valuable change. By intervening early, you get tangible results and also help Gerhard to feel good about his work again. Real-time feedback also positions you to check in later for progress.

By making praise and constructive criticism a routine part of your managerial approach, you create countless new opportunities to track improvements, make adjustments, share resources, and offer support. Here are some scripts to try:

- "This work is excellent. Here's what I like about what you've done . . ."

- "I think you can do even better. Here's what I'm thinking of specifically . . ."

- "Can you help me understand your thought process here?"

- "Can I offer you another way of thinking about this?"

Giving difficult feedback

One of the reasons that we avoid giving corrective feedback in the moment is that it can be unpleasant to deliver criticism. Many managers worry that:

- Criticism will set off a heightened emotional reaction, like anger or crying, or the person will shut down and fail to engage in the conversation.

- The problem they need to address touches too closely on the employee's identity and will challenge this person's sense of self as a competent professional.

- They may have to tell an employee that their paycheck or job security is at stake.

To mitigate these factors, follow these steps:

Step 1: Understand the situation objectively

INSEAD professor Jean-François Manzoni suggests you begin by examining why you need to give feedback in the first place. Too often, he says, we draw strong conclusions about a situation without entertaining alternatives. For example, if we suspect that one person's difficult personality is causing a team conflict, we rarely look into secondary theories, such as whether the employees in question have clashing work styles.

We also tend to see the stakes of our feedback in win-lose terms. Because we have a hardened preconception of what the source of the problem is, we think we know the only solution. And if a feedback interaction ends without the employee accepting that solution, it must be a failure.

Once you're aware of these biases, you can correct for them. Start by analyzing what you actually know about the situation:

- What have you observed firsthand? What biases might be coloring your memory?

- What have other people told you? What are their biases?

- What other cues are you interpreting—tone, body language, a sequence of events? How much weight should you give these interpretations?

- What *don't* you know? What *didn't* you witness? Whose perspective *haven't* you heard?

- What are other possible explanations for the employee's actions and behaviors?

In general, the fewer conclusions you draw from these facts, the better. Instead, identify questions you want to ask your employee.

Step 2: Plan the conversation

Write down your key points before you go into the meeting—questions raised in step 1, or any other information you want to convey, like the behavior that needs to change or the goal of the change. That way you'll know what you want to say as you begin the conversation. These notes can also help you reorient yourself in the middle of the meeting if you get distracted.

Rehearse ahead of time if you can, by yourself or with a colleague. Role-playing can help you see the situation from your direct report's perspective and figure out what approach will work best.

Also let your employee know ahead of time what you'll be discussing, so they don't feel blindsided: "I'd like to speak to you tomorrow about the efficiency of the production process lately."

Step 3: Lead the meeting

When the meeting begins, it's generally best to jump into the negative feedback right away. Sometimes managers try to ease into an unpleasant conversation by asking leading questions ("Are you happy with your performance right now?"), but if your employee doesn't know how to play along, or chooses not to, you'll both feel frustrated. Another common tactic to diffuse the awkwardness is the feedback sandwich: open with praise, move to criticism, close with praise. But if you don't have any genuine accolades to offer, your employee will see this for the trick it is. Instead, start by simply naming the topic you want to discuss: "I'd like to talk about your production output and the bottlenecks that have been coming up."

Talk about the employee's behavior, not motivations.

Often if an employee's productivity slows down, we're more likely to blame them for being lazy than to investigate other factors, like a process change. That's because, according to Manzoni, "most people tend to overestimate the effect of a person's stable characteristics . . . and underestimate the impact of the specific conditions under which that person is operating." But often we're wrong. And even when we're not, analyzing personal traits tends to alienate your employee.

When you give feedback, focus instead on behaviors and skills. Avoid making global statements ("You're X kind of person") or speaking in absolutes ("You always do Y"). Instead, use language like:

> "I'm concerned about this *behavior*."

> "When you *did* this . . ."

> "When you *said* that . . ."

> "As a *result* of your actions . . ."

> "The *impact* of this behavior on your coworkers/the company/ me is . . ."

> "The *outcome* I want to address is . . ."

Elicit the employee's point of view.

The preparation that you did about your biases and your knowledge of the situation allows you to approach your employee with questions instead of an accusation, Manzoni says. "I don't know if you're aware of this—or if it's true or not—but I've heard that we're behind where we want to be with production. What do you think?"

Asking for your employee's take on a problem means you might learn something important—perhaps they are involved in an interpersonal conflict in the office that you weren't aware of, or maybe they're dealing with a technical problem that's more complex than you realized—or, as in Gerhard's case in the example, they may have some misconceptions about what is expected.

Second, by giving the employee the opportunity to explain what's going on, you're communicating that you see them as a person. Your employee probably feels very vulnerable in these moments, and they need to believe that you want to treat them fairly and care about how they perceive the situation.

Consider phrases such as:

> "What's your view on this issue?"

> "How does what I've said track with your experience?"

> "Have I left out anything important?"

> "I hear what you're saying."

> "That's an important perspective."

> "You and I are on the same page here."

> "Thanks for sharing this information with me."

Don't escalate.

If your employee challenges you by contesting your facts or pushing back against your interpretation, take a deep breath before you respond. Too often, managers dig in their heels at these moments because they think their authority is being tested. In fact, you'll gain more personal power by being honest, fair, and emotionally generous in a trying situation. Try to locate specific points of agreement and then also disagreement, and keep asking questions about them:

> "Can you help me understand this point more clearly?"

> "It sounds like you're hearing me say X. I must not be communicating very clearly, because that's not what I want to say to you. My point is Y."

"We're on the same page about *X*, but I think there's a gap in how we're thinking about *Y*. I think that gap is coming from this . . . What do you think?"

Step 4: Look ahead

As with coaching and performance reviews, move the conversation toward an agreement about next steps: "So you'll use the more streamlined approach to the production recordkeeping going forward." If you can't reach an agreement or if the conversation gets too heated, it's OK to press pause: "Let's stop here for now. I think we both need some time to process everything we've talked about. We can meet again in a week." With a little time, you both might calm down enough to reach an accord or it can give you time to solicit others' input.

Coaching and developing employees

Coaching is a proactive dialogue between you and your team members intended to foster high performance and long-term development. Coaching is less transactional than feedback, which tends to focus on specific situations and outcomes. Ed Batista, an executive coach and instructor at the Stanford Graduate School of Business, argues that coaching as a practice is broadly applicable and that managers at all levels can benefit from working with their direct reports in this way.

Batista describes coaching as the practice of "asking questions that help people discover the answers that are right for them." Asking questions instead of offering solutions pushes your employees to develop critical thinking skills and the confidence to act on their own. It also puts the onus on them to solve problems and own the results. Ultimately, your aim is to help employees become more adaptive and self-sufficient.

Coaching requires time, effort, and an emotional openness from *both* participants; it's a true partnership. You can compel a direct report to attend a meeting about their performance, but you can't make them think critically about their work, try new techniques, or persevere through failure. Employees who aren't willing to do these things aren't good candidates for coaching. But when you and your employee approach this relationship with enthusiasm and mutual respect, it's one of the powerful strategies you have for developing talent.

When to coach

Most managers approach coaching as a semiformal arrangement, with regular meetings and discussions, sometimes involving goals, action items and follow-ups. That said, you can use coaching strategies in your daily interactions—when a direct report hails you in the hallway with a problem, for example. To determine if you're in a situation where coaching is likely to work, look for these cues:

- Your employee genuinely wants to improve their performance.

- They're frustrated or bored because they're not working from their strengths.

- They're professionally stymied by personal obstacles, like a fear of public speaking.

- They've formulated specific professional goals and need help reaching them.

- They're good at their job, but don't know how to manage themselves.

If you think coaching could help a member of your team, talk to them about what you'd like to do. Now is the time to explain how it will work: "I'd like to work with you as a coach to help you address X problem/work on X behaviors/develop X competency. If you agree, we'll meet periodically to do goal setting and problem solving together around this issue. My role here would be to support your growth, not to give you tactical direction. Think of it as a dedicated half hour when I can serve as a sounding board and a resource. Is this something you could commit to?" If your employee agrees, schedule your first coaching session.

How to hold a coaching session

Coaching sessions are a special kind of conversation, says executive coach Amy Jen Su. Compared with a performance review or a one-on-one meeting, they take the broadest view, looking at past performance, current projects, and future development.

Step 1: Prepare for the meeting.

Coaching sessions require forethought and planning on your part or else your direct report won't put in the work either. Identify specific performance issues you'd like to address, skill gaps you'd like to fill, or a new role you're preparing your employee for. How are *your* aims likely to tie in with theirs?

Step 2: Begin by inviting your employees to take the lead.

Your employee brings their own agenda to the table, so ask them about it. "What do *you* want to achieve during these sessions?" "What do you want to make sure we get to?" The kind of help you offer will depend on the needs they express, so listen for these three categories:

- **Long-term development.** They want to build new skills or work toward major career goals.

- **Debriefing an event or project.** They want to learn from recent experience and come up with strategies for handling similar situations in the future.

- **Short-term problem solving.** They have an imminent issue and need an action plan right now.

As you listen, look for links between their goals and yours. What connection exists between their long-term career strategy and the performance issue you want to fix? How can you address a skill gap during a problem-solving session? By finding commonalities, you can shape the purpose of these sessions in concert with your employee.

Step 3: Build a shared understanding of the issues.

At this stage, build a shared narrative with your employees about what is and isn't working in their current situation. "Your employee very likely still knows more about it than you do," says Jen Su, and certainly they know more about their point of view. Bring all of that information out into the open by asking questions, such as:

- Long-term development

  "What's your comfort level in this area? How do you *want* to feel about it?"

  "How have you performed in the past? What should success look like?"

  "How do you prepare for this now? How could you prepare differently?"

- Debrief on an event or project

  "How did things go? In an ideal world, what would have happened?"

  "How would you describe your impact? What worked well? What didn't?"

  "How would you prepare or handle this differently for this next time?"

- Short-term problem solving

  "Tell me more about the situation, your tasks and deadlines."

  "Which of these are tied to our group's highest priorities?

  "What courses of action are available to you? How feasible are they?"

Use active listening techniques and ask open-ended questions. Keep a lid on your reactions, if you can; your employee will feel safer sharing their vulnerabilities if you maintain a neutral, sympathetic demeanor, and let them talk without interruption.

Step 4: Reframe the issue.

Once your employee has laid out their point of view, it's time to start working on solutions and next steps together. Instead of offering advice ("Try X. Here's how I do it . . . "), help them think more critically about the assumptions and choices that are already driving their behavior. You can do this by helping them see themes in what they've said, and by offering competing lenses through which they can see the issue at hand. Consider language like:

"You seem worried about . . ." or "It sounds like your main concern is . . ."

"I notice you've used this same phrase a couple times in this conversation. Why is that important to you?"

"I see a pattern in how you deal with ___ issue. What's going on there?"

"It sounds to me like your current outlook emphasizes X, but doesn't allow much room for Y. How could that be holding you back?"

"Have you seen someone else be successful with this issue in the past? How did they approach it?"

"What if you looked at it from this angle/tried this tactic? How would that play out?"

Step 5: Close with an action plan.

End with a clear action plan for your employees, something that will help them make meaningful progress and hold them accountable going forward. Ask them to articulate their main takeaways orally, or write up their to-do list in an email after the session. Your role in this stage is to ensure that the goals are realistic, help them prioritize tasks, highlight obstacles and brainstorm solutions, and provide additional support as needed.

Step 6: Follow up.

After the session ends, check up on your direct reports to make sure that they continue to improve. Schedule more coaching sessions, if they're needed. And touch base casually to learn what's working and what isn't, modify the action plan, secure additional resources, and give feedback—whether to praise or to improve. Even if you are pressed for time, still put these check-ins on your calendar. A one-line email or quick word of encouragement can go a long way toward sustaining your employees' motivation as they grow.

Performance reviews

While coaching requires more planning than a casual, one-off feedback conversation, performance reviews generally occur annually. As with coaching sessions, you'll use them to discuss goals, provide feedback, and correct performance problems. Unlike coaching, these appraisals directly affect salary decisions and promotions. That can make them time consuming and stressful for manager and employee alike.

If approached with the right frame of mind, they're well worth the effort. You don't often have the chance to sit down with your people, face to face, and say: "Here's where you stand." "This is what I need from you." "Thank you for your outstanding work." During these meetings, you can address all the critical issues that get lost in the daily grind.

Your formal feedback will give your direct report the opportunity for growth. Moreover, a yearly review offers them some protection when they're struggling with performance issues. If you address their problems head on in regular, formal meetings, they won't be blindsided by bad news when it's too late to do anything about it.

Performance reviews are also valuable to your organization. The information you collect and codify will help the company make valid decisions about pay and developing talent. And when it comes to difficult employees, performance reviews protect your organization again lawsuits by employees who have been fired, demoted, or denied a merit increase.

There's no one right way to conduct a performance review: every organization has its procedures, and each situation presents a different set of challenges. Here is a set of general steps:

Step 1: Prepare your employee

It's important to involve your employees in every stage of the process, so that their point of view is incorporated. Start by asking them to complete a self-appraisal. In many companies, HR provides a checklist for this purpose, with the goals, behaviors, and functions associated with each employee's role. If you're making your own list, include questions like:

- How well do you feel you've achieved your professional goals?

- What accomplishments are you proudest of? What contributed to your success?

- Which goals are you currently struggling with? What's holding back your progress?

Whether you're using a template from HR or making your own, make sure that the performance goals you reference are items that you've already shared with the employee at their last review or when they were hired. You can use this list to prepare your own appraisal, too. Look through the notes you've collected about each person's performance—projects they've worked on, feedback you've given them, any complaints or commendations from their colleagues. If possible, solicit feedback from others in the company who have worked with your direct report.

Dick Grote, who has created performance management systems for hundreds of the world's biggest organizations, recommends giving your employees a copy of your appraisal an hour or so before your review meeting starts. "When people read someone's assessment of them, they are going to have all sorts of churning emotions," he notes. "Let them have that on their own time, and give them a chance to think about it."

Step 2: Open with a tone of partnership

Your employee may have an emotional response to reading your review, so as your meeting begins, do what you can to put them at ease as you settle in; don't let them feel as if they're in the prisoner's dock, about to receive judgment. Next, invite your employee to share their self-appraisal: "I'd like to start by asking you to talk a little about how you feel you're doing." Listen carefully and don't interrupt. This phase of a performance review, like a coaching session, will help you understand your direct report's point of view and tailor your remarks later in the conversation.

Step 3: Share your appraisal

Traditionally, performance reviews are treated as a place to focus on what's *not* working with a direct report. But exclusively or dominantly focusing on the negative can be hugely discouraging. Be clear in highlighting the strengths you appreciate about employees. If they highlighted the same area of strength in their self-assessment, reinforce their perception. If they didn't, share why you value a particular talent or skill.

Carefully choose the areas of development that are most important to discuss in the performance review. Use a conversational tone to review the expectation, the gap, and the opportunity to demonstrate improvement. As with all corrective feedback, don't be vague ("You're not a team player") or make it about your feelings ("I'm so disappointed"). Instead, talk about specific behaviors: "When you do X, it is causing a problem for the team" or "You're not meeting Y performance target." Being clear and succinct in these moments is actually the most respectful thing you can do: you're treating your employee like a mature adult and giving them the information they need to do better.

Step 4: Probe for the root cause of performance gaps

Once you've given positive or corrective feedback, encourage your employee to reflect their perceptions. Pay close attention to how they respond by:

- **Listening actively.** Concentrate on your employees' message and its implications rather than on your response. In particular, listen to the elements of the critique that they've honed in on, and pay attention to the images and metaphors they use. If you don't understand something, ask.

- **Noticing nonverbal cues.** Observe your employee's body language and tone. Do their voice and facial expressions match what they're saying? Comment on what you see and ask them to tell you more about it: "Bill, you seem angry. Did something I say seem unfair to you? Tell me about it."

- **Paraphrasing what your employee says.** By restating a response in different words, you show them that you understand their point. If anything is unclear, ask more questions until you are on the same page.

Step 5: Create a new performance plan

Give your employee the first opportunity to develop a plan to close any gaps between their current and required performance: "What would you propose?" They'll be more committed to a solution they've authored and more explicitly responsible for carrying it out. As with coaching, you can challenge questionable assumptions or offer ideas to strengthen the plan. In some cases, you'll need to be very directive. For staff with major performance gaps, the product of this conversation will be part of their record and should include:

- Specific goals

- A timeline

- Action steps

- Expected outcomes

- Required trainings or resources

You don't need to limit this conversation to strengths and problem areas. Since an entire year may have passed since their last performance review, take this opportunity to reexamine their overall performance goals, too. Do they still make sense—for the individual team member, for your unit, and for the organization as a whole?

Step 6: Get it on the record

Document whatever agreements you make and include:

- The date

- Key points from your employee's self-appraisal

- Key points from your appraisal

- A summary of the performance plan

- Agreed-on next steps

- Performance goals for the coming year

Your company will likely require you to provide copies of this record (as well as the review itself) to your direct report and HR. Keep a version in your own files, too. In most cases, you and your employee will both have to sign the review, and your employee has a legal right to append their own comments.

Step 7: Follow up

After your annual performance review discussions, make note of the follow-up that's required with each of your team members. For high performers, it might include coaching discussions to prepare them for new responsibilities. Employees who are struggling should be monitored carefully around the performance plan you jointly developed. Consider these options for your follow-up:

- Planning monthly or quarterly meetings to check progress

- Checking in virtually on a more frequent basis—for example, with weekly email updates or a digital performance log

- Initiating a coaching relationship

- Helping them connect with a mentor

- Auditing their needs for more resources or training

Giving feedback during a performance review is more formal and therefore requires steps, like more elaborate documentation and preparation. But in delivering your review, the same principles apply as in the informal feedback you supply more frequently: listen actively and maintain a tone of partnership.

———————

Both corrective and positive feedback, given well, can solve imminent problems and also help your employees grow in their careers. By giving feedback in a way that your employees can hear and act on, you'll build their trust in you as a guide and advocate, and provide value for your organization as well.

Recap

- Giving your team members feedback is critical to helping them succeed in their jobs.

- *Positive* feedback reinforces good work. *Corrective* feedback urges the recipient to change course or adjust practices that aren't working.

- Sharing feedback in real time gives you and your employee the best chance to resolve the issue in question.

- Following a process in which you ask questions and have an open view of the outcome of your feedback will make it more effective and easier for your colleague to hear.

- *Coaching* is a proactive dialogue between you and your team members intended to foster high performance and long-term development.

- Though coaching is not just for your stars, not all situations are right for coaching.

- Similar principles hold for delivering performance reviews as for other forms of feedback, though performance reviews also call for more-formal documentation.

Action items

When giving feedback:

- ❏ Seek an objective understanding of the situation you want to address by examining your own biases and assumptions.

- ❏ Plan what you want to say in the conversation and rehearse with a colleague if you can. Let your employees know ahead of time what the topic of your meeting is, so they don't feel blindsided.

- ❏ During the meeting, talk about behaviors, rather than motivations.

- ❏ Elicit your employee's perspective on the issue and resist the urge to escalate the interaction if you feel challenged; ask more questions.

- ❏ Close the meeting by looking ahead: What agreement can you make about next steps and future expectations?

When coaching:

- ❏ Check the list of cues given earlier to determine if the situation you are facing now is right for coaching.

- ❏ Prepare for a coaching session by thinking through your own goals for the coaching relationship.

- ❏ Open the meeting by asking your employee to take the lead. Listen to what's currently on *their* mind, and look for links between their goals and yours. Use that common ground to define a shared goal for your partnership.

- ❏ Build a shared understanding of the issue you're working on by asking open-ended questions. Resist the urge to correct or override the employee's point of view.

❏ Reframe the issue by helping them see themes in what they've told you and offering new lenses on the problem.

❏ Close with a concrete action plan for what they'll do next. Let them take the lead here, but offer advice about what's realistic.

❏ Follow up afterward with a formal coaching session or in casual conversation.

When conducting a performance review:

❏ Ask your employee to conduct a self-appraisal. Use this, along with other records of performance, to create your own comprehensive review of their work.

❏ Open the meeting with a tone of partnership by asking your employee to share a self-appraisal. Maintain a professional, friendly tone throughout.

❏ Next, go over your assessment of their performance. Balance positive and constructive feedback, described in straightforward language.

❏ Probe for the root cause of a performance gap by asking for their perspective on a problem. Continue to discuss until you both understand the underlying cause.

❏ Invite your employee to take the lead in creating a new performance plan with specific goals and a timeline. Get plans on record and distribute appropriately.

❏ Identify your own follow-up items, including regular check-ins, coaching sessions, or other support as needed.

11.

Developing Talent

The world is constantly changing, and your organization along with it. Your team—the company's human capital—drives that change and shapes your company's future. Your role as a manager is to develop talent that meets the needs of your business. It is fundamentally future-oriented, ensuring you can deliver exceptional performance both today and tomorrow. Whereas feedback aims to improve performance now, talent development expands your employees' capacities for the future.

The best managers know how to balance the needs of the organization with the interests of its employees. As you work with your employees to identify new skills, new experiences, and new responsibilities of interest, you're helping them find work that's fulfilling. As their manager, you must also look for the resonances between their desires and your company's needs. In this chapter, you'll learn about the benefits of employee development, as well as how to spot those opportunities and help your employees take advantage of them.

Employee development as a priority

One of the most important and rewarding responsibilities you have as a manager is to develop the capabilities of your direct reports. That means helping them:

- Discover their passion and purpose

- Identify their work values

- Understand the organization's priorities and politics

- Improve their skills

- Expand their competencies

- Challenge themselves with new experiences

- Acquire mentors and build their professional network

- Discover how to manage others

You've already thought about how to do many of these things for yourself and sought to negotiate opportunities for growth with your own boss (see chapter 8, "Self-Development"). You asked yourself, "How does my work fit into the vision I have for my life and my career purpose?" Now you're looking at the issue through the eyes of your employees and your motivation is a little different: you want to help others grow and align to their greater purpose, but with a focus on how that growth will intersect with the business goals of your unit.

The company benefits greatly from your investments in talent development. Many managers assume that the personal happiness of their employees conflicts with the needs of the business, and that they must choose between the two. But that's a mistake. Employee development is one of your core responsibilities for a reason: It directly serves your business's interests. By encouraging your direct reports to think strategically about their career and helping them become more capable and content, you're creating tangible value for your organization.

Developing your employees also benefits you. If you can improve your team's performance and move promising players to the next level, you'll enhance your reputation with upper-level management. What's more, your staff's expanding networks can enrich your own professional connections. New experiences bring them into contact with people you might be glad to know. And you'll refresh your existing network, too, as they develop new relationships with *your* old colleagues, like other managers in your company. It is incredibly rewarding to invest time and energy to develop the talents of others in the organization.

Of course, your employees are the most obvious beneficiaries here. The payoff is clear with star performers, who will rise to higher and higher levels of responsibility with your help. But it's just as important to spend time with all of your employees. Even people with more modest professional goals will perform better in their current role if they feel that you respect and support their growth. Nearly all employees have a basic human need to keep learning. Frederick Herzberg, a psychologist who studied employees' motivation, argued that money is a less powerful motivator than opportunities to learn, advance in their responsibilities, and be recognized for their achievements. Employee development doesn't need to be about facilitating your employees' meteoric rise to the top; it's more about helping them achieve this fundamental satisfaction in their everyday work and reach their highest potential, whatever that might be.

Creating career strategies with your staff

Effective managers help employees discover what they *really* want out of their work and how they can use their present situation as a springboard to reach those goals. That means talking to your direct reports about their hopes and dreams, but also engaging in some practical brainstorming about where they can find opportunities for growth in your organization and how their present role could be reengineered for the better.

In the past, when many companies had more defined career paths for advancement, this conversation would have gone a little differently. Most companies had a career ladder of some form, a logical series of stages that moved a talented and promotable employee through progressively more challenging and responsible positions. Managers propelled their employees to the next rung when the manager and HR colleagues judged them ready. The path for growth was mostly unidirectional: up, in whatever stream of the business they'd already landed in.

Today, the map for each employee's development is more complicated. You can move up, but also *over* through a lateral career move—for example, from customer service representative to user-experience (UX) researcher. And because many companies have adopted flexible organizational structures, employees can also grow in the same position by reinventing their responsibilities.

All this means that career advancement requires more initiative and more imagination than ever before, from employee and manager alike. That's great, because it gives you and your employee the opportunity to craft a strategy that's responsive to the company and the individual's needs, something you couldn't do when organizational structures were more rigid.

Take the example of the customer service rep who wants to transition to UX. That's a difficult jump to make if each business division has a strictly regimented pecking order ("UX researchers must have at least three years' experience as a UX research assistant"). But if you and your counterpart in the other unit can work together to bring a bright rep over to UX quarter-time, both departments will benefit tremendously. The UX team can use their direct line into customer service to identify design problems, and customer service can use the employee's new expertise to improve internal tools, from rewriting agendas to customizing software settings, as well as customer-facing scripts and services. Similar opportunities to this one abound.

Step 1: Talk to your direct reports

Start with your employees. To support their growth, you need to understand their aspirations and their current state of development. The more you know about the people who work for you, the more you'll be able to motivate them, coach them, and help them grow. The coaching sessions,

Employee development interview

To help your direct reports create and implement a career strategy, sit down with them to learn how they see their current situation and future path. This is an intimate conversation, so prepare them ahead by letting them know what you'd like to discuss, and share any questions you'd like them to give special thought to. Use these questions from psychiatrist Edward Hallowell, who has studied the brain science of high performance:

INTERESTS AND SKILLS

Learn about what kind of work they enjoy and what direction they'd like to keep growing in by asking the following questions:

- "What are you best at doing? What do you most like to do?"

- "What do you wish you were better at? What talents do you have that you haven't developed?"

- "What skills are you most proud of? What do others say are your greatest strengths? What have you gotten better at?"

- "What are you just not getting better at, no matter how hard you try? What do you most dislike doing? The lack of which skills most gets in your way?"

- "Can you think of ways to incorporate more of what you do best and what you most enjoy into your job?"

- "Can you think of ways to build on your strengths and accomplishments to date in your current role?"

- "Everyone has weaknesses and dislikes. How do you think you can continue to compensate for yours? How would your work have to evolve to accommodate them?"

ORGANIZATIONAL FIT

Understand what kind of environment they need to thrive by asking:

- "What sorts of people do you work best and worst with? Do you hate to work with highly organized, analytic people, or do you love it? Do creative types drive you crazy, or do you work well with them?"

- "What sort of organizational culture brings out the best in you? What tweaks would make this organization a better fit? What aspects trouble you the most?"

WORK VALUES

Find out what they think a good career looks like by asking:

- "What was the most important work-related lesson you learned from your parents?"

- "What lesson did the best boss you ever had teach you about yourself?"

- "What one lesson about managing a career would you pass along to the next generation? How would you apply that lesson to yourself right now?"

- "What are you most proud of in your work life? What regrets do you have about how you have run your career? Could you make any changes based on those regrets?"

performance reviews, and feedback meetings discussed in chapter 10, "Giving Effective Feedback," provide many opportunities to gain this understanding. If you haven't yet discussed these bigger-picture issues with them yet, look at the box "Employee development interview" for possible scripts.

Step 2: Suggest training opportunities

Close out the conversation by suggesting a few next steps for them:

- "In an ideal world, what would your work-life balance look like? Looking forward over the next six months, one year, and five years, how do you see yourself achieving that balance?"

- "What were you doing when you were happiest in your work life? How could you incorporate that into what you're doing now?"

VISION OF THE FUTURE

Discover what ambitions they already have for their development by asking:

- "What are your most cherished hopes for the future, workwise? What stands in the way of realizing those hopes?"

- "What are your short-term and long-term professional goals?"

- "Do you have other, big-picture personal development goals that dovetail with your professional ambitions? How do these personal and professional goals relate to each other?"

- "How could we better structure your current role to add value to the organization? Are there other opportunities in the company you'd like to explore?"

Source: Adapted from Edward Hallowell, *Shine: Using Brain Science to Get the Best from Your People*. Boston: Harvard Business Review Press, 2011.

- **Meet with HR** about formal skill trainings, a mentorship program, or other opportunities for growth. Can you connect them to someone you already have a relationship with?

- **Find informal training opportunities.** Encourage them to search for online courses, local conferences or seminars, or books that could help them develop specific skills.

- **Schedule informational interviews** with other people in the company. Can you introduce them to any colleagues who might be able to act as a mentor or offer a learning opportunity, like a temporary or part-time assignment?

- **Pitch you on a job redesign** that would solve a specific problem for your unit or improve its performance, while creating new growth opportunities for them. Can you identify your top problems for them, or share other information about the organizational priorities that are driving your business strategy right now?

Step 3: Refresh responsibilities

While your employees are following up on your initial discussion, there are a few things you can do to make their current role align better with the trajectory they're charting:

- Redefine their job so that they do more work they'll enjoy and learn from.

- Find a mentor for them within your team who can teach them the skills they want to know.

- Delegate stretch assignments that will help them grow, or expose them to different parts of the company.

- Make them the point person on your team for dealing with another business unit that's relevant to their interests.

- Negotiate temporary or part-time assignments for them with colleagues in other units.

- Involve them in your silo-busting efforts (see chapter 5, "Becoming a Person of Influence") to coordinate with other parts of the organization.

Some of these options will require your employees to spend time away from your team, working in other parts of the company with other managers. Don't look at this as losing their time. A well-conceived assignment will benefit your group, too. If, down the line, you do end up grooming a particular employee for a promotion within your unit, the experience in a different area will serve them well. And if they ultimately choose to move into another role outside the team, you'll benefit from having a colleague who understands and values what your staff does.

Developing high-potential talent

High performers, who typically make up about 5 to 10 percent of your team, have unique needs. These employees exhibit strong performance and show great potential to do even more for the organization. This group requires a commitment from you to develop and promote their talent in the organization.

To identify your high performers, look for the team members who:

- Exceed your standards on multiple measures

- Act on constructive feedback in order to improve performance

- Show potential to perform at a higher level within the next year or two

- Make key contributions to the team

- Work hard under pressure and pick up slack from others

- Act as a positive role model for others

High performers typically place a high value on their own development and see it as a sign that your company is a good place to build a career. When you meet star employees for development interviews, start by offering specific, detailed praise about their work; they may not know how good it is or what kinds of effort are most valuable to you and the rest of the team.

Come prepared to talk about specific opportunities you think they might benefit from, for example, skill training through HR or a temporary assignment with another team. (Your preparation for this meeting might include touching base with your own boss to talk about how employees' development could meet larger needs in the unit, or coincide with your own plans for advancement.) Then follow up within the company in a timely way to make sure that these resources and opportunities come through. Even if everything doesn't pan out, you want to be able to tell high achievers that you're doing everything you can for them. Your advocacy as their boss is important to them.

In addition to promoting your direct reports' career goals, you should also make sure you—and they—understand the cost of what it takes them to achieve those great results. If their work habits aren't sustainable, they risk burning out and maybe quitting your organization altogether. So check in frequently to make sure work isn't disrupting important life functions like health, family, and leisure. Ultimately your employees' work-life balance is up to them: if they choose to forgo their hobbies and their kids' sports games in the name of work, you can't stop them. But you can make sure that you're communicating clear expectations and empowering them to work well. Make a habit of asking, "How can I continue to support you?" and "What can we do as an organization to get better at supporting your great work?"

High performers put themselves under a lot of pressure, but there are a few things you can do to help them grow in a healthy way:

Set boundaries with compassion.

When your employee interrupts you in front of your boss to show off their expertise, you might feel angry. But expressing these negative feelings to a star player may cause a backlash. Instead of saying "That was out of line!" wait until your feelings have calmed and then try a compassionate question that pushes them to reflect on their own motives:

"Your interjection earlier surprised me. What were you hoping to accomplish there? What do you think the effect was?"

They'll probably say something like, "I wanted to make a point I thought you were missing."

Don't argue. Instead, probe their response gently: "I thought I had explained to you my plan for how to approach this meeting. What made you think I wasn't going to carry it off?" Then state your expectations clearly: "Here's how I'd like to handle that next time." Help them stay true to their motivation to present themselves in the best possible light and encourage them to do so without stepping on or around anyone else.

Praise personally, praise often.

High performers often second-guess praise, even when they need it badly. So it's important to make your accolades as specific as you can, tailored to their own self-perceptions. For example, if they pride themselves on being a good writer, don't tell them the graphics in the presentation were top-notch. Instead, point to writing details: "Your phrasing on the closing slide was very powerful. We should consider incorporating that language into our team's vocabulary." Keep your comments authentic by avoiding exaggeration or clichés.

You may find the constant pressure to produce praise exhausting. That's only natural; it *is* exhausting. But remember that however unimportant these compliments seem to you, they're fulfilling a genuinely vital psychological need in your employees. You can help them by digging deep in yourself to share the real gratitude and admiration you feel for their exceptional performance.

Stretch assignments

Stretch assignments give employees an opportunity to assume new responsibilities that will challenge current competencies and provide an opportunity for growth. This might be a temporary or part-time assignment covering for a coworker on leave or running a short-term project. Or perhaps you're delegating an important leadership function, like acting as a liaison with another department. The ultimate stretch assignment, of course, is a full-time promotion to another role in your unit or elsewhere in the company.

Whatever the particulars, these assignments are a calculated risk on everyone's part: the company, your employee, and you. If your employee succeeds, the company benefits from their talent, and they get an impressive new responsibility. You get the satisfaction of seeing your direct report shine, a reputational refraction of their success, and (depending on the assignment) the use of their talents in a brand-new way. If they fail, though, everyone feels the downside. Your company might incur losses in productivity or profit; your employee, deeply demoralized, may take a big step back in their career path; and you must manage the fallout to your unit *and* your good name.

All this means that you'd better choose carefully, says Claudio Fernández-Aráoz, a senior adviser at the global executive search firm Egon Zehnder. Whether you're recommending your employee for a position elsewhere in the company or reassigning them on your own team, there are a few questions you should ask yourself:

Do they really have what it takes?

Their intelligence, creativity, and work ethic are probably well known to you. But other intangibles, more difficult to evaluate, matter just as much. Are they motivated by a desire to help others succeed or chiefly by a selfish ambition? Do they have the right leadership assets—resilience, sociability, and the willingness to learn? Are they really prepared to accept the personal costs of a more strenuous position?

Is it the right opportunity?

Fernández-Aráoz argues that "the sweet spot of development for high achievers is when you have a 50–70% chance of success." You're looking for an assignment that the employee has a real shot of completing, but where they will genuinely have to fight for their success. As you evaluate the match, don't limit yourself to considerations of skill and experience. What about the cultural fit? Will your direct report have any social capital to draw on in this posting? Review, too, the consequences for your company (and yourself) if this assignment doesn't pan out. How much damage could a failure inflict? Would you be able to recover?

Can you make it happen?

Securing a stretch assignment can be difficult, especially if you need to get senior management or executive approval. Start by choosing the right sponsor—someone with the right mix of power and credibility who can cosign your recommendation. When you make the pitch, don't overjustify the candidate's background. Instead, focus on the core competencies that you think make them a good fit for the role. Be prepared to speak in detail about your own experience managing them and present the risks honestly, so that nothing comes out later to make a liar of you. Finally, have a plan for how your unit will accommodate this change. Who will perform your employee's current responsibilities? If the assignment will split their time, how will you help them manage their time?

Over the course of your career, some of these assignments will backfire. As long as everyone is prepared for that possibility and understands the risks, that's OK.

————————

Developing talent is incredibly rewarding for managers. It isn't easy to find the time required to do this well. But you need to make time. The work you put into the manager-employee relationship, from delegating assignments to giving effective feedback and coaching, all positions you for success with the longer-term responsibility of talent development. Your company is counting on you to ensure the future needs of the business will be met. When you're pressed for time and you feel as if your own performance is under a microscope, you may shy away from making the necessary investments in your people's development. Challenge yourself here and not only will your employees benefit, you and your organization will, too.

In part four, "Managing Teams," you'll learn how to channel these individual abilities into a coherent and creative team.

Recap

- One of the most important and rewarding responsibilities you have as a manager is to develop the capabilities of your direct reports.

- Your organization also benefits greatly from your investments in talent development. Help others grow with a focus on how that growth will intersect with the business goals of your unit.

- Today's world of lateral career moves means you and your employees can be creative about crafting career strategies that are responsive to their—and the company's—needs.

- High performers, who typically make up 5 to 10 percent of your team, place a high value on their own development and therefore have a unique set of development needs and risks.

- Stretch assignments are a calculated risk on everyone's part—the company, your employees—and you. But they will also give your employees new responsibilities and the opportunity for growth.

Action items

- ☐ Consider all of the actions you've taken in the past year to further employee development on your team—coaching, stretch assignments, and so on. Which of these activities are paying off right now? What more can you do?

To create a career strategy with one of your direct reports:

- ☐ Talk to your direct report about their interests and skills, organizational fit, work values, and their vision of the future; conduct an Employee Development Interview (see questionnaire in the box given earlier).

- ☐ Based on their response, suggest training opportunities for them. Urge them to meet with HR, conduct informational interviews in the company, or pitch you on a job redesign.

- ☐ Refresh their responsibilities so that their day-to-day work is better aligned with their larger aspirations.

To develop high-potential talent:

- ❏ Scope out the prospects for a high-potential employee's development in your company by talking to your boss and to other colleagues in the organization. What opportunities are available for someone with their talents?

- ❏ Talk to your high performers regularly about their stress levels and work-life balance: "This week has been very busy for you, and your performance at Thursday's meeting was fantastic. How are you feeling after all that? What do you need to recharge your batteries?"

- ❏ Recognize and embrace the need to validate high-potential talent on a regular basis. High achievers will respond favorably to recognition of their efforts.

To create stretch assignments:

- ❏ To evaluate an employee for a stretch assignment, ask yourself: Do they have what it takes? Is it the right opportunity? Can I secure it for them?

- ❏ Choose a sponsor to cosign your recommendation and prepare a pitch about why this person can succeed in the role, what your experience with them has been, and what risks the company assumes if the sponsor approves the assignment.

- ❏ Provide as much support as necessary to ensure the employee can shine in their stretch assignment. Check in regularly and support their success.

PART FOUR

Managing Teams

12.

Leading Teams

Leading a team means managing multiple people who come together to achieve a shared goal. Whether your team is project-focused, functional, or cross-functional, you face a common set of opportunities and challenges that come with bringing together unique individuals in the workplace. You're uniting people with fundamentally different points of view, distinct skill sets, and varying backgrounds and requiring them to work together closely.

These differences, of course, are exactly why teams have the potential to achieve impressive outcomes. When you assemble a group of people who think differently, you put ideas into competition with each other. You look at problems from multiple angles and find solutions together that no single person could have come up with. You build productive relationships with stakeholders who have different viewpoints, expertise, and needs. And you motivate all team members to bring their best, because they know their expertise counts and their individuality is valued.

Your job is to make sure all members of your team contribute to their full potential, making the team as highly effective as possible. In this chapter, you'll learn how to put together a well-balanced team that can execute its mission, whether they're collaborating across cultures, virtually, or in the face of conflict.

Team culture and dynamics

As the group's leader, your goals here are twofold. First, you must make sure that your team captures the right mix of competencies required to achieve its objectives, without duplication or gaps. Second, you must create a work environment that allows people to contribute fully, so that they can bring their unique abilities and viewpoints to bear on the work itself. The result: a supportive, collaborative team culture, where diverse individuals can interact productively in pursuit of the group's shared purpose.

If you're working with an established team, use the team audit in exhibit 12-1 to learn as much as you can about how the team currently functions, its strengths and weaknesses, and where you may need to focus your efforts.

Whether you are starting a new team from scratch or assessing the needs of a group you've inherited, here's what you can do to build a strong, supportive team culture:

Step 1: Assemble your team

Begin by evaluating the diversity of your team's composition relative to the competencies you need. Learn as much as possible about team members, including their training and skills, professional background, work style, motivations and goals, and life experience. This allows you to plan for how to maximize each individual's contributions.

Use the information you've gathered to evaluate whether your team has the right balance of competencies. Use exhibit 12-2 as a starting point.

If you're creating a new team, use these insights to find people who can carry out these tasks; if you have inherited an existing team, you may need to present a proposal to your boss to get approval to add members. As you look for the right individuals, ask for referrals and recommendations

EXHIBIT 12-1

Prompt: Team audit

Use this audit to gather information from each team member about the current strengths and weaknesses of your team's culture. Ask each person to complete the audit privately and then compile anonymized responses into a group profile and share with the group. During a meeting, ask the team to discuss the results and come up with priorities for future growth.

Cultural dimension	Rating: 1 = ineffective; 5 = very effective					Comment/ Example
	1	2	3	4	5	
Achieving our goals and purpose						
Improving our work processes						
Feeling a sense of team identity						
Making decisions						
Communicating						
Resolving conflicts						
Participating in the team						
Generating creative ideas and solutions						
Combating groupthink						
Ensuring effective team leadership						

The biggest challenge we face as a team is:	
Our greatest strength as a team is:	
The one thing I would most like to see the team do is:	

Source: Mary Shapiro, *HBR Guide to Leading Teams (ebook + Tools)*. Boston: Harvard Business Review Press, 2015.

from your colleagues, your network, your management team, and subject-matter experts. Seek out other people who have run teams like this in your company, or outside it, and touch base with your HR career office. If you already have a few key, founding members of the team, involve them in this process, too.

EXHIBIT 12-2

Making the most of diversity

To complete the tasks at hand, you need members who bring:	To get everyone working well together, enlist members who excel at:
• Relevant functional expertise (for example, in engineering, accounting, marketing, finance, or customer service) • Relevant industry knowledge (for example, in manufacturing, technology, health care, or financial services) • Relevant professional networks (for example, relationships with clients, partners, or vendors) • Relevant task experience (for example, project management, event planning, client services) • Technological skill • An appetite for research • The ability to mine and analyze data • A knack for writing and presenting	• Facilitating meetings • Building consensus • Giving feedback • Communicating in groups • Resolving conflicts • Negotiating • Motivating others • Exercising emotional intelligence • Influencing others—and accepting influence in turn • Networking with people outside the team who can provide resources

Source: Adapted from Mary Shapiro, *HBR Guide to Leading Teams (ebook + Tools)*. Boston: Harvard Business Review Press, 2015.

Step 2: Hone your sense of purpose

"The essence of a team is common commitment," say Jon Katzenbach and Douglas Smith, organizational consultants formerly with McKinsey & Company. "Without [a common commitment], groups perform as individuals; with it, they become a powerful unit of collective performance. This kind of commitment requires a purpose in which team members can believe."

Your role as a leader is to develop this common commitment, a purpose that vests individuals to the team's success. Even if your team has been in existence for some time, this exercise is very helpful to ground everyone in your mission. Leadership teams review their purpose regularly to accommodate any shifts or adaptations, for example.

One way to get started is to call a team meeting, preferably with a whiteboard. Start by having everyone comment on why the team exists, what demand or opportunity brought the team together. Why did upper management create your group, and what mandate do you have? (If you don't have a clear answer to this question yourself, pose it to your boss and anyone else responsible for the group.) Next, ask team members to elaborate on this bare-bones mission. Ask questions like:

- How does our work support the strategic goals of the company?

- How will we define success? What does "a job well done" look like?

- How do we want to work to affect the people who come in contact with us—customers, clients, others in the company?

- How will being part of this team make us feel? What group ethos will we have?

- How will our team's outcomes affect the larger world—our industry, or community, and so on?

Write down ideas and draw out themes until you have a coherent mission statement that embodies a common perspective. Then invite the team to endorse it.

Step 3: Set team performance goals

Every team in the company should have goals that support the organization's strategy. These goals describe specific, attainable short-term objectives that pertain to the team *as a unit.* Katzenbach and Smith suggest, "Getting a new product to market in less than half the normal time," for example, or "responding to all customers within 24 hours." They translate the high-level purpose you defined in the previous step into concrete action.

With these goals in place, individuals cannot measure their contributions against one another, counting beans and keeping score. Instead, they need to measure their success as a unit. "*We* met this goal," or "*We* failed." Success redounds to the whole team, no matter their internal divisions, and failure can't be assigned to any one subgroup.

To achieve this effect, you need to choose goals that involve *everyone's* work. Don't specify outcomes that mainly depend on salespeople and that

Rules inventory

RESPECT AND TRUST

- Keep conversations confidential.

- Be punctual to work and to meetings.

- Avoid sarcasm, snide remarks, or melodramatic body language (such as eye rolling) when conveying disagreement.

- Listen without interpreting people's motives. Ask why they said, did, or asked for something.

- Respect other people's ways of accomplishing tasks; don't redo work or impose your way on others.

MEETING DISCUSSIONS AND DECISION MAKING

- Share "airtime," listen, and don't interrupt others.

- Invite quiet people to speak.

- Stop advocating for your position after a decision has been made.

- Support the team's final decision, even when it's different from the one you proposed.

FEEDBACK AND REPORTING

- Give the team status updates according to the prescribed processes (which the team determines).

- Give a heads-up and be responsible for the consequences if you have to miss a deadline.

- When giving or receiving feedback, put it in the context of helping the team move toward its goals. Give positive feedback frequently and negative feedback constructively.

- Admit your own mistakes.

(continued)

CONFLICT RESOLUTION

- Assume that every team member is working in good faith toward the team's goals.

- Discuss conflict with the goal of identifying what is best for the team's future.

- Discuss the conflict first with the person involved; avoid talking behind anyone's back.

- Don't yell, use profanity, make threats, or walk out of discussions.

Source: Adapted from Mary Shapiro, *HBR Guide to Leading Teams*. Boston: Harvard Business Review Press, 2015.

the finance people have nothing to do with. For each goal, go through a mental list of everyone on your team: How will each person contribute?

Step 4: Define group norms

Diversity of thought and perspective is your best bet when developing a high-functioning, high-achieving team, but it doesn't come without its challenges. That's because difference breeds conflict. If someone works best under a fixed plan, the colleague who insists on improvisation is going to stress him out. Likewise, if someone is used to looking at a certain task through a sales lens, she's not going to appreciate it when a marketing expert waltzes in with his own way of doing things.

More insidious are conflicts that arise from cognitive biases about racial, gender, and ethnic differences. These biases can cause us to discount the contributions of people who don't mirror our way of thinking or our sense of self. Lack of communication and mutual respect can ultimately lead to intolerable frictions and even collective failure.

To preserve diversity and reconcile differences, everyone should have a clear picture of what being a good team member looks like. These rules "make team members' behavior more predictable," says Mary Shapiro, an expert on teams and professor at the Simmons School of Management. Providing guidelines means that "you won't have to play bad cop as often." Group norms also settle some of the social uncertainty that can accompany diverse personalities coming together. An additional benefit is that you'll spend less time talking about group processes, such as how to deliver status updates. And you'll have clear, uniform ways of handling difficult interactions like giving feedback or resolving conflict. These rules apply to you, too, says Shapiro: they "clarify what others may expect of you as leader."

Build this list in a group brainstorming session. Use the box "Rules inventory" as a menu of options to get the conversation started.

Step 5: Build relationships within the team

Teams run on trust—in each other and in you. To overcome communication and coordination barriers, your team members need strong personal relationships. If they see each other as human beings, they're more likely to reach out for help, share ideas, and assume good faith when conflict does arise. In particular, strong relationships will help you keep valued team members who might otherwise feel marginalized by the group.

To build trust on your team, include social face time in all group interactions, and dedicate a communication channel like group chat for casual check-ins and banter. Encourage team members to set up weekly office hours, when their colleagues can swing by their office or video chat them without going through the hassle of making an appointment. Pair team members on a rotating buddy system for regular one-on-one lunches. It's OK to do something cheesy—doing something silly together is sometimes the best team-building exercise of all.

The work you do at the beginning of your tenure as team leader will make a big difference to the group's trajectory. By calibrating competencies and adding structure to the group's work, you can help your people work together toward a shared goal and succeed *because of* their differences, not in spite of them.

Managing cross-cultural teams

Cross-cultural teams allow you to call on the best specialists worldwide and capture valuable insight into local markets, customer bases, manufacturing conditions, and more. But leading a team with people from different nations and backgrounds comes with special challenges. Left unattended, these differences can become major sources of conflict. (For an example of what can go wrong, read the box "Case study: Manager in the middle.") Even worse, your company can't compete and grow globally if its employees are unable to collaborate across cultures. But you have more maneuvering room in this situation than you may think.

Observe closely

Understand potential sources of conflict *before* they erupt. Professors Jeanne Brett (Northwestern), Kristin Behfar (University of California, Irvine), and Mary C. Kern (Baruch College) identify four key areas you should address in teams that span different cultures:

- **Direct versus indirect communication.** Some team members use direct, explicit communication, while others are indirect, asking questions instead of pointing out the problems with a project, for example. When members see such differences as violations of their culture's communication norms, relationships can suffer.

- **Trouble with accents or fluency.** Members who aren't fluent in the team's dominant language may have difficulty communicating their knowledge. This can prevent the team from using their expertise and create frustration or perceptions of incompetence on both sides.

- **Differing attitudes toward hierarchy.** Team members from hierarchical cultures expect to be treated differently according to their status in the organization. Members from egalitarian cultures do not. Failure of some members to honor those expectations can cause humiliation or loss of stature and credibility.

- **Conflicting decision-making norms.** Members vary in how quickly they make decisions and in how much analysis they require beforehand. Someone who prefers making decisions quickly may grow frustrated with those who need time.

To combat these issues:

Foster open-mindedness

Encourage your people to look at cultural conflicts from the other side's perspective: "Why do you think [colleague] is doing that?" "Could there be a cultural issue at play here? What might it be?" Where appropriate, use one of the four cultural lenses just discussed to identify problems: "I wonder if this is a communication problem. Here's why . . ." If it's not possible to hold a full discussion on the topic, you can still push people to frame their problems as cultural, and not personal, differences: "I understand why you're frustrated. But everyone on this team doesn't share the same attitude toward authority, and that's a difference we have to work around if we're going to succeed."

The goal is for your team members to become self-aware enough to manage their frustrations without forming implacable grudges. Ultimately, you may decide that some cultural norms actually *benefit* the group in different circumstances. If so, these practices of open-mindedness may help your team become psychologically nimble enough to bounce back and forth between styles depending on the context.

Intervene judiciously

In general, it's best if your team members learn to adapt to these differences on their own. But sometimes you may need to intervene directly to resolve an issue or at least moderate its impact on the rest of the team. If you're in this situation, use the conflict-resolution techniques discussed later in this chapter. With cross-cultural teams, you may not always know when conflict is brewing, because team members may not feel comfortable opening up to you (as in the "Manager in the middle" case). If you suspect this is happening, talk to someone with firsthand experience of the culture in question. Ask for their take on what might be happening and for advice about how to approach the affected team members.

CASE STUDY

Manager in the middle

When a major international software developer needed to produce a new product quickly, the project manager assembled a team of employees from India and the United States. From the start, the team members could not agree on a delivery date for the product. The Americans thought the work could be done in two to three weeks; the Indians predicted it would take two to three months. As time went on, the Indian team members proved reluctant to report setbacks in the production process, which the American team members would find out about only when work was due to be passed to them.

Such conflicts, of course, may affect any team, but in this situation, they arose from cultural differences. As tensions mounted, conflict over delivery dates and feedback became personal, disrupting team members' communication about even mundane issues. The project manager decided he had to intervene, with the result that both the American and the Indian team members came to rely on him for direction regarding minute operational details that the team members should have been able to handle themselves. The manager became so bogged down by quotidian issues that the project careened hopelessly off even the most pessimistic schedule, and the team never learned to work together effectively.

Source: Jeanne Brett, Kristin Behfar, and Mary C. Kern, "Managing Multicultural Teams," *Harvard Business Review*, November 2006.

Managing virtual teams

Just as cross-cultural teams have become increasingly common, virtual teams have become almost ubiquitous. You're leading a virtual team if your people don't consistently share a location. Maybe some members of your team are permanently anchored in Singapore, while others are in Seattle, or maybe frequent travel means that *someone* is always calling in from the road. Perhaps some individuals work from home a few times a month or are scattered across so many different floors that even though you all work in the same building, you're more likely to meet over Skype than in a conference room.

While leading any team involves a mix of managing people and processes, virtual leaders must perform these functions without face-to-face accountability. Although you may have more technological options to keep connected than ever before, these tools don't always empower strong virtual connections. Here's how to stay on top of the work, even when you can't see the people doing it:

Pick the right tools.

The technologies you use will have a tremendous impact on your team's ability to function in a virtual environment. First, figure out what your team needs, what resources are presently available to you, and the security policies and restrictions of your company. Evaluating existing resources involves looking at what your team members have in place on their end, but also at the tools your organization brings to the table. Run through the list in the box "Checklist for technology setup" to find the issues that will be most relevant to your needs.

Checklist for technology setup

CHOOSING HARDWARE AND SOFTWARE

- What quality of internet access do team members need and are their current setups sufficient? Ask them to perform an internet speed test.

- What will be your primary means of team communication—email, phone, IM? How will you conduct meetings—phone, video?

- What hardware and software will team members need to communicate, create, and share content? What compatibilities will you require?

- What capacities do team members need to have on their phones? Do team members need to be on the same mobile operating system (Android versus iOS)?

- Will you need project management or issue tracking software (such as Asana, Smartsheet, SharePoint, JIRA, Microsoft Project, or Basecamp)?

STORING AND SYNCHRONIZING TEAM MATERIALS

- How much storage capacity will you need? Should it be scalable?

- Will you store content on hard drives, company servers, or in the Cloud (such as Dropbox or Google Drive)? What are security concerns, risks, and rules?

- Will you synchronize content, updating files automatically across the whole team? Will you need versioned documents or an ability to track who made changes?

- Will you need to share or synchronize calendars?

BUDGET AND SECURITY

- What is your budget for all technology—purchase, installation, storage, and maintenance? What capital expenses do you have to plan for, versus operational expenses?

- What costs will the organization bear, and what will individual team members pay for?

- What security requirements or protocols does your company have for transmitting and storing sensitive data?

Clarify expectations for engagement.

Everyone who's worked with virtual collaborators has experienced "ghost-ing" in some form, when a colleague just stops answering emails and phone calls. Remote work can lend plausible deniability to wrongdoing with this sort of behavior: "I just didn't see your email!" Remove that veil by setting clear expectations for what an engaged team member looks like. Ban mul-titasking on calls, and make a point of calling on people who aren't contrib-uting. Set an email policy, stipulating how quickly people should answer emails and return calls. When team members travel, encourage them to set aside extra time after their trip to catch up on missed connections. Then enforce these rules with low-touch, regular check-ins over text or IM: "I haven't heard much from you this week. Where are you on X project? Do you need anything from me to keep things moving?"

Technology crisis card

Ask all team members to keep this basic information on hand (on their desktop, in their purse) for when things go wrong.

- Name of your internet service provider and a helpline phone number
- Name of the account holder and your account number
- Account information for your most important tools (the email ad-dress or name it's registered under, password hints, security ques-tions, purchase information)
- Name and version of your computer's current operating system
- Name and phone number of an in-home IT service

Have a backup plan.

At some point, your teleconference app *will* crash. The colleague who's supposed to give a presentation *will* lose their internet access ten minutes into your meeting. Help your people take these obstacles in stride by asking them to make a "technology crisis card" ahead of time, so they can quickly sort out problems as they arise (see the box). Encourage them to use the buddy system, too, so that when something goes wrong, they can turn to a designated colleague for help or an update.

Foster social bonds.

Remote work can be very isolating. Without regular face time, team members may struggle to build trusting relationships and may wonder if anyone really sees—and appreciates—their work. To keep motivation high, make low-stakes social time a priority in your team's routines. Friday afternoon check-ins over video chat, regular "office hours" on IM, even an ice-breaker routine at the beginning of each meeting can make all the difference. Don't always worry about keeping things focused on work during these mini-interactions. Your team members need to learn to relate to each other at the personal level, too.

It's equally important for you as a manager to engage effectively with all employees, especially if some are co-located with you and others are virtual. Make a special point to connect with virtual team members personally to build and maintain strong relationships over time. Use Skype or other video tools as often as possible to connect personally and hold yourself accountable for engaging virtual employees fully in team discussions.

Virtual teams require a lot of organization up front, especially from you. But once you've covered these basics, your people will be working as effectively apart as they ever could together.

Productive conflict resolution

Conflict is an unavoidable, even necessary, part of collaboration, and all teams experience it, not just cross-cultural or virtual ones. "There will, even should be, conflict in a group with a task that has even a minimum of complexity," according to Jeanne Brett, a professor at Northwestern's Kellogg Graduate School of Management and director of its Dispute Resolution Research Center. Teams that don't disagree also don't challenge assumptions, investigate ideas, point out mistakes, and motivate each other to their highest performance. Indeed, the whole point of fostering diversity on your team is to bring different viewpoints to the table. To some extent, you *want* these viewpoints to come into conflict; that's how creativity and learning happen.

But, of course, not all conflict is useful. Personality clashes and task-related disagreements can bring a destructive toxicity.

Many managers believe that their role is to minimize all conflict on the team. Not so. The trick is to encourage *healthy* conflict. That means facilitating constructive conflicts and resolving harmful ones. Here's the difference: healthy disagreements result in a better work product and/or stronger intrateam relationships. Unhealthy disagreements undermine your shared accomplishments and damage the team's working relationships.

It can be a tough call to make in the moment—"Should I let my employees pursue this disagreement, or is it time to intervene with a conflict resolution?" You'll have to go with your instinct a lot of the time, but when you're really torn, ask yourself: Is this productive? Is this moving us closer to or further from a positive outcome?

If your answer to the first questions is yes, your best bet is probably to encourage debate and discussion so that each side can confront the other's point of view. This isn't a free-for-all: you still need to be actively involved as a moderator, so that the conversation stays respectful and on track. But if your answer is no, your people may need the structure of a conflict-resolution process to reach closure. Here's how to handle both situations:

How to facilitate constructive conflict

It's not easy to fight well, but shared processes help. Clarify your expectations with the team before a major conflict arises, either by posting your own rules somewhere (in a meeting room, on the team site) or by leading the group in a shared discussion of norms. Address these key topics:

Set ground rules.

Naming the behaviors that are and aren't OK during a conflict will keep disagreements from spiraling out of control. Every team is different, and the specific personalities and organizational culture at play will dictate what makes sense in your particular environment. One rule, though, applies universally: conflict should be handled openly. Disagreeing with someone isn't inherently disrespectful, and if team members choose not to voice their opinion, they should be prepared to let it go. For other potential guidelines, see the earlier box "Rules inventory."

Establish a shared process for resolving conflict.

If team members know what to do when friction arises, they won't shy away from necessary disagreements, and more often than not, they'll be able to solve their own problems. Clear, step-by-step protocols for handling conflict should be a central part of your team's normal processes. One such protocol should deal with formal conflict resolution, addressed later. But spell out the lower-stakes alternatives, too. For example, team members should:

- Respectfully confront the colleague they disagree with before they bring in anyone else, including you.

- Talk about complicated issues face-to-face or over video chat, not over email.

- Prepare on their own before they open a discussion with each other, so they come ready to explain their concerns and discuss alternatives.

- Take turns summarizing each other's ideas or concerns—in good faith. By forcing themselves to articulate each other's point of view, they might find new ground for compromise.

- Put the discussion on pause when they feel themselves losing track of the argument or their own self-control.

- Escalate the argument without becoming vindictive or angry. When disagreements prove intractable, frame it as "We need help sorting this out," not "The team leader will decide who's right and who's wrong."

Provide criteria for contentious trade-offs.

When zero-sum decisions arise for a team, it's helpful to have some well-defined criteria for making trade-offs. Fortunately, your team has these at hand, in the form of your organization's overall strategy and the purpose and objectives this strategy has already defined for your group's work. Clarify these points with your people and be specific about your goals and highest priorities. For example, "Meeting the deadline for this assignment is more important than fulfilling its scope" or vice versa.

How to resolve destructive conflict

With practice, your team members may learn to manage constructive conflict mostly on their own, with little intervention from you. By contrast, a formal conflict-resolution process always involves you. Sometimes your employees will bring an issue to your attention and ask for your help. But if they're not self-aware enough to do this, you may need to take the initiative and ask them to participate. However you start off, the process should have three phases:

Step 1: Find the root cause.

This step may require some research on your part. If the conflict is complicated or long-standing, you'll want to know what's going on before you invite two tense people to a meeting to hash it out. If you do decide to involve other people in your inquiry, try to talk to all parties involved in the conflict separately. And follow up with anyone else on the team whose perspective could clarify the problem, if you can do it sensitively. The questions you want to clarify *for yourself* through these interviews are:

- Why are team members arguing with each other?

- Is there a deeper personality conflict here?

- Are there organizational causes of this conflict?

- Is this a recurring pattern?

- Why does one member always insist on getting his or her way?

- Is the cause of this conflict a behavior? A clash of opinions? An external situation?

When you have some answers to these questions, you'll be able to start generating ideas for negotiating a resolution. For example, if the conflict is caused by a personality clash, you'll probably need to help the team members learn to communicate better with one another and be more respectful when they disagree. If the conflict is caused by project circumstances, you and your team can brainstorm fixes like hiring additional resources, redefining roles, or modifying the scope of the work.

Step 2: Facilitate a resolution.

You may have a few ideas for how this situation should evolve, but it's best to avoid dictating a solution. Solutions don't work simply because they make sense or because you said so; they work when they have buy-in from the people who have to execute them. For this reason, compromises that are imposed from above tend not to be as thorough or as resilient as the ones a team arrives at by itself.

Frustrating as it may be, play no more than a facilitating role. Your listening-to-telling ratio should be 4:1, and the "telling" part should mostly be active listening tactics to help team members understand underlying assumptions. That means asking open-ended questions, restating and reframing team members' perspectives, and encouraging the other people in the room to do the same. Set the tone for this discussion by reminding people to stick to the facts, to talk about behaviors instead of traits, and to follow the team's ground rules for conflict.

If the team members resist coming to a resolution despite your best efforts, you may need to steer the conversation a little more decisively. Leadership coach Lisa Lai recommends using these five questions to facilitate the conversation:

1. What does each person *really* want?

2. What matters to them, personally and professionally?

3. What motivates them? What fears do they have?

4. Where is there common ground?

5. What's the difference between their stories?

If the conversation really seems stuck, try these tactics:

- Ask each team member to share their BATNA. In negotiation parlance, a BATNA is your "best alternative to a negotiated agreement"—basically, what your team members think will happen if they can't resolve their dispute. Then ask them how their BATNAs will affect the rest of the team. Articulating consequence to the group may help them recommit to finding a solution.

- Refocus the discussion on the team's strategic objectives. Sometimes, the team members' shared interests are strong enough to compel a resolution on their own (see the box "Case study: Focusing team members on a shared goal"). Other times, you may need to push a little harder. Ask the team members to identify together the key priorities that their agreement should address and then limit the scope of the discussion to these issues alone: "This is a very complicated situation, and I can see it's wearing on everyone involved. But if we can't resolve *all* of it right now, that doesn't mean we can't resolve *any* of it. For now, let's focus on coming up with a solution for *X* issue."

CASE STUDY

Focusing team members on a shared goal

Kelley Johnson, the owner of an eco-lodge in Belize, regularly has to deal with team dynamics. Since the lodge is in a remote location, it employs over twenty-five full-time staff who live onsite for weeks at a time. This close-knit work situation can often lead to conflict if not managed correctly. The lodge has four managers, including Katja, a German expat who runs the front office and oversees the staff when Kelley is off-site; and Carlos, a Belizean who is in charge of client services. Katja is incredibly organized and meticulous about her work. Carlos is a genius when it comes to client service, making each guest feel special. "He has an ability to make every guest feel as if they are the first one to ever see a snake," says Kelley.

But last winter, Katja asked Kelley to fire Carlos because she felt he wasn't doing his job. He regularly forgot to do tasks and was sloppy with his paperwork. She was frustrated and felt as if she was working twice as hard as he was. Carlos had also previously complained about Katja. He resented her criticism and felt she was too cold to their clients.

As Kelley saw it, they were both failing to understand each other's talents. Kelley responded to Katja by asking her to take a step back and look at the situation. Carlos was failing to do part of his job description, but he was invaluable to the lodge. Katja conceded that his job description should be changed so that he could live up to expectations.

Kelley spoke to both employees, explained why each one was extremely valuable to the team, and asked them to appreciate what the other brought. They were part of a profit-sharing plan, which meant a piece of their salary hinged on the business. She asked them to focus on the larger purpose and to put their disputes behind them. With expectations reset, Carlos and Katja found a way to work together by accepting they had completely different styles but both cared ultimately about the same thing—making the lodge successful.

Source: Adapted from Amy Gallo, "Get Your Team to Stop Fighting and Start Working," HBR.org, June 9, 2010.

Step 3: Get back to work.

"[T]he best way to heal war wounds is to start working again," says Amy Gallo, the author of the *HBR Guide to Managing Conflict at Work*. "Get a relatively easy task in front of the group to help them rebuild their confidence as a team. As the leader, you can model moving on and focusing on work." You can also model forgiveness. Hurt feelings and damaged egos are collateral damage at these times, and people may need to be reminded that it's possible to let their anger go and that, in fact, you expect them to. "Going forward, it will be useful to establish a practice of regularly checking on how you all are working together," adds Gallo. "This will help you identify problems before they turn into full-fledged disputes."

So much of what you do as a manager is empowering diverse individuals to come together as a team and deliver shared results. Along the way, you need to bond team members to your purpose, establish shared norms, and navigate disagreements. Creating this kind of strong team culture is an essential prerequisite to the hard work you do as a high-performing team.

In the next chapter, you'll learn how to leverage all of this hard-won teamwork to get the creative juices flowing.

Recap

- Bringing unique individuals with different points of view together in the workplace brings opportunities and challenges.

- Effective teams have a mix of competencies and backgrounds.

- Your role as a team leader is to create a work environment that allows each person to contribute fully.

- Defining group norms helps everyone understand how a good team member acts despite their differences and makes team members' behavior more predictable.

- Building strong relationships on the team will help you engage valued team members who might otherwise feel marginalized by the group.

- Cross-cultural and virtual teams run higher risks of conflict and misunderstanding because communication is more difficult and cultural assumptions may be different.

- Team conflict can be constructive or destructive, depending on whether they produce better work and/or stronger intrateam relationships.

Action items

To build a team and its culture:

- ☐ Use the team audit in exhibit 12-1 to evaluate the strengths and weaknesses of the team's culture, and exhibit 12-2 to evaluate.

- ☐ Recruit a team that has a mix of training and skills, professional background, work style, motivation and goals, and life experience.

- ☐ Hone your sense of purpose together, asking the questions given earlier.

- ☐ Set team performance goals that you can be accountable to as a group, not as individuals.

- ☐ Define group norms that describe what it means to be a true team player, drawing from the "Rules inventory."

- ☐ Build relationships within the team that can sustain your work together going forward.

To manage a cross-cultural team:

- ☐ Observe closely. Be proactive in identifying potential sources of conflict, *before* they erupt. Areas likely to cause trouble are: direct versus indirect communication; trouble with accents or fluency; differing attitudes toward hierarchy; and conflicting decision-making norms.

❑ Foster open-mindedness. Help your team members become aware of opposing cultural norms and encourage them to embrace new ways of doing things.

❑ Intervene judiciously. If your team members can work things out on their own, reorganize their work or take direct action to resolve indecision.

To manage a virtual team:

❑ Pick the right tools. Make sure your team's technology infrastructure matches their real needs.

❑ Clarify your expectations for engagement. Explain what behavior you expect from engaged team members and then hold people accountable.

❑ Have a backup plan. Ask your people to make their own plan Bs for when technology runs amok.

❑ Foster social bonds. Institute routines that help team members connect on a personal level.

To manage conflict on your team:

❑ Manage constructive conflict by setting clear ground rules, establishing shared processes, and providing criteria for how to make contentious trade-offs.

❑ Resolve destructive conflict by finding its root cause, facilitating a resolution, and normalizing any remaining tensions by getting right back to work.

13.

Fostering Creativity

Creativity is the ability to generate novel ideas. Creativity isn't just about developing innovative products and product features for your customers: a creative team can identify better ways to execute internal processes, find better ways to market a product, come up with better options in a negotiation, and solve problems more effectively. Enhancing team creativity is a goal-oriented, collaborative process that draws on each team member's skills, experience, and expertise.

Some people think that creativity only comes from "creative" people. But it responds to concrete cues, too. In this chapter, you'll learn how to lead productive idea-generating sessions and build a creative culture on your team.

Plan a creative session

You know you need a new idea—maybe you're trying to come up with a name for a new product or a feature for an existing one, or to imagine the possibilities for a new business model entirely. Leading a brainstorm session isn't your only option. By planning how you'll facilitate your creative session, considering the timing, space, and rules, you can ensure that participants are energized, focused, and productive.

Find the right time

Plan the timing for your idea-generation session carefully. Depending on the scale of what you're trying to achieve, you may not be able to imagine a wide range of ideas, winnow down options, and come up with a plan all in one meeting. So before you send an invite, create an overarching timeline. When do you need your fresh idea to come to fruition? What milestones will you achieve in the meantime, and what scheduling constraints do you need to work around?

Once you have your timeline, do you best to schedule the initial session far in advance of your final deadline. Many people assume that creative minds come up with their best ideas when time is tight, but that's rarely true. Teams that are pushed to work creatively within an arbitrarily short time will burn out, and their performance won't be consistently great.

Creative sessions are mentally demanding, however, so keep each meeting to thirty minutes. If you decide that your team needs more time, you can reconvene, but it's better to stop and schedule a follow-up meeting than to force your group to keep grinding away unproductively.

Pick a time when people are likely to be at their peak energy, but not immersed in other distractions. First thing in the morning and late in the day are not ideal; likewise, avoid scheduling sessions right before a long break or a major work event. People won't pay attention.

Set the scene

If possible, choose a location where your team rarely meets in order to stimulate new thinking. If you need to use your regular space, play around with the room setup. Instead of sitting around a conference table, position chairs in clusters.

Ask your team to leave all laptops, tablets, phones, and other devices behind at their desks. Instead, supply the room with tactile tools beyond the traditional whiteboard: huge pieces of paper, small colorful sticky notes, or a blackboard with colorful chalk. Cover any tables with paper that can be used for note taking, doodling, or drawing, and provide colored pens or pencils, markers, crayons, pipe cleaners, even clay. Even if people don't end up using these supplies for the work at hand, playing around with art can help bypass inhibition and ignite the imagination.

Don't limit these measures to game-day preparations. You can enrich your team's everyday physical environment, too. Encourage casual conversations and spontaneous meetings by setting up open seating and planting a few gathering places around the office: coffee machines, water coolers, relaxed seating, games. Take note of the places people are already gathering informally and make them more comfortable. Stock these places with creative tools like whiteboards, markers, flip charts, and art supplies, so that these fortuitous interactions can easily transition to something more creative.

Establish rules of conduct

In the last chapter, you saw how group norms help teams overcome difference and mitigate conflict. That's especially true when it comes to generating ideas, where these differences may be most on view and everyone's feeling exposed.

To create a sense of safety, set out ground rules at the start of your meeting. Write them on the whiteboard or where everyone can see them. You might invite the rest of the group to contribute their ideas, but be firm about the behaviors you expect. If these expectations aren't already a part of your team's ground rules, consider reinforcing them:

- **Respect all members of the group.** Ideas and assumptions may be attacked; individuals may not.

- **Be a good listener.** Everyone will have an opportunity to speak and should actively listen to others.

- **Value varying points of view.** Everyone has a right to disagree and challenge assumptions. Conflicting views are a valuable source of learning and should be welcome when raised at an appropriate time in the discussion.

- **No idea is a bad idea.** No idea should be labelled "stupid," "useless," or any other negative descriptor. No one should be shamed for participating in the creative process.

These items may already be a part of your team norms and you can simply remind team members at the start of the session. Be sure to empower everyone in the group to help you enforce these guidelines by calling out bad behavior when it happens.

Tools for generating ideas

Successful idea-generating sessions may feel loose and spontaneous, but they actually have a lot of structure. That's because our brains all need some help breaking free from their normal pathways.

Creative ideas arise from *divergent thinking*, when your team strikes out in a new thought direction, away from the familiar ways of seeing and doing things. This type of thinking allows your team to view a problem from novel perspectives, discover new connections between facts and events, and explore questions that have never been asked before. The goal is to quickly generate a wide variety of solutions for a given problem, without prejudging the merit of those options.

You can approach this process in a *solution-centric* or a *problem-centric* way, says innovation expert Thomas Wedell-Wedellsborg. In a solution-centric session, the group focuses on generating ideas around a broadly defined issue, such as "How can we improve our marketing plan?" By focusing on potential, future actions, instead of present conditions, you keep the group from locking in too tightly on just one point of view. You'll generate a handful of highly original ideas, but a lot of nonviable ones, too. And if you end the session with a long list of options, you may not have the resources to process which one's which.

By contrast, a problem-centric session focuses on solving a specific, clearly-defined issue. Because these sessions are grounded in making real problems better, they generate fewer, higher-quality ideas that are easier to follow up on. But it's important to have someone in the room who really understands the problem, or the conversation can go off the rails.

How do you get a room full of professionals to think freely in this way? There are several different ways to structure your idea generation:

Brainstorming

This is probably the most well-known option for divergent thinking. The basic goal is to quickly solicit a lot of ideas from a group, and it's especially useful when you want to engage everyone on the team in an informal way. Especially with a solution-centric approach, you want quantity over quality, so encourage even the wildest ideas, no matter how strange. You never know where they may lead. If your team easily comes up with five ideas, push for twenty.

Help the team along by toggling between these three techniques:

- **Modifying.** How could your team members change or adapt the way they already do things to achieve some different outcome? Start by asking them to set some priorities: "We want to make this work process more responsive to changing information" or "We want to increase our sales conversion rate." Then ask them to diagram all the tasks, roles, processes, and protocols involved in the problem. What margin does the team have for changing each of these elements? What are all the possible fixes you could make? Put the subject-matter experts for each issue in conversation with other members of the team, and invite nonexperts to explain how they experience the problem. You might be surprised to hear what your IT specialist has to say about your sales strategy, or what the person who sits next to the copier all day has observed about the way the team prepares for major presentations.

- **Visioning.** For a more solution-centric conversation, ask group members to imagine an ideal solution to the problem or question before you in great detail and then work backward to figure out how they might achieve it. Start with an open-ended question like,

"If our consulting company could provide *any* services, what would they be?" Assume that money, time, and resources are no object. Write every idea down (on sticky notes stuck to a window, for example) and invite the team to group related suggestions. Then ask, "What would we need to know and do to make each of these alternatives happen?"

- **Experimenting.** Create a complete matrix of all the elements at play in a problem—clients, services, resources, and so on—and then systematically combine and re-combine them to find new business possibilities. For example, if a car-washing company were looking to break into a new market, the team members might list the products they could wash, the equipment they could buy, and the products they could sell at the top of the matrix. Then, under each category, they would list all the possible variations they could think of, no matter how outrageous. The resulting table lets the team mechanically combine components to come up with new ideas: selling microfiber cloths for motorcycles, letting boaters wash their boats in company stalls, and power-washing homes with sprays and hoses. This exercise works well for solution- *or* problem-centric conversations, depending on how pie-in-the-sky the variables in your matrix are and whether there's a subject matter expert on hand to guide the group toward viable combinations.

There's no one right technique or right order to try them in. The trick is to keep things moving, so that when one line of thought goes stale, you're ready with another prompt.

Mind mapping

This is a free-association activity that gets your team thinking visually to develop a constellation of interconnected ideas. Your team members may be able to generate more connections using this method than they would simply by listing ideas.

Begin by writing a keyword or concept in the center of a blank page or whiteboard. Hand out a bunch of sticky notes and have your team members write down as many words related to the original ideas as they can in a fixed amount of time—say, ten in two minutes or twenty in five minutes. Then invite them to come up and add their words to the map. Don't evaluate or judge any of their notes yet, just put them on the board. Next, connect the ideas by moving the sticky notes around and drawing lines between them. Encourage the team to use colors to indicate action items, insights, doubts, and other important factors. (See exhibit 13-1.)

If there are ideas that don't connect to the original thought, that's OK. Leave the map up for everyone to see. And as new words and ideas emerge, add them. Someone might be inspired to offer a full-blown theory or plan: annotate the map with that information, too.

This technique is exploratory: you're working toward a shared understanding of an issue, and not a tidy list of next steps. To make the

EXHIBIT 13-1

Mind map

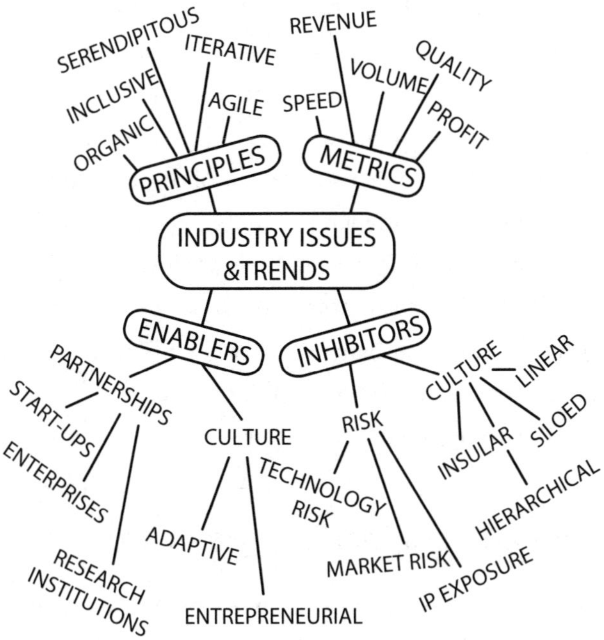

Source: Nancy Duarte, *HBR Guide to Persuasive Presentations*. Boston: Harvard Business Review Press, 2012.

conversation more problem-centric, try "question-storming," say Jeffrey Dyer, Hal Gregersen, and Clayton Christensen, authors of *The Innovator's DNA: Mastering the Five Skills of Disruptive Innovators*. Make the key-word for your exercise a specific problem, and then have people write down related questions on their sticky notes.

Catchball

Both mind mapping and brainstorming are great options for a team that's starting the idea-generation process from scratch. If your team already has an idea or two on the table (such as an existing product or the typical solution to a common problem), consider using the "catchball" approach. Catchball has two goals: to improve on an existing idea and to gain buy-in from participants. You'll need a single, focusing idea to get things started, so it works well in problem-centric sessions.

In this exercise, someone on the team "tosses" the initial idea to some-one else. Whoever "catches" the idea must understand it, reflect on it, and improve on it in some way. Then that person tosses the modified idea back to the group, where it's caught by someone else and improved further. (If anyone freezes up, the rest of the team can help them out.) As each person participates, they have the opportunity to tinker with the idea and enrich the conversation. The result is a shared sense of responsibility and commit-ment, regardless of where the idea originated. To see catchball in action, read the box "Case study: "Playing catchball with traffic safety."

As your team builds ideas, assign someone to write down each and every one so you can discuss them later. Catchball tends to push people to move from generating ideas to narrowing them down too fast, but a note taker can help the group separate these processes.

Making sure all perspectives are heard

Whether you're still generating ideas or you've moved on to evaluating them, as the team leader, you're in a position to modulate the loud voices and amplify the soft ones. If the conversation really seems to be moving, it may feel awkward to interrupt the flow. But you need to get everyone's

CASE STUDY

Playing catchball with traffic safety

Members of a neighborhood association are concerned about the large number of bike accidents at a certain intersection and want to gather ideas to take to city officials. Jake is the first to get the ball: "The traffic light pattern needs to be changed." He passes the ball to Sonia, who elaborates: "There needs to be a 'left on green arrow only' signal." Next, to Vijay: "I like that. Can they shorten the yellow light, too?" Finally, to Alessandra: "And maybe reprogram the traffic light pattern for a few blocks in each direction, so fewer cars end up fighting through that intersection at once." The team now has some ideas to present at the next city council meeting.

point of view and stop the team from coalescing around an idea or solution before that happens. Here's how to do it:

Ask people to talk—or to stop talking

- Call on quiet participants directly. "Felicia, we haven't heard from you yet. Are we missing any big issues here?" "Vijay, what's your biggest concern about this approach?" Some people might turn red, but at least you'll get their opinion. And they'll get to practice speaking in a group if that's something they're working on.

- Make sure your virtual participants are heard. Spend the first five minutes of the meeting on chitchat that specifically engages them—about the weather, sports, weekend activities, and the like. As the session unfolds, make sure to check back in with them. A sticky note on your computer or at the top of your tablet can help; you might also deputize someone else in the room to keep track of virtual participants. You can even set a vibration alarm on your smartphone to go off every ten to fifteen minutes as a prompt to engage virtual attendees.

- When you've hit upon a particularly fruitful line of thought, watch for body language that indicates someone is eager to jump in. Leaning forward and making eye contact with the speaker are big cues. Acknowledge these participants with eye contact or a nod, signaling that you see them and that you'll call on them in a minute. This will help them focus on what's being said, not whether they'll get the chance to speak.

- Keep louder attendees from dominating. Try scripts like "Thanks for those comments. Now let's hear from someone who hasn't had a chance yet." "Before we hear from you, Akila, I'd like to hear from Young-Ju."

Structure the conversation so it feels safe to take risks

- If your meeting has a dozen or more participants, break the group into pairs or trios, and have each unit report back about a particular aspect of the problem. You might ask them to run different idea-generating exercises—one group does mind mapping, while another does visioning. This arrangement ensures that people who wouldn't speak up in front of the whole group can still be heard.

- Appoint someone to play devil's advocate. This role is about challenging assumptions, not attacking other people for the sport of it. Pick someone with tact and humor for this role, and make sure the rest of the group knows what's going on. Incorporating this person's contributions into the general discussion will show that you're open-minded and ready to make space for unpopular ideas.

Push for "second thoughts"

- Ask general questions such as "Have we forgotten anything?" "What's our blind spot?"

- Give the group a little time to think things over. If the ideas don't come rushing right away, don't give up on a particular technique. Pause and scan the room, looking for people you can make eye contact with. Then address them in a friendly way: "What's the first thing that came to mind for you?" As the conversation advances, let people circle back to earlier ideas. Revisiting old comments doesn't mean the conversation is losing focus; it means people are making connections.

- Let people know they can share feedback after the meeting too, once they've had more time to reflect.

Your role throughout this process is to be as supportive of the wide range of ideas as possible. Never show that you think an idea is silly, and thank everyone for their contributions at the end of the meeting.

Dealing with negativity

When you make an effort to bring all perspectives to the table, you're going to hear some negativity. People won't like everything that's said, and they may not like the very idea of changing how they do things. You might hear:

- **It's not needed.** "Our product sells well, and customers report a high level of satisfaction. Why do we need a new formulation?"

- **It's too risky.** "There are too many unknowns about how this alternative will work. We may lose customers if it's not as good as our current product."

- **It's too expensive.** "We don't have money to invest in a new initiative."

- **It won't work.** "Two years ago, we reformulated this program. It was a total flop, and we lost a lot of customers."

- **It's not technically feasible.** "The new product can't be done to our quality standards."

EXHIBIT 13-2

Techniques for overcoming resistance

Tactic	Method	Scripts
Persuasion	• Invite everyone to respond with data, evidence, facts, and logic. • Throw the idea back to the person who originated it: What does the person see as the key benefits?	• "You raise some important issues. If I'm hearing you right, your main concern is X. Can anyone respond to that?" • "Help us understand why you think this won't work. Then someone else in the group can explain why they think it will."
Participation	• Engage the resister by asking for the person's ideas or other contributions. • Connect the attractive parts of the idea to other options this person has already embraced. • Show your appreciation for the person's contributions.	• "I can tell you have strong opinions on this, and that's great. What other alternatives do you have in mind? How would you adapt this idea to make it work?" • "This idea is building on your earlier suggestion that we do X. How could your suggestion be better realized here?" • "I think it's great that we challenge each other productively. Thanks for bringing up these issues."
Facilitation	• Ask the person what would make them comfortable with this idea. • Ask what downsides the person is concerned about, and invite the team to brainstorm how you could mediate those effects.	• "Wow. I didn't know this was something you cared so deeply about. Tell us more about your thoughts on this." • "I appreciate your perspective, and I'm happy we're having this conversation. Can you share more specifics about your concern or help us understand what we may have missed?"
Negotiation	• Push the group to consider compromises or trade-offs in the design to address the resister's concerns. • Push the resister to engage with new suggestions.	• "I think [team member] has done a good job explaining their concerns. Everyone, what fixes could help resolve this issue?" • "[Team member], we've heard a couple ideas for resolving this issue. What seems most workable to you?"
Direction	• Use your power to redirect harmful comments.	• "We can always count on you to tell us what you think. For now, though, we need to move on." • "I appreciate that you're not afraid to say what's on your mind. Let's circle back to this later."

Source: Adapted from "Innovation Implementation" in *Harvard ManageMentor*. Boston: Harvard Business School Publishing, 2016. Electronic.

- **It will change the group's culture.** "We've never done things that way before. It's just not how we work."

Don't let these comments discourage you. You can head them off in part by putting in place strong group norms that emphasize respect and positivity. But when someone violates these norms, or if they have other objections, you'll need to respond promptly to keep their comments from derailing the rest of the room. Exhibit 13-2 describes five tactics for keeping the conversation productive: persuasion, participation, facilitation, negotiation, and direction.

Keeping the conversation positive isn't about ignoring serious challenges to an idea; it's about keeping everyone engaged in coming up with solutions and coming to new ideas with an open mind.

Trying new tools and techniques for generating new ideas can help your team become more creative when you have a particular problem to solve. But creating a supportive, safe environment will help your team members perform at their best in their other work as well. If they trust you and their peers to engage with their ideas in good faith, they're more likely to lean into hard problems and develop creative, effective solutions.

Recap

- *Creativity* is the ability to generate novel ideas, whether innovative products or features, better ways to execute internal processes, or unexpected solutions in a negotiation.

- Creativity doesn't just come from "creative" people.

- Planning the timing and setting of a creative session can make it more productive.

- There are a number of different tools and approaches for generating new ideas; brainstorming isn't your only option.

- Getting everyone's perspectives is very important; creative ideas come from unexpected places.

- Feeling psychologically safe helps individuals take risks and generate new ideas.

Action items

Plan an idea-generating session:

❏ Pick a time for your idea-generating session when people will be at peak energy and that also gives you a chance to hold follow-up sessions.

❏ Create a space that is both stimulating and allows the team to focus.

❏ Establish rules of conduct that reinforce respect for all ideas and points of view.

Lead an idea-generating session by deciding if you want a solution-centric or a problem-centric approach, and then considering the following options:

❏ Invite your team to envision an ideal future for the problem, absent any constraints. Then work backward to figure out how it could happen.

❏ Ask your team to find fixes to the current situation. Put experts and non-experts into active dialogue about each solution.

❏ Conduct a mind-mapping exercise, connecting how each team member sees the issue in a single, unified schema.

❏ Orchestrate a game of catchball, where one idea is passed from person to person and each team member contributes a new twist.

Encourage everyone to participate:

❏ Before your next idea-generating session, take five minute to write down your go-to scripts for those awkward moments when you need to interrupt someone or solicit a silent participant.

❏ Create a dedicated online space where team members can debrief after the meeting or register their follow-up thoughts—the team site, a group chat, something that's easy for everyone to access and that won't result in a lot of annoying email spam. Monitor the site regularly so that when people contribute, you can acknowledge their comments.

Manage resistance to new ideas:

❏ Listen for the root cause of the resistance. Does the person think the innovation is unnecessary? Unworkable? A threat to their position?

❏ Invite the group to make a persuasive case for the idea in play.

❏ Engage a person in an active conversation about their concerns. Push them to participate in a real dialogue, and facilitate a back-and-forth discussion between them and the idea's champions.

❏ Redirect the conversation when the negative comments can't be productively addressed.

14.

Hiring—and Keeping—the Best

You've heard it often: employees are your organization's most important assets. Their skills, institutional knowledge, and motivation to work are the key factors differentiating your company from the competition.

As a manager, your role is to bring the best, most promising talent into the organization. To some extent, this is work you must do daily—helping team members find their place and creating opportunities for them to shine. But it also requires some big-picture thinking about how you find the right people, design satisfying jobs for them, and maintain their motivation through the ebb and flow of daily work life, particularly when you have the opportunity to make a new hire.

Crafting a role

Before you can make a good hire, you need to know what you're hiring *for.* You also need to determine which skills and personal attributes will make a candidate a good fit with the requirements of the job and the organization—and with the culture of your team. It's the difference between hiring an accountant and hiring an accountant with the technical knowledge, creative mindset, and leadership skills to lead the overhaul of the billing systems you have planned.

This isn't just a matter of filling vacancies. Your team can and should evolve, depending on the people who join it. A new team member who's highly disciplined and driven may push the group to streamline its work processes, while someone with strong interpersonal skills can strengthen collaborative relationships. To get the most value from the recruitment process, approach it as a practical *and* an aspirational exercise. Let your guiding concerns be "Who can do this job the best?" and "Who will help our team continue to grow?"

To answer these questions, gather information about the job itself, the kind of person who can do it well, and the environment in which they be working.

Step 1: Define the job's primary responsibilities and tasks

If you're rehiring for an existing role, look at what the incumbent is doing and evaluate that person's job description. Is it still accurate and relevant? To find out, talk to other team members who work closely with this person: "How would you describe this role? What are the most important things this person does, from your perspective?" Also talk to your own boss: "Going forward, what strategic objectives would you really like to see this role support? What responsibilities do you put the most emphasis on?"

Finally, read through old performance evaluations. When past employees performed well in this role, what accomplishments were most important? What failures had the worst impact on the rest of the team?

Step 2: Describe the ideal candidate

Education and experience are two of the most critical pieces of information you'll consider when evaluating candidates. In the case of education, you may wish to specify a certain type of degree or a certain level. Ask yourself when these specifications are truly necessary. Can you be flexible in this area, or is industry or functional experience an adequate substitute?

Establishing criteria for personal characteristics is more difficult. It may help to talk to your coworkers and review your own files. What traits and abilities made past employees successful? What weaknesses were the most difficult to compensate for or to reform? Think about analytic and creative abilities, decision-making style, interpersonal skills, and motivation. The right characteristics aren't absolute; they depend on the rest of the team members and how they work. Consider following up with a group session, in which you all can reach a consensus about the ideal candidate.

Step 3: Evaluate the environment: team culture

Naturally, you want to hire someone who can get along with the group—who will understand its sense of humor, fall in line with its norms, and share in its identity. But you also want someone who fills any gaps on your team in behaviors or competencies. Maybe you're all creative problem solvers, but you don't have strong communication habits. See chapter 12, "Leading Teams," for more on identifying competency and cultural gaps on your team.

Step 4: Write the job description

Once you've studied these three categories—the job's responsibilities, the ideal candidate, and the cultural fit—you're ready to create a job description. This is a profile of the job, its essential functions, reporting relationships, hours, and required credentials. Having all this information in one succinct description will make it possible for you to explain the job both to potential candidates and to any recruiters you may be using to identify candidates.

In some cases, your organization may have a required format or standard job description you can use as a model. If you're writing one from scratch, include the following information:

- Job title, business unit, and the name of the organization

- Job responsibilities and tasks

- Hiring manager and reporting manager

- Summary of the job tasks, responsibilities, and objectives

- Hours, location, and any information about compensation that you can provide

- Experience and training required

Your description should not be discriminatory and should comply with all relevant legal restrictions. In the United States, for example, stated job requirements must clearly relate to getting the job done and must not unfairly prevent racial minorities, women, people with disabilities, or other protected classes from being hired.

Many of these items will probably have to be cleared with your HR department before you're ready to move on to the next stage: recruitment.

Recruiting for potential

Recruiting actually works best when you aren't hunting too strictly for competency and experience, but rather for *potential*, according to Claudio Fernández-Aráoz.

Fernández-Aráoz, a senior adviser at the global executive search firm Egon Zehnder, has spent thirty years evaluating and tracking executive performance. He explains:

> In a volatile, uncertain, complex, and ambiguous environment, competency-based appraisals and appointments are increasingly insufficient. What makes someone successful in a particular role today might not tomorrow if the competitive environment shifts, the company's strategy changes, or he or she must collaborate with or manage a different group of colleagues. So the question is not whether your company's employees and leaders have the right skills; it's whether they have the potential to learn new ones.

Recruiting world-class talent

You've determined the competencies and experience that candidates should bring to the position you're trying to fill. Now that information will help recruiters, applicants, and everyone else involved in the hiring process understand, "What *is* this job?"

The purpose of the recruitment process is to find a candidate who embodies the traits you defined earlier and who meets the basic requirements outlined in your job description. Beware, however, of focusing *too* narrowly on the description (see the box "Recruiting for potential").

To identify high-potential candidates, Fernández-Aráoz looks at five traits:

- **Motivation**—a fierce commitment to excel in the pursuit of unselfish goals

- **Curiosity**—a penchant for seeking out new experiences, knowledge, and candid feedback and an openness to learning and change

- **Insight**—the ability to gather and make sense of information that suggests new possibilities

- **Engagement**—a knack for using emotion and logic to communicate a persuasive vision and connect with people

- **Determination**—the wherewithal to fight for difficult goals despite challenges and to bounce back from adversity

If you emphasize these intrinsic qualities in your search, you'll prioritize candidates who have the internal resources to succeed in unfamiliar and rapidly changing environments

Source: Claudio Fernández-Aráoz, "21st-Century Talent Spotting," *Harvard Business Review*, June 2014.

Step 1: Get the word out

Gaining access to qualified candidates is critical to the success of your hiring effort. To do so, push information about your search through as many appropriate channels as possible. Work with your HR department to get the job posted on your company careers site, as well as with recruiting agencies, job websites (the more narrowly targeted, the better), industry conferences, trade publications, and campus recruiting. Also get referrals from colleagues.

Often the best candidates come from personal connections, so complement HR's efforts by sharing the posting through your social media network. Ask your colleagues to also spread the word (see whether your company offers rewards to employees whose referrals are actually hired).

Step 2: Screen résumés

The cover letter and résumé are the candidate's first introduction to you. When you have a large number of résumés to review, a two-pass process will make the task more manageable. In the first pass, eliminate candidates who fail to meet the basic requirements of the job. In the second pass, look for résumés that include:

- Signs of achievement and results: for example, a profit orientation, stability, or progressive career momentum

- Confidence and aptitude for complex environments

- Diversity of experience and skills

- Language that mirrors the cultural norms of the organization

- Clear packaging or presentation via the résumé and letter

Be on alert for red flags, too, such as:

- A lengthy description of the applicant's education or personal background versus experience

- Unexplained employment gaps

- A pattern of short-term employment, especially after the applicant has been in the workforce for more than a few years

- No logical job progression or continuity

- Lack of results or accomplishments

Your goal here is to narrow down the list of contenders, but don't be too strictly bound by what you've said you're looking for in the job description. Résumés and cover letters by their very nature tell you more about experience and competency than about someone's potential for growth. So keep an eye out for applications that, while they may not match your needs perfectly, show sparks of promise: a personable, dynamic cover letter, or a résumé with an irregular but intriguing job progression. These might be signs of a candidate who's responded creatively—and successfully—to an increasingly unstable job market. You can ask about these anomalies at the interview.

Step 3: Conduct interviews

Ask each candidate the same core questions, but leave yourself room to follow up on promising lines of inquiry. To get the best sense of your candidate, chart a middle path between a structured and unstructured interview. The conversation should proceed in three phases:

- **Opening.** This should take 10 percent of the allotted time. You want to make the candidate feel comfortable so that they'll answer your questions openly, so start on time and be friendly. Introduce yourself, explaining what your role is and offering something about yourself: how you got started at the company, or how you made a personal connection with a certain detail in their cover letter or résumé. If other people are sitting in on the interview, they should also introduce themselves. It's OK to acknowledge some of the awkwardness of the situation. A little humor can put interviewees at ease.

- **Body.** Plan to use 80 percent of your allotted time in this phase. Here you must gather the information that will help you evaluate candidates and also to "sell" your organization. Using your core questions as a guide, pursue a direct line of questioning based on the applicant's résumé. Identify similarities and patterns of behavior consistent with your idea profile, ask directly for details, and probe for tangible measures of success. You should ask most of the questions and do most of the listening, around 80 percent of the time. After all, you'll learn nothing while you're talking. Take good notes with concrete details, not just your overall impression. They'll help you recall significant facts and make your case for your preferred candidate to the rest of the hiring committee. Also ask the interviewee if they have any questions, especially ones that might affect their understanding of the position or their decision to participate in the next step of the hiring process.

- **Close.** Use the last 10 percent of the interview to wrap up the conversation. Thank the candidate for coming in and explain how and when they'll hear about follow-up interviews or decisions. Briefly remind them of the strengths of your organization, tailored to the issues you've learned are most likely to affect their decisions. Ask if they have any final questions, then shake hands and walk out with them.

Your success in this format will depend on whether or not you ask good questions. See the box "Interview questions" for scripts to use as you prepare.

During or immediately after the interview, you or your HR recruiter should ask the candidate for references. When you speak to these people, as well as any other managers, coworkers, or supervisees you know who are connected to the applicant, verify the basic claims the interviewee has made. But you can also employ variants of the questions in the "Interview questions" box to gain a more complete picture of the candidate.

Step 4: Evaluate candidates

Judging other people for a job is always a subjective exercise. How smart are they, really? Will they get along with the rest of the team? Do they seem genuinely motivated to succeed, or are they just putting on a show? Before

Interview questions

TO GAUGE EXPERIENCE AND COMPETENCIES

- "What three things in the past six months are you the most proud of?"

- "Tell me about your experience with X group in X industry. How is this relevant to this position?" (Repeat)

- "What was your role in achieving X outcome described on your résumé?"

- "How did you gauge success in X role?"

- "What is the most challenging goal you've ever been given?"

- "What connects all the jobs on your résumé?"

TO LEARN MORE ABOUT THEIR PERSPECTIVE

- "Which of your roles did you enjoy the most and why?"

- "How would your peers describe you, using five adjectives?"

- "What's the biggest failure you've experienced and how did you handle it?"

- "Given industry trends, how do you think this role will evolve over the next three to five years?"

TO GAUGE POTENTIAL

- "What do you do to broaden your thinking, experience, or personal development?"

- "What steps do you take to seek out the unknown?"

- "How do you invite input from others on your team?"

- "How do you react when someone challenges you?"

- "Why do you think you were selected for a growth opportunity?"

(continued)

TO GAUGE THE CULTURAL FIT

- "What type of culture do you thrive in, and why?"
- "What values are you drawn to and what's your ideal workplace?"
- "Why do you want to work here?"
- "Tell me about a time that you disagreed with a colleague or your boss and how you handled it."

you make a decision based on your impressions, determine as clearly as you can what biases you may have that could inappropriately affect your decision. Seek outside validation from references and others on the hiring committee, and come to a decision that uses your subjective judgments in the best possible way. That means picking someone because you think he's really determined to succeed, not because you went to the same college or because he is cheerful or easy to talk to.

To organize your evaluation, create a decision-making matrix like the one in exhibit 14-1. For each category, rate the candidate on a scale of 1 to 5, with 5 indicating "excellent." (It's best to do this immediately after the interview; if you can't, use your notes.) Then, in the "Notes" section, write down what seemed truly outstanding to you about this candidate, what worried you, what confused you or seemed anomalous, and finally, what personal biases might be affecting your point of view. Do not overlook this last step. Acknowledging your own biases is a critical part of any decision-making process. Doing so doesn't invalidate your judgment; it helps you double-check and, ultimately, defend the validity of that judgment.

Ask the other members of the decision-making team to fill out a chart like this, too. As a shared starting point, this information will help members corroborate their subjective opinions and work through any conflict in an organized manner.

EXHIBIT 14-1

Candidate evaluation worksheet

Job title:

Candidate name	Education	Previous experience	Job accomplishments	Personal attributes	Cultural fit	Potential	Total
Notes:							
My biases:							
Notes:							
My biases:							
Notes:							
My biases:							

Ratings, 1 (poor) to 5 (excellent)

Source: Harvard Business Review. *Harvard Business Essentials: The Manager's Toolkit.* Boston: Harvard Business Review Press, 2004.

Ultimately, you all must answer two questions: "Do we have enough information to make a good decision?" and "Do we want this person to work for us?" If the answer to both is yes, congratulations! It's time to make an offer.

Step 5: Make an offer

Be sure that you understand your organization's policy on who makes the job offer. In some companies, the immediate supervisor or manager does this; in others, it's the job of the HR department.

Job offers are usually made in person or by telephone. After extending a verbal offer, you should also send a written confirmation. In both cases, make the offer with enthusiasm and a personal touch, perhaps by referring to something positive that you recall from the interview. Probe candidates for information about any concerns, the timing of their decision, and other positions they may be considering.

An offer letter is an official document, so be sure to seek advice from HR before you send it. Do *not* imply that the offer is an employment contract. Include important facts in the letter, such as:

- Starting date

- Job title

- Expected responsibilities

- Compensation

- Benefits summary

- Time limit for responding to the offer

If your candidate accepts the offer, your responsibilities as a talent manager are far from over. Now that you've hired the talent, you need to figure out how to keep it.

Retaining employees

The retention of good employees matters for two bottom-line reasons. First, when employees leave, your company loses their knowledge and their (often expensively) acquired skills. When those employees go to a competitor, the loss is compounded.

A low retention rate also imposes high costs on your organization in terms of job searches. The US Department of Labor estimates the total costs of turnover at about one-third of the new person's yearly salary. Among managerial and professional employees, or people with rare and difficult-to-acquire skill sets, that proportion increases dramatically. In emerging markets, according to the researchers, "the supply of experienced managers is the most limited, and the shortage is expected to continue for another two decades." Strong retention practices would help these companies keep talented employees in a competitive environment.

Understanding why employees come or go is critical to creating stability on your own team. Five issues tend to underlie employees' decisions to stay with an organization:

Issue 1: Pride and trust in the organization

People want to work for well-managed companies with strong missions and skilled, resourceful leaders. When they don't trust the leadership or when they feel the organization is squandering their work, they'll leave.

What to do.

Look for ways to communicate your company's leadership to your team in a positive, concerted way, and connect your team's work to the overall mission of the organization at every possible opportunity. That might mean including an agenda item at each meeting where you discuss how the meeting's business connects to the company mission and your team's strategic objectives.

Encourage your employees to attend companywide events where they can observe and talk to company leadership and, when appropriate, invite them along in small groups to your meetings with higher-level management. If events in your organization, like layoffs or poor quarterly performance, shake employee trust, talk to your team proactively about what the company is doing to turn things around. Highlight the opportunities these turbulent times create for your people.

Also invite your own boss and others to visit your team's work space in informal walk-throughs or meet-and-greets. This sort of interaction can build trust in both directions.

Issue 2: The relationship with their supervisor

People want a boss whom they respect and who supports them. They become alienated from the company when this relationship becomes stressful or problematic, and they don't see any other options in the organization.

What to do.

Although it's your job to manage up and build influence within your organization, in your team's eyes your relationship with them is primary. Employees are highly sensitive to whether you see them as assets that need to be managed for maximum output or people whose development you genuinely care about; hence the importance of the strategies in chapter 3, "Emotional Intelligence," and chapter 11, "Developing Talent."

Issue 3: Meaningful work

People want to work for companies that let them do the kinds of things that appeal to their deepest interests. Satisfying and stimulating work makes all of us more productive. When their responsibilities shift to something less favorable, they seek out better opportunities.

What to do.

Talk to your employees regularly about the fit of their role. When there's a pervasive misfit ("I've always felt I do my best work as a strategic thinker, but lately my job has shifted mainly to execution"), it's time for a job redesign. If you can identify the elements that are generating satisfaction and dissatisfaction in a particular job, you may be able to split off the unwelcome tasks entirely and give them to other people who will appreciate the work. If you can't completely reformat the role, consider other measures that might alleviate your team member's unhappiness: setting up a job rotation or stretch assignment (see the section "Stretch assignments" in chapter 11), adding variety to a repetitive job, or engaging isolated employees in occasional team projects. If a job involves some truly repugnant tasks, consider eliminating or outsourcing those tasks. The cost of outsourcing might actually be lower than the cost of a high turnover rate.

Issue 4: Work-life balance

People want to work in an environment that doesn't cut them off from the other sources of meaning in their life—family, community, extracurricular activities. They look elsewhere when work isolates them from these touchstones, or when it imposes unbearable mental and emotional burdens.

What to do.

Many jobs have periodic rough patches, when work-life balance is just *hard*. As you coach your team, share with them the techniques in chapter 7, "Personal Productivity." Make sure your employees understand the business priorities that are making life so difficult for them right now and the personal payoff for them. Above all, acknowledge the sacrifice. The dismissive attitudes of "Chin up" or "This is just how we do it" are deeply alienating for someone whose home life is in crisis. You should also experiment with new ways to get work done, like remote work and flexible hours.

Outside of these crunch times, set a tone that normalizes a fulfilling life outside work. Encourage people to talk about how they spent their weekends, what their vacation plans are, how their kids are doing, and what new hobbies have caught their interest. Make it clear that you approve of healthy work-life boundaries, and that you don't see them as a threat to your team's dedication.

Issue 5: Fair compensation

People want to work for companies that pay them fairly for their labor. This includes not only competitive wages and benefits but also intangible compensation in the form of opportunities to learn, grow, and achieve.

What to do.

This is a complicated issue to finesse. On the one hand, if talented employees feel undervalued, they'll leave. Even people with strong intrinsic motivations see their compensation as an indication of the organization's appreciation for their contributions and abilities. But compensation isn't a completely reliable motivator. Years ago, Frederick Herzberg, a founder of motivation studies, found that pay raises produce temporary performance improvements at best; other research corroborates that simply offering more money isn't a powerful retention tool.

So what should you do? Claudio Fernández-Aráoz (a senior adviser at the executive search firm Egon Zehnder), Boris Groysberg (a professor at Harvard Business School), and Nitin Nohria (dean of Harvard Business School) collaborated on an analysis of how companies assess and manage their rising stars, and first and foremost they suggest offering a fair and market-wise salary. Any money you save with a below-market rate, you'll lose in depressed profits and turnover costs. But don't go overboard. Even if you can afford "excessive" financial incentives, they might backfire. "While companies need to pay people well to attract and retain high potentials in the first place, they should be careful not to overdo it, because that is the surest way to demotivate employees who are not classified as high potentials, who may feel unfairly paid."

For any individual on your team, some issues will matter more than the others. As you work with your team members, determine which motivations matter the most to each person so you can tailor your retention strategy to their needs.

Motivation and engagement

In the previous section, you considered employee retention from a strategic standpoint: "Where are the most important pressure points? What can I do to make these work in the company's favor?" All of the concerns outlined earlier, from organizational pride to fair compensation, are different expressions of the same underlying issue: employee motivation.

What makes people want to belong to your team? What makes them want to do what you ask, to the very best of their ability? These questions seem so fundamental that it's easy to imagine they don't have real answers. They do. Decades of research (starting with Herzberg, mentioned earlier) have given us a remarkably coherent picture of what truly engages people in their jobs: interesting, challenging work; and the opportunity to achieve and grow into greater responsibility.

Recent research by Teresa Amabile, a Harvard Business School professor, and her collaborator Steven Kramer bear this out. Amabile and Kramer studied how to drive innovative work in organizations and found that "of all the things that can boost emotions, motivation, and perceptions during a workday, the single most important is making progress in meaningful work. And the more frequently people experience that sense of progress, the more likely they are to be creatively productive in the long run." They call this the *progress principle* and encourage managers to provide "catalysts and nourishers" that help people feel as if they're advancing every day, for example, by setting clear, achievable short-term goals and giving team members autonomy as they pursue them, expressing respect to team members, and so forth.

Herzberg's own original recommendation to "enrich" your team's work includes seven strategies for keeping your employees motivated (see exhibit 14-2).

As a manager, you must constantly balance the needs and desires of individuals with those of the company. Whether you're hiring a new candidate or trying to reengage a dissatisfied worker, you need to understand and maximize the value they bring to your team. But you must keep their

EXHIBIT 14-2

Principles of job enrichment

Principle	Motivators involved
Removing some controls while retaining accountability. *For example, limit the number of times employees need to bring a decision to you for a sign-off. Instead, schedule a standing meeting where they can update you about their work and you can offer guidance.*	Responsibility and personal achievement
Increasing the accountability of individuals for own work. *For example, attach clear goals to specific tasks and then ask employees to report to you on their progress toward that goal.*	Responsibility and recognition
Giving a person a complete, natural unit of work (module, division, area, and so on). *For example, give your salespeople responsibility for different geographic regions or customer segments.*	Responsibility, achievement, and recognition
Granting additional authority to employees in their activity; job freedom. *For example, invite employees to redesign a work process that they think could be better.*	Responsibility, achievement, and recognition
Making periodic reports directly available to team members themselves rather than to supervisors. *For example, convene a team meeting to discuss quarterly results, share credit, and discuss next-quarter goals.*	Internal recognition
Introducing new and more difficult tasks not previously handled. *For example, delegate selected leadership tasks or create a stretch assignment.*	Growth and learning
Assigning individuals specific or specialized tasks, enabling them to become experts. *For example, ask employees to study an issue on the team, perhaps one that resonates with their job description or past experience, and to make a recommendation to you about a course of action.*	Responsibility, growth, and advancement

Source: Frederick Herzberg, "One More Time: How Do You Motivate Employees?" *Harvard Business Review*, January 2003.

interests in mind as well—how best to motivate, reward, develop, and advocate for them. One does not take clear precedence over the other; rather, they're symbiotic. Companies depend on satisfied and dedicated employees to succeed; employees depend on strategic leadership for their own happiness and sense of worth.

In this section, you've learned how to think about the employee side of this equation. In part five, "Managing the Business," you'll learn how to think about the business side.

Recap

- Your role as a manager is to bring the best, most promising talent into the organization.

- Before you can make a good hire, you need to know what you are hiring *for*.

- Instead of just filling vacancies, consider how you want your team to evolve. What new competencies are you looking for?

- As you recruit candidates, beware of focusing *too* narrowly on the description. It can be more important to find someone who can grow.

- Retaining talent is vital to the organization because turnover costs are roughly one-third of the person's salary.

- Understanding what makes someone want to stay with your company and belong to your team can help you motivate your employees.

Action items

To define the role you are hiring for:

- ❏ Use the current job description and talk to the incumbent, their colleagues, and even your boss to define the primary tasks and responsibilities associated with the role you will fill.

❏ List the personal and professional attributes your ideal candidate should have. Talk to your team and your colleagues and review past employees' performance reviews to pinpoint the most important qualities.

❏ Synthesize all this information in a job description and run it by your HR department.

To recruit talent:

❏ As you begin your search, get the word out through the people and channels that are most likely to produce high-quality candidates.

❏ In interviews, listen much more than you speak. Ask questions that allow you to understand all facets of a candidate's professional experience and perspective.

❏ Evaluate candidates in a standardized way, so that you can identify your biases and compare opinions meaningfully with your colleagues.

❏ Find out who in your company is authorized to make a formal offer. Issue the offer over the phone or in person, and follow up with a letter.

To retain employees:

❏ Build connections between your team and the organization's leadership, whether that means talking about the vision and activities of leaders or arranging in-person meetings.

❏ Be open to redesigning a job when it goes stale.

❏ Actively coach team members through difficult stretches in their work-life balance, and encourage them to find fulfillment outside work.

❏ Pay your employees fairly, but don't expect money to make up for other, fundamental dissatisfactions.

To motivate your employees:

❏ Initiate informal conversations about what Amabile and Kramer call the "inner work life" of your team, one-on-one or with a group of people who share the same role. Ask "How interested in and challenged by your work do you feel right now? In what parts of your job do you think you're really growing? What parts seem stagnant?"

❏ Review the total distribution of tasks and responsibilities across your team. How could you shift these elements between different roles to deepen individual team members' opportunity for expertise or sense of ownership?

❏ Overcommunicate about changes in plans. When priorities shift, deadlines change, or assignments get axed, talk to your employees up front about why this is happening and what it means for them. Emphasize the value of the work they've already done and explain how that value will be carried forward in the new scheme.

PART FIVE

Managing the Business

15.

Strategy: A Primer

As a manager, you're focused on making your unit as operationally effective as possible—doing things right. But as a leader, you have another charge: to do the *right things*. That means making strategic decisions about how your group should contribute to your organization's overall success.

To maximize your team's contributions, you must align their work with your company's strategy and the actions of others in the company. When your people see that they can truly drive change, their confidence in your leadership and their commitment to your decisions will deepen. And this trust will boost performance down the line.

In chapter 4, "Positioning Yourself for Success," we discussed how you can begin to align your and your team's work with organizational strategy and objectives. In this chapter, you'll discover the role you can play in the strategic thinking of your organization as you grow throughout your career, what strategy *is*, how to formulate it, and how to lead your team through the ensuing change.

Your role in strategy

If you are a beginning or midlevel manager, strategy formulation may not be part of your job, but it will be as you move higher in the organization. So it's never too early to begin thinking strategically about the business. Every day you make decisions—choices that can help or hurt your organization, depending on how well they align with the broader strategy. To generate the best possible results overall for your organization, you need to consider the implications of each course of action. In other words, you need to think strategically.

When you analyze a business process, for example, the part of you that cares about "doing it right" will look at how to improve cost and time effectiveness, or the quality of the output. But as a strategic thinker, you'll also ask yourself: Should we even be doing this process? Is it more or less important to the company's goals than a new process you'd like to introduce? When you ask these higher-order questions and challenge assumptions, you make smarter long-term decisions. And your team makes more meaningful contributions to the organization at large.

The further you advance in your career, the more important your grasp of strategy becomes. As you take on more responsibility, you'll be expected to steer your team in a way that draws on your company's unique competitive advantages, and to formulate plans that build the company's competitive advantage even further. You can build these muscles now by learning what strategy is and how to develop it. Your mastery of these topics will help you stand out in the future.

What is strategy?

Bruce Henderson, founder of Boston Consulting Group, wrote that "strategy is a deliberate search for a plan of action that will develop a business's competitive advantage and compound it." Competitive advantage, he continued, is found in differences: "The differences between you and your competitors are the basis of your advantage." Henderson believes that no two competitors can coexist if they seek to do business in the same way. They must differentiate themselves to survive.

For example, two men's clothing stores on the same block—one featuring formal attire and the other focusing on leisure wear—can potentially prosper. But if the two stores sell the same things under the same terms, one or the other will perish. More likely, the one that differentiates itself through price, product mix, or ambiance will survive. Harvard Business School professor Michael Porter, whose work inspires modern corporate strategy, concurs: "Competitive strategy is about being different. It means deliberately choosing a different set of activities to deliver a unique mix of value." Consider these examples:

- Southwest Airlines didn't become the most profitable air carrier in North America by copying its rivals. It differentiated itself with a strategy of low fares, frequent departures, point-to-point service, and customer-pleasing service.

- Toyota's strategy in developing the hybrid-engine Prius car was to create competitive advantage within two important customer segments: people who want a vehicle that is environmentally benign and cheap to operate, and those who covet the latest thing in auto engineering. The company also hoped that the learning associated with the Prius would give it leadership in a technology with huge future potential.

Strategies may center on low-cost leadership, technical uniqueness, or focus. Porter also argues that you can think about them in terms of strategic position, "performing *different* activities from rivals' or performing similar activities in *different* ways." These positions emerge from three, sometimes overlapping sources:

- **Need-based positioning.** Companies that follow this approach aim to serve all or most of the needs of an identifiable set of customers. These customers may be price sensitive, demand a high level of personal attention and service, or may want products or services that are uniquely tailored to their needs. Target's focus on image-conscious shoppers is an example of this type of positioning.

- **Variety-based positioning.** Here, a company chooses a narrow subset of product/service offerings from within the wider set offered in the industry. It can succeed with this strategy if it delivers faster, better, or at a lower cost than competitors. Walmart's past decision not to stock big-ticket items like appliances and electronics is an example of this type of positioning.

- **Access-based positioning.** Some strategies can be based around access to customers. A discount merchandise chain, for example, may choose to locate its stores exclusively in low-income neighborhoods. This reduces competition from suburban shopping malls and provides easy access for its target market of low-income shoppers, many of whom don't have automobiles. Target's decision to locate stores in urban environments is an example of this type of positioning.

Simply being different, of course, won't keep you in business. Your strategy must also deliver value. And customers define value in different ways: lower cost, greater convenience, greater reliability, faster delivery, more aesthetic appeal, easier use. The list of customer-pleasing values is extremely long. As you evaluate your own company's strategy for gaining competitive advantage, ask yourself these questions:

- Do we differentiate ourselves based on need, variety, or access?

- How does our positioning attract customers away from rivals? How does it draw new customers into the market?

- What value does our strategy aim to provide? Does it deliver?

- What tangible advantage does this strategy provide for our company?

Understanding your company's approach here will hone your ability to think strategically. And it will also allow you to formulate your own group's strategy from the ground up.

Developing strategy

If you haven't had much experience developing strategy, know that most managers are in the same position. That's because it isn't an everyday activity. "Executives hone their management capabilities by tackling problems over and over again," notes Harvard Business School professor Clayton Christensen. "Changing strategy, however, is not usually a task that managers face repeatedly. Once companies have found a strategy that works, they want to use it, not change it. Consequently, most management teams do not develop a competence in strategic thinking."

Whether you're revitalizing your team's business model or building a new business unit from scratch, you need to analyze how your company's external circumstances relate to its internal resources. That's the essence of strategy building: finding unique links between the opportunities and threats that present themselves to your business and your particular capacity to respond.

The order in which you perform this analysis is important. It yields the best results when you begin by identifying a problem out in the world, then work toward a solution inside your company. The process rarely succeeds in the opposite direction: a strategic initiative that's not grounded in a real business need is likely to make you *less* competitive rather than more.

Over the past few decades, a number of frameworks for building strategy have emerged, from the work of Porter and others; for a summary of the major developments, see the box "Navigating the schools of strategic thought" at the end of this chapter. The following steps are a generalized outline of these processes, which may prepare you to contribute to your company's strategy, as well as ensure your team's plans are well constructed.

Step 1: Look outside to identify threats and opportunities

There are always threats in your organization's outer environment: new entrants, demographic changes, suppliers who might cut you off, substitute products that could undermine your business, and macroeconomic trends that may reduce the ability of your customers to pay. Opportunity also lurks in a new-to-the-world technology, an unserved market, and so forth.

Deepen your understanding of this landscape by gathering the views of customers, suppliers, and industry experts you may interact with in your role. Have conversations with others in the organization to identify current threats and opportunities. Some firms, particularly in technological fields, enlist teams of scientists and engineers to analyze markets, competitors, and technical developments. It's their job to look for anything that could threaten their current business or point toward new directions that their business should follow. Gain exposure to this work if possible.

Whether you're contributing directly to strategy development in your role or simply trying to understand the environment in which you operate, consider the following questions:

- What is the economic environment in which we must operate? How is it changing?

- What will our customers want/expect from us in five to ten years? How will the world have changed?

- What major threats do we face now or are we likely to face soon? What aspects of the current environment are our competitors struggling to adapt to?

- What opportunities for profitable action lay before us? What are the risks associated with different opportunities and potential courses of action?

Step 2: Look inside at resources, capabilities, and practices

Internal resources and capabilities can either frame and support or constrain your company's strategy, especially for a larger company with many employees and fixed assets. And rightly so. A strategy to exploit an un-served market in the electronics industry might not be feasible if your firm lacks the financial capital and human knowledge to carry it off. Likewise, a strategy that requires entrepreneurialism from your employees probably won't get off the ground if your company's management practices reward years of service over individual performance.

These internal capabilities—especially the human ones—matter greatly, but strategists often overlook them. To whatever degree you participate in organizational or team strategy development, consider questions like:

- What are our competencies as an organization or team? How do these give us an advantage relative to competitors?

- What resources support or limit our actions?

- What attitudes and behaviors do our employment practices encourage?

- What is our workforce good at, and what does it struggle to accomplish?

- What does it take to implement real change here?

Step 3: Consider strategies for change

Once you have a picture of how the changing external world affects your business and what the company or your team looks like right now from the inside, it's time to think about directions for change. Christensen has advocated that strategy teams first prioritize the threats and opportunities they find (he calls them "driving forces" of competition) and then discuss each one in broad strokes. Like all idea-generation sessions, these conversations will be most successful if you push your team to create many alternatives (see more on brainstorming in the section "Tools for generating ideas" in chapter 13). There is seldom one way to do things, and in some cases, the best parts of two different strategies can be combined to make a stronger, third option.

As you're working with your boss, your peers, or your own team, don't be too attached to your new ideas at this stage. Check your facts and question your assumptions. Some information is bound to be missing, so determine where your knowledge gaps are and how to fill them. As your options start to take shape, vet the leading strategy choices with others, including longtime employees, subject-matter experts, and other industry players in your network. (You'll have to be careful how much information you share with each person, of course.) Collecting a wide range of reactions will help you counter groupthink.

Step 4: Build a good fit among strategy-supporting activities

Good business strategies, according to Porter, *combine* activities into a chain whose links are mutually supporting and lock out imitators. Take the rise of Southwest Airlines as an example: as Porter describes, the company's breakthrough strategy was based on rapid gate turnaround that allowed Southwest to make frequent departures and get the most out of its expensive aircraft assets. The emphasis on gate turnaround also dovetailed with the low-cost, high-convenience proposition the airline offered its customers. Critical activities across the company's operations supported these goals: the highly motivated and effective gate personnel and ground crews, a no-meals policy, and no interline baggage transfers. All made rapid turnarounds possible. "Southwest's strategy," wrote Porter, "involves a whole system of activities, not a collection of parts. Its competitive advantage comes from the way its activities fit and reinforce each other."

To systematize the strategy in your own organization, focus on these issues:

- What activities and processes are involved in carrying out our strategy? Which are most (and least) important to the success of the strategy?

- How could we modify each activity and process to better support the strategy? How can we organize these changes to compound our advantages?

- What resources and constraints should we plan for? How will we implement the highest-priority and highest-impact changes?

Step 5: Create alignment

Once you've developed a satisfactory strategy, your job is only half done. The other half is implementation. You'll need to create alignment between your people and operations, and your strategy. This is critical for managers at any level. Ideally, employees at every level in your company will understand (1) what the strategy is; (2) what their role is in making it work; and (3) what the benefits of the strategy will be to the organization and to them as individuals. Only when your people have a strong grasp of all three points will they be able—and willing—to carry out their work.

Managers like you play two roles in this process. As a *coordinator*, you must organize work in your department so that those everyday efforts support the business's strategic intentions. That means drafting assignments, streamlining processes, and reshaping roles so that no one's time is wasted and everyone feels connected to the shared sense of purpose. And as a *communicator*, you must help people understand the strategy and how their jobs contribute to it. Even your entry-level employees should be able to articulate the goals of the organization and explain how their efforts every day fit in.

———————

It's important for you as a leader to ensure that your employees understand your strategy and instinctively agree that it's in their interests to support it. Sometimes this comes easy, but at other times, organizational change requires a more deliberate effort on your part.

Leading change and transitions

If you're leading your team through strategic change, you'll likely get a range of responses, from "This is exactly what we need! I'm on board!" to quizzical stares and tight-lipped smiles. Some employees may respond with open doubt, fear, or anger. Too often, these reactions take managers by surprise. To overcome resistance, you must actively seek buy-in through-out the process. You've learned how to do this generally in chapter 5, "Be-coming a Person of Influence," but let's discuss how to approach strategic change specifically.

Articulating a vision that others will follow

David Bradford and Allen Cohen, both scholars of business leadership, have observed that significant change only happens when someone pres-ents a compelling vision to draw out and channel the group's energy. "Peo-ple need to see that change will be worth all the effort," they write. "It is difficult to visualize interactive changes in the abstract." Think of a vision as a picture of the hoped-for end result of your new strategy: what it will look like, how it will function, what it will produce. It also helps to tie into something your followers already innately care about.

To share that vision in a way that encourages buy-in:

Focus on people.

"A vision always goes beyond the numbers that are typically found in five-year plans," says John Kotter, a professor at Harvard Business School and author of the classic book *Leading Change: Why Transformation Efforts Fail*. To connect with your team at an emotional level, he suggests, tell a story about how the change you're seeking will affect real people connected with your company—customers *and* employees. Draw this picture in some detail: For example, what will an improved customer interaction look like? How will the customer and the employee feel during these interactions, and how will it make their lives better?

Practice, practice, practice.

You probably won't get your vision statement right the first time. As you gain more experience with the change process and learn about your peo-ple's responses, modulate your pitch. Kotter offers this benchmark: "If you can't communicate the vision to someone in five minutes or less and get a reaction that signifies both understanding and interest, you are not yet done."

Weave your vision into everyday management.

Your employees need repeated exposure to your ideas in order to really internalize them. "Executives who communicate well incorporate messages into their hour-by-hour activities," says Kotter. "In a routine discussion about a business problem, they talk about how proposed solutions fit (or don't fit) into the bigger picture. In a regular performance appraisal, they talk about how the employee's behavior helps or undermines the vision." By orienting employee interactions around your vision, you show your people how the strategic change will work and why it matters—and that you want them to take it seriously.

Find the right allies.

People must accept the messenger before they accept the message. Chances are you aren't that messenger for everyone, and that's OK. Find people who are. Look up and down the chain of command for individuals whose colleagues see them as trustworthy and competent, and who themselves seem open to change. Focus on persuading these people, and ask them to play a leadership role with their peers. That could mean facilitating a meeting with the rest of the team, playing backup for you in a Q&A, or simply supporting your plan in regular interactions with their colleagues.

Court the uncommitted.

Ronald Heifetz and Marty Linksy, who teach leadership at the John F. Kennedy School of Government at Harvard University and are in private practice with Cambridge Leadership Associates, advise that "the people who will determine your success are often those in the middle." These employees don't have anything against your initiative per se, but "they do have a stake in the comfort, stability, and security of the status quo," write Heifetz and Linksy. "They've seen change agents come and go, and they know that your initiative will disrupt their lives and make their futures uncertain. You want to be sure that this general uneasiness doesn't evolve into a move to push you aside." To recruit these players, sincerely acknowledge their accomplishments, as well as the loss and sacrifice that change entails.

Help them understand the personal upside to adapting to change. Also make it clear that only those who can and will adapt will have a future on your team.

Overcoming resistance

Even if you take all these steps to gain support for your vision, your team members may still have some legitimate reservations. If you're asking them to do something new, they may worry about risking failure or about changing their status from master to apprentice. Perhaps you're asking them to throw out comfortable assumptions—that they provide a certain kind of value to the company, that the work they do is stable and prosperous. Maybe change upends the established balance of power, bringing some skill sets and experiences to new prominence and devaluing others.

Dealing with these reactions is tough, but your leadership can survive some discontent. Here are two approaches you can try:

Cook the conflict.

While it's important to confront the fear and doubt that's driving resistance, you can't always afford to bring conflict to a head. Sometimes, open clashes can help resolve disagreements and channel your people's passion in a constructive way. Other times, they simply put too much stress on the group's morale.

To balance this delicate equation, Heifetz and Linksy recommend two techniques: "First, create a secure place where the conflicts can freely bubble up"—maybe an off-site retreat with an outside facilitator, or an on-site conversation governed by a special set of rules for respectful, open dialogue. Insulate these conversations from your discussions about actually implementing and executing change. That means holding separate meetings, at separate times, with separate agendas. "Second, control the temperature" of the conflict by pushing people to tackle a tough issue when you think they can resolve it constructively, and by backing away from disagreements or slowing the pace of change when the group's morale becomes fragile.

Engage others in problem solving.

When everyone is looking to you for answers, you may feel you need to provide them all yourself. But your employees must own this change, too, and they need to feel competent in the new regime. That means "forc[ing] yourself to transfer . . . much of the work and problem-solving to others," say Heifetz and Linsky. If ever there was a time to delegate, it's now. Encourage discussion, collaboration, and creative thinking among team members around specific problems or challenges that arise.

Creating a change-ready culture

It's easier to lead change in an organization that embraces change as a matter of course. Your company is such an organization if it has effective and respected leaders, doesn't luxuriate in the status quo, and is accustomed to collaborative work. To foster this kind of environment, Harvard Business School professor Michael Beer has recommended four approaches for challenging the complacency:

Educate employees about the organization's competitive situation.

Your employees may not be concerned about productivity, customer service, or costs because they simply don't know what's wrong. Share the data that's driving your decisions with your employees and explain the short- and long-term implications for the company.

Solicit input about employees' dissatisfactions and problems.

You may be out of touch with weaknesses of the business or emerging threats—things that front-line employees understand through daily experience. If this is the case, you can't be a credible agent of change. To better understand how your people see the business, ask them what they think and then communicate that information up the chain of command. By opening communication between the front lines and the C-suite, you'll invite your team to think more critically about how the organization can change and make them coauthors of the new strategy. Encourage your employees to be open about the challenges, as well as ideas and solutions that might solve the issues at hand.

Create dialogue about the data.

One-way information sharing is important, but real alignment happens when employees and management develop a joint understanding of the company's problems. Stage conversations where each group can pose questions and offer ideas, incorporating different points of view in a single, coherent discourse.

Set high standards and expect people to meet them.

The act of stating high standards by itself creates dissatisfaction with the current level of performance. Stage "stretch goals" for your team that are difficult but achievable, and backed up with real resource commitments from upper management. Your employees need to believe that they truly can master the new skills and tasks you've set for them, and that you're committed to their success.

Change management is an important skill in today's business world, where strategy-formulation initiatives, reorganizations, and audacious goals are increasingly the norm. If you lead your team through change successfully—at any level—you'll increase the group's productivity and deliver new benefits to your organization.

The more you incorporate a strategic mindset into your everyday life as a manager, the more benefits you'll see in your own career and on your team. By emphasizing the strategic value of team members' contributions and inviting them into a larger conversation about the future of the company, you deepen the meaning of their work.

Recap

- Although you may not formulate strategy, strategic thought is already a part of your job when it comes to managing the company's resources properly.

- Your role as a strategist will evolve as you assume more responsibility. But because few companies explicitly train managers for this sort of work, even experienced managers will benefit from a review.

- Strategy aims to develop a business's competitive advantage and compound it. The basis of this advantage is difference—the unique value your company alone can deliver.

- Your company can create difference in three different ways: need-based, variety-based, or access-based strategic positioning.

- You can evaluate your company's strategic position by analyzing its business with these three lenses.

Action items

- ☐ Begin having informal discussions with customers, suppliers, and industry experts to learn about how they view your industry and the opportunities you may have to better partner with them.

- ☐ Review the major initiatives or projects your organization has launched in the past five years. What does their success or failure reveal about the company's competencies?

- ☐ Map out the major functions and processes in and around your area of responsibility. Is this a "system of activities" or a "collection of parts," in Michael Porter's phrasing? How could you reorganize these processes to better support your company's strategy?

- ☐ Block out a half hour in your schedule to draft *and practice* a short summary of your vision for a new project for your business unit. Try it out on a mentor, colleague, or trusted employee.

❏ Next time an employee comes to you with a complaint about a controversial assignment, put on your coaching hat. Instead of jumping in with solutions or gearing up your pep talk, ask: "What are your priorities here? What possible courses of action do you see?"

❏ Make your company's competitive situation an agenda item for your next team meeting. Invite your boss or another higher-up to deliver an update and field questions from the group.

Navigating the schools of strategic thought

In this HBR article, editor Andrea Ovans lays out the evolution of strategic thought and its best-known thinkers, most persistent ideas, and most influential articles and books.

If you read what Peter Drucker had to say about competition back in the late fifties and early sixties, he really only talked about one thing: competition on price. He was hardly alone; that was evidently how most economists thought about competition, too.

It was this received opinion Michael Porter was questioning when, in 1979, he mapped out four additional competitive forces in his seminal article "How Competitive Forces Shape Strategy." "Price competition can't be all there is to it," he explained to a *Harvard Business Review* editor when asked about the origins of the five forces framework.

So, after much theoretical and empirical labor, he famously argued, in addition to the fierceness of price competition among industry rivals, the degree of competitiveness in an industry (that is, the degree to which players are free to set their own prices) depends on the bargaining power of buyers and of suppliers, as well as how threatening substitute products and new entrants are. When these forces are weak, as in software and soft drinks, many companies are profitable. When they are strong, as in the airline and hotel industries, almost no company earns an attractive return on investment. Strategy, for Porter, is a matter of working out your company's best position relative not just to pricing pressures from rivals but to all the forces in your competitive environment.

For many, it seemed, that was pretty much the last word on the subject. But that wasn't exactly so.

In "What Is Strategy?"—published seventeen years after he burst on the scene with his original five forces article—Porter argues against a bevy of alternate views, both old and then new, that were circulating in the intervening years. In particular, he takes issue with the views that strategy is a matter of:

- Seeking a single ideal competitive position in an industry (as the dot-com wannabes were apparently doing at the time he was writing)

- Benchmarking and adopting best practices (a veiled reference to the book *In Search of Excellence*)

- Aggressive outsourcing and partnering to improve efficiencies (perhaps a reference to "The Origin of Strategy," published in 1989 by Boston Consulting Group founder Bruce Henderson)

- Focusing on a few key success factors, critical resources, and core competencies (maybe a reference to C. K. Prahalad and Gary Hamel's 1990 article, "The Core Competence of the Organization")

- Rapidly responding to ever-evolving competitive and market changes (perhaps a reference to Rita McGrath and Ian MacMillan's 1995 article on innovation strategy "Discovery-Driven Planning")

At a fundamental level, all strategies for Porter boil down to two very broad options: *Do what everyone else is doing (but spend less money doing it),* or *Do something no one else can do.* While either approach can be successful, the two are for him not economically (or, one might say, morally) equivalent. Competing by doing what everyone else is doing means, he says, competing on price (that is, learning to be more efficient than your rivals). But that just shrinks the pie as, in the rush to the bottom, profitability declines for the entire industry.

Alternatively, you could expand the pie by staking out some sustainable position based on a unique advantage you create with a clever, preferably complicated, and interdependent set of activities (which some thinkers also call a value chain or a business model). This choice is easy to see in the airline industry, where most airlines "compete to be the best," as Porter puts it, fighting over a very stingy pie indeed, while Southwest, among a handful of other airlines, built far more profitable businesses with a completely different approach, which targeted a different customer (people who might otherwise drive, for example) with a cleverly efficient set of interdependent activities, thereby expanding the entire market.

A tour de force by any measure, "What Is Strategy?" is certainly required reading for all strategists. But it is far from the final word. One could perhaps usefully divide the vast universe of subsequent strategy ideas into those that focus on:

- Doing something new

- Building on what you already do well

- Reacting opportunistically to emerging possibilities

In the *do something new* camp, then, would be W. Chan Kim and Renée Mauborgne's work on finding or creating uncontested new markets, first articulated in 1999 in "Creating New Market Space," and further fleshed out in 2004 in the now-classic "Blue Ocean Strategy," as well Alvin Roth's seminal 2007 work on "The Art of Designing Markets," and Mark Johnson, Clayton Christensen, and Henning Kagermann's "Reinventing Your Business Model." So, too, would be transformation strategies based on reconsidering your company or your industry's value chain. These include not only much of Porter's work but Ian MacMillan and Rita McGrath's "Discovering New Points of Differentiation."

In the *building on what you already do well* camp are "Finding Your Next Core Business," by Bain consultant Chris Zook, and "Growth Outside the Core" (about adjacency moves) by Zook and colleague James Allen, as well as the classic "Competing on Resources," by David Collis and Cynthia Montgomery. Also in this category are the myriad of articles on competitive responses, which include George Stalk and Rob Lachenauer's "Hardball: Five Killer Strategies for Trouncing the Competition," and its companion "Curveball: Strategies to Fool the Competition." Here, too, can be found articles on how to defend yourself against disruptors, like Richard D'Aveni's "The Empire Strikes Back: Counterrevolutionary Strategies for Industry Leaders," and "Surviving Disruption," in which Maxwell Wessel and Clayton Christensen detail a systematic way to determine when it's too soon to abandon your business to a disruptor.

It's tempting to think the third camp—*reacting opportunistically to emerging possibilities*—represents the field's most recent thinking. But, in fact, McGrath and MacMillan's work on discovery-driven planning was first introduced twenty years ago, and this camp includes other classic flexibility-as-strategy pieces that date from the 1990s, including Tim Luehrman's "Strategy as a Portfolio of Real Options," and David Yoffie and Michael Cusumano's "Judo Strategy." It also includes Michael Mankins and Richard Steele's more recent "Stop Making Plans; Start Making Decisions," which made the case for continuous strategic planning cycles. And, finally, it includes various approaches to running established companies as if they were startups, such as Steve Blank's "Why the Lean Start-Up Changes Everything."

Take a look at the richness of the ideas in all three camps, and it's hard to agree that strategy boils down to a discouraging choice between "do something so dauntingly original that no one can copy you" and "fight to the death with your rivals over the pie." Taken in all of its variety and complexity, this body of work suggests not the terrifying terrain of competitive jeopardy but a broad expanse of opportunity; in the face of rapidly changing technologies, globalization, and the inexorably accelerating pace of change, there remain endlessly clever new ways to make money, beat the competition, and nudge Adam Smith's invisible hand toward truly productive and profitable enterprises.

Source: Adapted from Andrea Ovans, "What Is Strategy, Again?" HBR.org, May 12, 2015.

16.

Mastering Financial Tools

You've probably heard the old adage that "you can't manage what you don't measure." Financial tools help you measure performance—of a product line, an investment, a functional team, or the health of the organization. They include commonly used financial statements, budgeting processes, and other diagnostic frameworks. By using these tools to assess the part of the business under your purview, you'll wield greater power with your colleagues in the finance department and with your leadership when you pitch a new idea or present a budget.

As a manager, you don't need to be a financial expert. But financial literacy, like strategic thinking, can improve your current performance, as well as your upward mobility. Financial literacy further supports your ability to understand your company's overall position and strategy, and how your piece fits into the bigger picture. That grasp of finance will help you make better decisions about how to allocate resources within your unit, and how to make the best possible contribution to the organization as a whole. Finally, if you can translate your own management goals and tactics into this language for your bosses, you'll signal to them that you're a savvy systems thinker with a feel for how the whole business works.

If you fear that your financial literacy is not very strong, don't worry. You're not alone. "In my experience, most senior executives find [measuring financial performance] an onerous if not threatening task," writes Andrew Likierman, dean of London Business School and former managing director of the UK Treasury. Because executives don't feel confident in their financial literacy, he explains, they leave this vital task "to people who may not be natural judges of performance but are fluent in the language of spreadsheets. The inevitable result is a mass of numbers and comparisons that provide very little insight into a company's performance and may even lead to decisions that hurt it." By becoming financially literate yourself, you can combine the numbers with your business insight in one powerful point of view on the company's actions, performance, and opportunities.

In this chapter, you'll first learn overarching principles of analyzing financial performance, and then we'll introduce you to the three key financial statements and how they relate to your work as a nonfinancial manager. Lastly, you'll learn about the budgeting process.

The basics of financial performance

True financial literacy requires more than facility with numbers and financial documents. First, you need to understand a few basic principles about how far the numbers can take you and what their limits are.

Principle 1: Look at context.

Measure more than just your company's or your team's performance at this moment. For example, it's useful to know that your business runs at a 30 percent margin. But that number will mean more if you also know that last year's margins were 35 percent, your peer's margins are 28 percent, or your industry's average margin is 45 percent.

Principle 2: Look forward as well as backward.

When you make important financial decisions, like a major capital investment, you need to think about not just what your past performance permits, but what the future will reward. Analyze forward-looking data like economic forecasts or predicted customer behaviors, in addition to your historical performance.

Principle 3: Question your data.

For all that your business relies on math, numbers can easily lead you astray. Indeed, many managers are surprised to learn that finance is as much an art as a science. Your information sources are often human—the procurement specialist who gathers quotes from vendors, for example—and their own biases may color the data or the way it's presented. If they have a personal interest in the outcome of a calculation, they may over- or underestimate a figure, even unconsciously.

There are some things financial tools simply don't measure very well. You can *try* to assign a dollar value to the benefits your team receives from a retreat or morale-building program, but if it feels as if you're pulling a number out of a hat, others in the company will probably find your "calculations" suspect too. "Think about this for a moment," urges Likierman. "How on earth can the presumed causal link [behind your number] be justified?" If the answer to this question is unclear even to you, Likierman urges a more qualitative form of measurement.

Keep these principles in mind as you use the financial documents described in the next section to measure the financial performance of your company or your group.

Understanding financial statements

To understand how your business works and whether it will keep working, consider these four questions:

- What does your company own, and what does it owe to others?

- What are its sources of revenue, and how has it spent its money?

- How much profit has it made?

- What is the state of its financial health?

You can find the answers to these questions in three main financial statements: the *balance sheet*, the *cash flow statement*, and the *income statement*. These are the essential documents of any business. Executives use them to assess performance and identify areas for action, shareholders look at them to keep tabs on how well their capital is being managed, outside investors mine them to identify opportunities, and lenders and suppliers examine them to determine the creditworthiness of the companies with which they deal.

Every manager, no matter where they sit in the organization, should have a solid grasp of these basic statements. All three follow the same general format from company to company, though specific line items may vary depending on the business. If you can, get copies of your company's most recent financials so that you can compare them with the samples discussed here. If your boss is reluctant to distribute the financial reports to you, tell her you're interested in expanding your financial understanding of the business and see if she will consider reviewing them with you.

The balance sheet

Companies prepare balance sheets to summarize their financial position at a given point in time, usually at the end of the month, the quarter, or the fiscal year. This document shows what the company owns (its assets), what it owes (its liabilities), and its book value, or net worth (also called owners' equity, or shareholder's equity). As a manager, it can help you understand how efficiently the company is operating.

Assets comprise all the physical resources a company can put to work in the service of the business. This category includes cash and financial instruments (such as stocks and bonds), inventories of raw materials and finished goods, land, buildings, and equipment, plus the firm's *accounts receivable*—funds owed by customers for goods or services purchased.

Liabilities are debts to suppliers and other creditors. If a firm borrows money from a bank, that's a liability. If it buys $1 million worth of parts and hasn't paid for those parts as of the date on the balance sheet, that $1 million is a liability. Funds owed to suppliers are known as *accounts payable*.

Owners' equity is what's left after you subtract total liabilities from total assets. A company with $3 million in total assets and $2 million in liabilities has $1 million in owner's equity. That definition gives rise to what's often called the *fundamental accounting equation*:

> *Assets – Liabilities = Owners' Equity*
>
> or
>
> *Assets = Liabilities + Owners' Equity*

The balance sheet shows assets on one side of the ledger, liabilities and owners' equity on the other. It's called a *balance* sheet because the two sides must always balance, as you'll see in the balance sheet of Amalgamated Hat Rack, an imaginary company whose finances we will consider throughout this section. The balance sheet describes not only how much the company has invested in assets but also what kinds of assets it owns, what portion comes from creditors (liabilities), and what portion comes from owners (equity).

Analyzing the balance sheet can give you an idea of how efficiently a company is utilizing its assets and managing its liabilities. This data is most helpful when compared with the same information from one or more previous years. Amalgamated Hat Rack's balance sheet (exhibit 16-1) shows assets, liabilities, and owners' equity for December 31, 2017, and December 31, 2018. Compare the figures, and you'll see that Amalgamated is moving in a positive direction: it's increased its owners' equity by $397,500.

Balance sheet elements.

Now let's take a closer look at each section of the balance sheet.

ASSETS.   Listed first are *current assets*: cash on hand and marketable securities, receivables, and inventory. Generally, current assets can be converted into cash within one year. Next is a tally of *fixed assets*, which are harder to turn into cash. The biggest category of fixed assets is usually *property, plant, and equipment*; for some companies, it's the only category.

EXHIBIT 16-1

Amalgamated Hat Rack balance sheet as of December 31, 2018 and 2017

	2018	2017	Increase (Decrease)
Assets			
Cash and marketable securities	$ 652,500	486,500	166,000
Accounts receivable	555,000	512,000	43,000
Inventory	835,000	755,000	80,000
Prepaid expenses	123,000	98,000	25,000
Total current assets	2,165,500	1,851,500	314,000
Gross property, plant, and equipment	2,100,000	1,900,000	200,000
Less: accumulated depreciation	333,000	290,500	(42,500)
Net property, plant, and equipment	1,767,000	1,609,500	157,500
Total assets	$ 3,932,500	3,461,000	471,500
Liabilities and owners' equity			
Accounts payable	$ 450,000	430,000	20,000
Accrued expenses	98,000	77,000	21,000
Income tax payable	17,000	9,000	8,000
Short-term debt	435,000	500,000	(65,000)
Total current liabilities	1,000,000	1,016,000	(16,000)
Long-term debt	750,000	660,000	90,000
Total liabilities	1,750,000	1,676,000	74,000
Contributed capital	900,000	850,000	50,000
Retained earnings	1,282,500	935,000	347,500
Total owners' equity	2,182,500	1,785,000	397,500
Total liabilities and owners' equity	$ 3,932,500	$ 3,461,000	$ 471,500

Source: Adapted from Harvard Business Review, *Finance Basics* (20-Minute Manager Series). Boston: Harvard Business Review Press, 2014.

Since fixed assets other than land don't last forever, the company must charge a portion of their cost against revenue over their estimated useful life. This is called *depreciation*, and the balance sheet shows the *accumulated depreciation* for all the company's fixed assets. Gross property, plant, and equipment minus accumulated depreciation equals the current book value of property, plant, and equipment.

Mergers and acquisitions can throw an additional asset category into the mix. If one company has purchased another for a price above the fair market value of its assets, the difference is known as *goodwill*, and it must be recorded. This is an accounting fiction, but goodwill often includes tangibles with real value, such as brand names, intellectual property, or the acquired company's reputation.

LIABILITIES AND OWNERS' EQUITY. Now let's consider the claims against a company's assets. The category *current liabilities* represents money owed to creditors and others that typically must be paid within a year. It includes short-term loans, accrued salaries, accrued income taxes, accounts payable, and the current year's repayment obligation on a long-term loan. *Long-term liabilities* are usually bonds or mortgages—debts that the company is contractually obliged to repay over a period of time longer than a year.

As explained earlier, subtracting total liabilities from total assets leaves owners' equity. Owners' equity includes *retained earnings* (net profits that accumulate on a company's balance sheet after payment of dividends to shareholders) and *contributed capital*, or *paid-in capital* (capital received in exchange for shares).

The balance sheet shows, in effect, how its assets were paid for—from borrowed money (liabilities), the capital of the owners, or both.

HISTORICAL COST. Balance sheet figures may not correspond to actual market values, except for such items as cash, accounts receivable, and accounts payable. This is because accountants record most items at their historical cost. If, for example, a company's balance sheet indicated land worth $700,000, that figure would be what the company originally paid for the land years ago. If it was purchased in downtown San Francisco in the 1960s, for example, now it is likely worth more than the value stated on the balance sheet. So why do accountants use historical instead of market values? The short answer is that it's the lesser of two evils. If market values were required, then every public company would be required to get a professional appraisal of every one of its properties, warehouse inventories, and so forth, and would have to do so every year—a logistical nightmare.

How the balance sheet relates to you.

Though accountants prepare the balance sheet, it's filled with important information for nonfinancial managers. Here are a couple ways you can use a balance sheet to see how efficiently your company is operating.

WORKING CAPITAL. Subtracting current liabilities from current assets gives you the company's *net working capital*, or the amount of money tied up in current operations. A quick calculation from its most recent balance sheet shows that Amalgamated had $1,165,500 in net working capital at the end of 2016.

Financial managers give substantial attention to the level of working capital, which typically expands and contracts with the level of sales. Too little working capital can put a company in a bad position: it may be unable to pay its bills or take advantage of profitable opportunities. But too much working capital reduces profitability since the capital must be financed in some way, usually through interest-bearing loans.

Inventory is a component of working capital that directly affects many nonfinancial managers. As with working capital in general, there's a tension between having too much and too little. On the one hand, plenty of inventory solves business problems. The company can fill customer orders without delay, and the inventory provides a buffer against potential production stoppages or interruptions in the flow of raw materials or parts. On the other hand, every piece of inventory must be financed, and the market value of the inventory itself may decline while it sits on the shelf.

FINANCIAL LEVERAGE. Using borrowed money to acquire an asset is called *financial leverage.* People say that a company is highly leveraged when the percentage of debt on its balance sheet is high relative to the capital invested by the owners. (*Operating leverage,* by contrast, refers to the extent to which a company's operating costs are fixed rather than variable. For example, a manufacturing company that relies on heavy investments in machinery and very few workers to produce its goods has a high operating leverage.)

Financial leverage can increase returns on an investment, but it also increases risk. For example, suppose that you paid $400,000 for an asset, using $100,000 of your own money and $300,000 in borrowed funds. (For simplicity, we'll ignore loan payments, taxes, and any cash flow you might get from the investment.) Four years go by, and your asset has appreciated to $500,000. Now you decide to sell. After paying off the $300,000 loan, you end up with $200,000 in your pocket—your original $100,000 plus a $100,000 profit. That's a gain of 100 percent on your personal capital, even though the asset increased in value by only 24 percent. Financial leverage made this possible. If you had financed the purchase entirely with your own funds, you would have ended up with only a 25 percent gain. In the United States and most other countries, tax policy makes financial leverage even more attractive by allowing businesses to treat the interest paid on loans as a deductible business expense.

But leverage can cut both ways. If the value of an asset drops, or if it fails to produce the anticipated level of revenue, then leverage works against the asset's owner. Consider what would have happened in our example if the asset's value had dropped by $100,000—that is, to $300,000. The owner would still have to repay the initial loan of $300,000 and would have nothing left over. The entire $100,000 investment would have disappeared.

FINANCIAL STRUCTURE OF THE FIRM. The negative potential of financial leverage is what keeps CEOs, their financial executives, and board members from maximizing their companies' debt financing. Instead, they seek a financial structure that creates a realistic balance between debt and equity on the balance sheet. Although leverage enhances a company's potential profitability as long as things go right, managers know that every dollar of debt increases risk, both because of the danger just cited and because high debt entails high interest costs, which must be paid in good times and bad. Many companies have failed when business reversals or recessions reduced their ability to make timely payments on their loans.

When creditors and investors examine corporate balance sheets, therefore, they look carefully at the debt-to-equity ratio. They factor the riskiness of the balance sheet into the interest they charge on loans and the return they demand from a company's bonds. A highly leveraged company, for example, may have to pay two or three times the interest rate paid by a less leveraged competitor. Investors also demand a higher rate of return for their stock investments in highly leveraged companies. They will not accept high risks without expecting commensurately high returns.

The cash flow statement

The *cash flow statement* is the least used—and least understood—of the three essential statements. It shows in broad categories how a company acquired and spent its cash during a given span of time. For managers, the status of the company's cash flow can affect budgeting, so it's good to have a sense of whether cash is tight or plentiful.

As you'd expect, expenditures show up on the statement as negative figures, and sources of income figures are positive. The bottom line in each category is simply the net total of inflows and outflows, and it can be either positive or negative. (See Amalgamated's cash flow statement in exhibit 16-2.)

The statement has three major categories. *Operating activities*, or *operations*, refers to cash generated by, and used in, a company's ordinary business operations. It includes everything that doesn't explicitly fall in the other two categories. *Investing activities* covers cash spent on capital equipment and other investments (outgoing), and cash realized from the sale of such investments (incoming). *Financing activities* refers to cash used to reduce debt, buy back stock, or pay dividends (outgoing), and cash from loans or from stock sales (incoming).

EXHIBIT 16-2

Amalgamated Hat Rack cash flow statement for the year ending December 31, 2018

Net income	$ 347,500
Operating activities	
Accounts receivable	(43,000)
Inventory	(80,000)
Prepaid expenses	(25,000)
Accounts payable	20,000
Accrued expenses	21,000
Income tax payable	8,000
Depreciation expenses	42,500
Total changes in operating assets and liabilities	(56,500)
Cash flow from operations	291,000
Investing activities	
Sale of property, plant, and equipment	267,000*
Capital expenditures	(467,000)
Cash flow from investing activities	(200,000)
Financing activities	
Short-term debt decrease	(65,000)
Long-term borrowing	90,000
Capital stock	50,000
Cash dividends to stockholders	—
Cash flow from financing activities	75,000
Increase in cash during year	$ 166,000

* Assumes sale price was at book value; the company had yet to start depreciating this asset.

Source: Adapted from Harvard Business Review, *Finance Basics* (20-Minute Manager Series). Boston: Harvard Business Review Press, 2014.

Again using the Amalgamated Hat Rack example, we see that in 2018 the company generated a total positive cash flow (increase in cash) of $166,000. This is the sum of cash flows from operations ($291,000), investing activities (minus $200,000), and financing ($75,000).

The cash flow statement shows the relationship between net profit, from the income statement, and the actual change in cash that appears in the company's bank accounts. In accounting language, it "reconciles" profit and cash through a series of adjustments to net profit. Some of these adjustments are simple. Depreciation, for instance, is a noncash expense, so you have to add depreciation to net profit if what you're interested in is the change in cash. Other adjustments are harder to grasp, though the arithmetic isn't difficult. If a company's accounts receivable are lower at the end of 2018 than they were at the end of 2017; for example, it took in "extra" cash from operations, so we would add that to net profit as well.

This document is useful because it indicates whether your company is successfully turning its profits into cash, and that ability is ultimately what will keep the company *solvent*, or able to pay bills as they come due.

How the cash flow statement relates to you.

If you're a manager in a large corporation, changes in your employer's cash flow won't typically have an impact on your day-to-day job. Nevertheless, it's a good idea to stay up to date on your company's cash situation, with your leader's support, because it may affect your budget for the upcoming year. When cash is tight, you will probably want to be conservative in your planning. When it's plentiful, you may have an opportunity to propose a bigger budget. Note that a company can be quite profitable and still be short of cash as a result of a lot of new investments, for example, or trouble collecting receivables.

You may also have some influence over the items that affect the cash flow statement. Are you responsible for inventory? Keep in mind that every addition there requires a cash expenditure. Are you in sales? A sale isn't really a sale until it's paid for, so watch your receivables.

The income statement

Of the three main financial statements, the income statement has the greatest bearing on a manager's job. That's because most managers are responsible in some way for one or more of its elements—generating revenue, managing profit and loss, or managing expense budgets.

Unlike the balance sheet, which is a snapshot of a company's position at one point in time, the *income statement* shows cumulative business results within a defined time frame, such as a quarter or a year. It tells you whether the company is making a profit or a loss—that is, whether it has a positive or negative net income (net earnings)—and how much. This is why the income statement is often referred to as the *profit-and-loss statement*, or *P&L*. The income statement also tells you the company's revenues and expenses during the time period it covers. Knowing the revenues and the profit enables you to determine the company's *profit margins*.

As we did with the balance sheet, we can represent the contents of the income statement with a simple equation:

Revenues – Expenses = Net Income

An income statement starts with the company's *sales*, or *revenues*. This is primarily the value of the goods or services delivered to customers, but you may have revenues from other sources as well. Note that revenues in most cases are not the same as cash. For companies that use an accrual method of revenue recognition (most larger companies), if a company delivers $1 million worth of goods in December 2018 and sends out an invoice at the end of the month, for example, that $1 million in sales counts as revenue for the year 2018 even though the customer hasn't yet paid the bill.

Various expenses—the costs of making and storing a company's goods, administrative costs, depreciation of plant and equipment, interest expenses, and taxes—are then deducted from revenues. The bottom line—what's left over—is the *net income* (or *net profit*, or *net earnings*) for the period covered by the statement.

Let's look at the various line items on the income statement for Amalgamated Hat Rack in exhibit 16-3.

The *cost of goods sold*, or *COGS*, represents the direct costs of manufacturing hat racks. This figure covers raw materials, such as lumber, and everything needed to turn those materials into finished goods, such as labor. Subtracting cost of goods sold from revenues gives us Amalgamated's gross profit—an important measure of a company's financial performance. In 2018, *gross profit* was $1,600,000.

The next major category of cost is *operating expenses*, which include the salaries of administrative employees, office rents, sales and marketing costs, and other costs not directly related to making a product or delivering a service.

EXHIBIT 16-3

Amalgamated Hat Rack income statement

	For the period ending December 31, 2018
Retail sales	$ 2,200,000
Corporate sales	1,000,000
Total sales revenue	3,200,000
Less: Cost of goods sold	1,600,000
Gross profit	1,600,000
Less: Operating expenses	800,000
Less: Depreciation expenses	42,500
Earnings before interest and taxes	757,500
Less: Interest expense	110,000
Earnings before income taxes	647,500
Less: Income taxes	300,000
Net income	$ 347,500

Source: Adapted from Harvard Business Review, *Finance Basics* (20-Minute Manager
Series). Boston: Harvard Business Review Press, 2014.

Depreciation appears on the income statement as an expense, even though it involves no out-of-pocket payment. As described earlier, it's a way of allocating the cost of an asset over the asset's estimated useful life.

Subtracting operating expenses and depreciation from gross profit gives you a company's *operating earnings*, or *operating profit*. This is often called *earnings before interest and taxes*, or *EBIT*, as it is on Amalgamated's statement.

The last expenses on the income statement are typically taxes and any interest due on loans. If you get a net profit figure after subtracting all expenses, as Amalgamated does, your company is profitable.

As with the balance sheet, comparing income statements over a period of years reveals much more than examining a single income statement. You can spot trends, turnarounds, and recurring problems. Many companies' annual reports show data going back five years or more.

How the income statement relates to you.

Let's look at the three managerial activities that the income statement captures:

GENERATING REVENUE. In one sense, nearly everyone in a company helps generate revenue, but it's the primary responsibility of the sales and marketing departments. If your revenues rise faster than the competition's, you can reasonably assume that the folks in sales and marketing are doing a good job.

It's critical that managers in these departments understand the income statement so that they can balance costs against revenue. If sales reps give too many discounts, for instance, they may reduce the company's gross profit. If marketers spend too much money in pursuit of new customers, they will eat into operating profit. It's the manager's job to track these numbers as well as revenue itself.

MANAGING A P&L. Many managers have P&L responsibility, which means they are accountable for an entire chunk of the income statement. This is probably the case if you're running a business unit, a store, a plant, or a branch office, or if you're overseeing a product line. The income statement you're accountable for isn't quite the same as the whole company's. For instance, it's unlikely to include interest expense and other overhead items, except as an "allocation" at the end of the year. Even so, your job is to manage revenue generation and costs so that your unit or product line contributes as much profit to the company as possible. For that, you need to understand and track revenue, cost of goods sold, and operating expenses.

MANAGING BUDGETS. Running a department means working within the confines of an expense budget. If you oversee a unit in information or human resources, for example, you may have little influence on revenue, but you will surely be expected to watch your costs closely, and all those costs will affect the income statement. Staff departments' expenses usually show up in the operating expenses line. If you invest in any capital equipment, like a complex piece of software, you will also add to the depreciation line. In the next section, you'll learn more about how to analyze the opportunities and constraints that shape your budget.

Budgeting

Budgeting season can be challenging for managers. The number-wrangling often causes stress and conflict and typically requires a time investment on frustratingly tight schedules. But good budgets are worth the time and trouble. They perform four basic functions, each critical to the success of a company in achieving its strategic objectives.

First, a budget forces you to *plan*—to set goals, choose a course of action, and predict the results. During this process, you must also *coordinate and communicate* with the different arms of your business to reconcile your collective priorities in a single, unified scheme. Once your plan has been set in motion, you rely on this scheme to periodically *monitor progress*, comparing actual results with the budget's projections. Eventually, your company will use this information to *evaluate performance*—yours, and other managers. And you'll use it to assess your own group.

Depending on your position in your organization, you may be required to deal with several different kinds of budgets:

- **The master budget** summarizes all the individual financial projects within an organization for a given period. It's the heart and soul of the budgeting process, incorporating the operating budget and financial budget of an organization in one comprehensive picture. Top management and financial executives are responsible for creating this budget.

- **The operating budget** collects the budgets from each *function* in the company, such as research and development, production, marketing, distribution, and customer service. This budget specifies revenues and costs for the coming period in a format much like the income statement every company generates. It's a target, not a forecast, a pact that top management and other members of the management team make with one another.

- **The financial budget** is a plan for the capital that will support the company's operating budget. It usually has three parts: a cash budget that plans for the level and timing of cash inflow and outflow; an operating asset investment plan that ensures that adequate capital will be available for assets such as inventory and accounts receivable; and a capital investment plan that budgets for proposed investments in long-term productive assets such as property, plant, and equipment expenditures and extended R&D programs. This budget is created by your organization's financial managers.

Master budgeting goes hand in hand with strategic planning at the highest level. The senior managers involved in this process consider questions like "Do the tactical plans we're considering support the larger and longer-term strategic goals of the company?" "Do we have, or have access to, the cash we need to fund these activities through the immediate budget period?" "Will we create enough value to attract adequate future resources —profit, loans, investors, and so on—to achieve our longer-term goals?" If you're not part of top management, you're more likely to engage with budgets at the *operating* level.

Preparing the operating budget

In a nutshell, the operating budget is structured as follows:

$$Revenues - (Cost\ of\ Goods\ Sold + Sales,\ General,\ and\ Administrative\ Costs) = Operating\ Income$$

You can balance this equation in five steps.

Step 1: Calculate your expected revenues (as appropriate).

If you have budget responsibility for revenue, you must apply some assumptions to forecast revenue growth (or decline). If you use the *incremental-budgeting approach*, you'll calculate this figure based on past performance and your future expectations for sales. If you use the *zero-based budgeting approach*, you'll create sales projections for each product or service from the ground up, using forecasted economic data, predicted consumer behavior, and other information.

Establishing projected revenue figures can create internal tensions. If managers are evaluated and rewarded for achieving their budgeted revenue targets, they may be tempted to put forward conservative numbers that will be easy to reach. This budgetary slack, or padding, provides a hedge for managers against downturns or inefficiencies. If actual revenues are higher than budgeted revenues (a likely outcome), the manager appears extremely effective. Ask your leader if they would prefer a more conservative or aggressive view of possible revenue, and then negotiate with them on a forecast that is achievable and reasonable, while still having to push your team in order to reach your goals. Be prepared to discuss what drivers are affecting your revenue forecast positively or negatively. Validating your assumptions behind the forecast with others may help you refine the numbers before you finalize your budget.

Step 2: Calculate the expected cost of goods sold.

As you'll recall, the cost of goods sold, or COGS, describes the direct costs of manufacturing a product or delivering a service. The total number of units to be produced will form the basis for determining these costs, including labor and materials. Ask team members most directly involved in production and sales to understand and capture all costs accurately.

Step 3: Calculate the expected other costs.

Other nonproduction costs include research and development, product design, marketing, distribution, customer service, and administration. Collaboration and sharing of your plans will be essential to your success in capturing a reasonable cost forecast. You don't want to miss costs that may come up throughout the year, as you'll still be responsible for your budget numbers.

Step 4: Calculate the expected operating income.

This is the difference between expected sales (step 1) and expected costs (steps 2 and 3). It's your target for the net profit (or loss) your unit will accrue during this financial period. Once you finalize your budget, you'll likely have intense scrutiny of your ability to achieve this number. Do your homework and check your work for accuracy.

Step 5: Develop alternative scenarios.

Budgeting is an iterative process, in which you constantly push yourself to ask, "What if?" Pose questions like: "How will a change in one part of this equation affect the expected outcome? For example, if we increase advertising, how will that affect sales?" "What are the major risks we're facing right now—for example, a labor shortage, production constraints, or falling prices? How can we incorporate that risk into the budget?"

To some degree, using financial tools is a matter of numerical calculation, a process that we leave more and more to financial modeling software and other technology. But numbers aren't always as objective as they seem. They're generated, collected, and interpreted by real people with materially different points of view. In this process, there's a lot of room for conflicting needs, dueling assumptions, and genuine disagreements about what's likely to happen.

By understanding how these tools work, you'll be better equipped to understand what the numbers are really saying. Financial literacy will improve your knowledge of the business and make you a better advocate for your team's needs and your own initiatives. Your management team lives and breathes these financial statements every day; when you ground your ideas in the language and results that matter to *them*, you'll gain credibility and influence in your organization.

Recap

- Financial data is most meaningful when you use it to compare your own performance to your competitors, and to future market conditions.

- Numbers aren't infallible. Question your data sources and be critical about the kinds of questions you apply financial techniques to.

- The balance sheet, income statement, and cash flow statement offer three perspectives on a company's financial performance. They tell three different but related stories about how well your company is doing financially.

- The *balance sheet* shows a company's financial position at a specific point in time. It provides a snapshot of its assets, liabilities, and equity on a given day.

- The *income statement* shows the bottom line. It indicates how much profit or loss was generated over a period of time—usually a month, a quarter, or a year.

- The *cash flow statement* tells where the company's cash came from and where it went. It shows the relationship between net profit and the change in cash recorded from one balance sheet to the next.

- Your own budgeting activities as a manager happen under the umbrella of your company's master budget, operating budget, and financial budget.

Action items

Financial statements:

- ❑ Review the balance sheet, cash flow statement, and income statement for your organization and your division to familiarize yourself with your company's finances.

❏ Bring any questions you have to your manager; this is a good opportunity to show them that you are engaged in learning more about the organization and to better understand their perspective.

Budgeting:

❏ Create an *operating budget* for your own unit by subtracting the expected costs of goods sold, and other expected costs, from your expected revenues.

17.

Developing a Business Case

To stand out as a manager, you can't just preserve the status quo. You need to pitch new ideas that create real value for your organization—and opportunity for you. Maybe you're responding to a pain point, like the rise of a disruptive new competitor or changing needs of your customers. Or perhaps you're chasing a positive opportunity, like a potential tax break. Whatever the motivation, you'll need to develop a business case that will mobilize others to support your plan.

This work draws on soft *and* hard skills we cover elsewhere in this book, such as strategy, influence, communication, and financial analysis. You'll need to gain the trust of many different actors in your organization, from decision makers to factory floor workers. These relationships, as well as the creative sessions you lead with your project team, will require great emotional intelligence. But you'll also need to perform and present clear, rigorous financial analyses to model your plans.

Stakeholder perspectives

Building a business case is about selling your idea and yourself to other people. If you're frenzied with pulling numbers and practicing a pitch, it's easy to focus only on the first two parts of that equation: "Is my idea compelling enough? Am I credible?" But as with any persuasive communication, your first question should be, "To whom?" Who is your proposal supposed to move? Whose buy-in do you need? You're not making your case to the void; you're making it to a particular group of individuals who all have their own interests and objectives. Understanding these decision makers will help you tailor your presentation and position yourself as compelling and credible to the people whose opinions matter.

Step 1: Identify your decision makers

Start by asking your boss who will be reviewing your idea, and how the final decision is likely to be made. Will a committee take a vote? Does one higher-up make the call? Corroborate this information by looking at projects that have gotten the green light in the past. If you notice that proposals from the finance department get a lot of traction, for example, you can safely conclude that the CFO has a lot of pull.

You may already have an instinct for where real influence lies in your company. "In most organizations, there's a dominant department, and its leader wields informal authority, regardless of title," write product development expert Raymond Sheen and HBR editor Amy Gallo in the *HBR Guide to Building Your Business Case*. "You can assume that the dominant department's objectives will trump others when decision makers review your case."

Step 2: Align with a champion

A champion is someone who advocates for your idea when you've left the room. In many cases, they're not the most influential person in the decision-making process, but they understand the value of your case and can articulate that value to everyone else. To find a champion, look for someone on the review committee who will directly and powerfully feel the benefits of your project. Then reach out, *before* you've fleshed out the details of your case and when you're still in an exploratory, information-gathering mode. Ask what this person's major priorities are right now, and what problems they're trying to solve. Then explain how your initiative could help, and use their feedback to make your plan an even better fit. If the person is willing, have them review your business case when it's ready. You want to build a case that speaks directly to your champion's motivations, so that they advocate for it as a favor to *themselves*, not to you.

Beyond providing feedback and a vote in your favor, this person can support you in a few different ways. Consider where their influence and interests lie in the company. Then make a specific ask. Can your champion:

- Provide a favorable introduction to key stakeholders and decision makers?

- Help you secure resources as you develop the project, like funding for field research?

- Knock down roadblocks or encourage others in the organization to cooperate with you?

- Strategize with you about how you'll win over holdouts?

- Play a role during the presentation itself, for example, by vocalizing a key point of view?

Step 3: Understand your audience's objectives

To ensure that your idea resonates with the other decision makers as well, review your division's or your company's strategic priorities. Understand how your idea supports these priorities and how it will help the judges achieve their goals.

Of course, each person you're pitching to likely has different objectives, depending on their position inside the company. Talk to your bosses and to your stakeholders directly to find out what these are. Ask questions like:

- What are your primary objectives this year? What barriers stand in your way?

- How do you measure success?

- What past projects have you supported, and what are your success stories? What made these initiatives work, in your opinion?

Your business case probably won't address each of the needs and preferences you surface. That's because you're trying to solve a problem for the business, not for any one person inside it. But you'll use this insight during the next stage of the process: clarifying the need you propose to meet.

Clarifying the need and value

Once you understand the goals and perspectives of your stakeholders, you can examine more closely the problem you want to solve and the value of your proposed solution.

First, identify the *need* behind your business case. What goals are at stake? What processes aren't working, what performance targets aren't being met? For example, if you're aiming to take advantage of a tax break, you might formulate the need this way: "Our wastewater treatment facility hasn't been updated in ten years and doesn't meet the latest state environmental standards. We're wasting $300,000 a year in operating costs on last-generation technology, missing out on $2 million in tax incentives, and risking our reputation as a green company."

Second, explore the *value* that your solution brings to the company. How will your idea contribute to the company's strategic objectives? How will it enhance performance, improve customer experience, increase profits, or lower costs? In the earlier example, you might urge the company to put the savings from its tax bill toward its new growth initiative, or to incorporate the upgrade into an environmentally conscious marketing strategy. The better you outline why your proposal is good for the business, your clients, and your employees, the more likely you are to get to yes.

Here's how:

Step 1: Talk to beneficiaries

These are the people whose job responsibilities bring them into immediate contact with the problem and who would be affected by your solution.

Sheen and Gallo suggest you ask them questions like: "When did the problem start (or when will it start)? How does it manifest itself? How often? How does the problem prevent their teams from doing their work effectively? Who else in the company does it affect? What customers are we not serving well?"

Ask for relevant data or documents (customer complaints, reports, surveys), and follow up on any referrals you receive. If you can, perform a little field work. Observe a manufacturing process, shadow a customer service rep, ask for a plant tour, sit in on a training session.

Sheen and Gallo urge managers to keep probing during these sessions. "The beneficiaries may not know the underlying reason for the problem . . . [or] they may have a solution in mind. But sometimes what they want isn't the best fix. Of course you need to look into this option, but it might not be your final recommendation, especially if it's costly or difficult to adopt." Instead of rushing to judgment, gather as much information as you can about these employees' experience of the problem, and make sure they understand that you value their insight and want to help them. Their support will make all the difference when it comes to implementing your idea, and it might influence the decision makers reviewing your case.

In some cases, you'll need to talk with clients or industry experts to understand needs and opportunities. As a manager, you benefit greatly from maintaining open dialogue with outside parties who can inform your strategy and business plans on an ongoing basis.

Step 2: Agree on what the solution should accomplish

Now that you know more about the issue at hand and the scope of a potential solution, go back to your stakeholders to check your understanding. Sheen and Gallo suggest using the following questions to guide your conversations:

- Where will the solution be used? In what offices and facilities? In how many countries?

- Who will be affected by the solution? A single department or the entire organization?

- How quickly does the solution need to be in place? Will we roll it out over time or all at once?

- How should we measure the solution's effectiveness? Do we have a baseline that we can compare against?

- Should we combine the solution with another related initiative?

It's important to have these conversations *before* you prepare your business case. You may find, for example, that you and the project's decision makers have very different expectations for a solution, or that there's a deep schism between how they view the problem and how the beneficiaries experience it. If a large gap exists, you need to figure out where your stakeholders are coming from and how negotiable their parameters are. If you tailor your plan to truly unreasonable expectations, you're setting yourself up for failure.

Cost/benefit analysis

Once you've defined the needs your business case will address and the goals it should meet, you can start to build a solution. If you're evaluating several different approaches, you can vet them in a few different ways, starting with a cost/benefit analysis. Your goal here is to create a detailed but holistic picture of how each alternative will affect the company's financial health. Decision makers will scrutinize this information to decide whether your business case is feasible and whether you're a credible advocate for it.

To perform the analysis, pick the two or three most viable options you're considering. "You'll drive yourself—and your team—crazy if you explore all the possibilities available to you," warn Sheen and Gallo. Run the analysis first for your most favored option and then adjust those numbers to see how each of the other choices compares. "Usually you'll change just a few figures," Sheen and Gallo advise. "For example, one option may be to do a phased rollout instead of a universal launch. Your project costs are likely to be similar, but some of your benefits won't show up until later—so you'll decrease those numbers for the first year or two."

So what numbers, exactly, are you looking for? Your analysis should cover these major categories:

Costs

- **Project costs** include project expenditures and capital expenditures. *Project expenditures* include development, testing and quantification, training and deployment, and travel costs. "I generally start by assessing how many people I need on the team and, using an average salary rate, I can project the personnel costs," Sheen says. "Then I do a rough estimate of travel and supplies to be purchased on the project."

  Capital expenditures pertain to assets you purchase or develop in the course of the project. As you saw in the previous chapter, assets depreciate—that is, they lose value over their use life. Your finance person will know whether you should represent assets costs as a single number in the year of acquisition or depreciated over several years.

- **Operating costs** capture how much it will cost to keep a project running after its initial implementation. Overhead like personnel, office space, and maintenance and licensing fees fall into this group. While your department will probably bear the project costs on its own, operating costs may be dispersed across the company. Keep an eye out for *transition costs*, too—the disruption caused by the process of implementing your solution.

Benefits

- **Revenue** is any additional money your initiative will bring in through sales. Your sales and marketing experts can help you with this figure. Ask them for three kinds of information: how much money you can expect, when it will appear, and how competitors will respond over the long term. Also, make sure to factor in the *cost of goods sold (COGS)* in this calculation, so you don't accidentally overestimate revenue. One way to estimate revenue gains from your business change is to examine a 2×2 grid that compares existing versus new clients on one side, to incremental versus net new revenue on the other. Are you expecting to increase revenue from existing clients and products (through new features as an example), or are you selling new products to new clients—or is it some mixture?

- **Productivity savings** is the money you'll save through efficiencies. Maybe your proposal lowers product costs by introducing more cost-effective materials, or perhaps you're cutting overhead by eliminating salaries or reducing your tax bill. "If you say your project will save personnel overhead costs, your stakeholders will probably ask, 'Who are we going to lay off?'" advise Sheen and Gallo. "Unless you get rid of people, you still have to pay them. Even if you make the argument that they'll do other things instead, you're not really saving money. You're just moving expenses around to other parts of the organization." Instead, look for personnel savings in more creative places, like diminished overtime payouts or time-wasting human errors.

Though you're just making rough estimates at this point, use your company's income statement to ensure that your projections are realistic. Limit your guesswork by talking to beneficiaries and experts inside and outside the company. Your marketing department, for example, can provide accurate information about how a new product line will affect revenue from other offerings, and procurement folks can tell you how much a contract with a new vendor will go for. Don't take these numbers for granted, though. Ask the specialists how they arrived at their figures, and consider what biases might drive someone to over- or underestimate a number. Track where every number is coming from in a master spreadsheet, and make sure that your sources are ready to back you up to your stakeholders.

Risk identification and mitigation

The cost/benefit analyses will narrow your field of potential solutions. But before you choose one, run another round of tests. "You've based every line of your spreadsheet on assumptions—which you've carefully documented," write Sheen and Gallo. "But what if they're wrong and things don't go as planned? What if the worse (or best) case occurs?" This "what if" process of analyzing your idea is invaluable.

To answer these questions, reexamine all of the beliefs that underwrite your estimates. What if a construction project runs over? What if a new competitor enters the market? What if there's a global economic slump next year? Estimate out how each alternative scenario affects the value of your project. You may find that your best plan is actually very vulnerable to risk and choose to redevelop your second-best option. Or perhaps the major threats to success on this project mirror a recent disaster within the company, and you need to show why your project won't fail in the same way.

Don't be gentle with your model. The decision makers certainly won't. They may not be as well versed as your team in the numbers, but they're probably experienced—and imaginative—when it comes to evaluating risk. If they have a fiduciary duty to the organization, they'll be extra cautious. Keep their perspectives in mind as you consider the box "Risk factors."

Generate a long list of potential risks and enter them into a spreadsheet. To identify the biggest threats and opportunities, Sheen and Gallo suggest scoring each risk on its probability and its potential impact. (Weather delays in winter: possible, but not likely to hold up a schedule by more than a few days. Asteroid collision: vastly more devastating, vastly less likely.) Multiply these two numbers together for each risk, then methodically comparing the results when you swap in the best- and worse-case values. Ultimately, says Sheen, "[y]ou're likely to choose a middle number for most lines, but you may have reason to be conservative or aggressive on certain items. If one of your critical stakeholders is risk-averse, for example, you may go with lower numbers on your benefit stream. If you face severe

Risk factors

- **Personnel.** What if the person running this project leaves the company? What if you don't get all the resources you requested? What if there's a labor shortage in a key specialty? Or conversely, what if you're able to pull together an all-star team or hire an outside expert? Assess this risk carefully given the impact that personnel have on any project's success.

- **Technology.** What if you encounter bugs when testing? What if employees struggle to adapt to the new system? What if your investment in technology becomes obsolete faster than expected; what is your plan to upgrade?

- **Quality/performance.** What if your solution doesn't perform as you expect it to—for better or worse? What if quality suffers because of a tight schedule? What if you're unable to deliver on the promise of the value proposition?

- **Scope.** What if the project needs to include more (or fewer) geographic regions, employees, or customers? What if the stakeholders change requirements? What if a regulatory change creates a new opportunity?

- **Schedule.** What if you aren't able to hit the launch date? What would allow you to get ahead of schedule? Does anything outside the project need to happen before you can complete it?

Source: Adapted from Ray Sheen and Amy Gallo, *HBR Guide to Building Your Business Case.* Boston: Harvard Business Review Press, 2015.

penalties for completing the project late, you may want to build some buffer into your timing assumptions."

Run your adjustments by subject-matter experts, like key beneficiaries or an advising specialist. They'll let you know where you need to be especially conservative in planning for risk, and where you can take a more aggressive approach. And for each set of assumptions, they'll help you decide whether your calculated return on investment is reasonable and adjust it if it's off.

Writing your business case

After all this research, analysis, and testing, you've settled on a single, well-justified solution. It sounds great in your head, in your notes, and in your conversations with collaborators. But to present it to decision makers, you'll need to organize all that scattered knowledge into one compelling document. This business case document should contain eight sections:

1. **Executive summary.** Open by briefly stating the problem or opportunity, the "how" and "why" of your solution, and the expected ROI.

2. **Business need.** Lay out the need in more detail, connecting it to your company's strategic goals. Use data to explain why this issue needs to be solved *now*.

3. **Project overview.** Outline the key elements of your solution. Describe its scope and how it will affect current business processes.

4. **Schedule, team, and other resources.** Sketch out an implementation plan, including deadlines, milestones, and personnel.

5. **Impact.** Detail the benefits for the company as a whole and for specific departments. Use numbers to make this section as specific as possible.

6. **Risks.** Give an overview of the major risks involved in doing—and not doing—the project. Explain how you'll capture potential upsides and minimize downsides.

7. **Financials.** Summarize the costs and benefits, and restate the ROI.

8. **Final pitch.** Restate the business need, the benefits of your solution, and, once again, the ROI.

You don't need to compose this as a Word document; the story you tell can ultimately take many forms, from a live presentation to an emailed Word document or slide deck. Make sure the document you create can stand on its own, however, whatever format you use to initially present it to stakeholders. That way it will be accessible to those who missed your presentation, or who want to revisit details afterward.

Once you've created the document, revisit it to make sure it compellingly answers the following questions: What exactly are you proposing? Why is it important? Why is it important *now*? (Remember that you'll be competing for the interest and investment others are seeking as well.) What results do you expect to achieve? What impact will those results have and on whom? Why should the company invest in this idea? What issues may come up and how do you intend to mitigate them to ensure the project is a success? What role will you play specifically to oversee and support the project's success? And finally, what specifically are you asking someone to approve, make a decision about, or otherwise support?

Getting buy-in for your plan

You've been building buy-in throughout this process by finding allies among your stakeholders, seeking out subject-matter experts, and cultivating trust with your project's beneficiaries. Now that your business case is complete, it's time to share it and mobilize that goodwill.

Before you submit the case for formal review, shop it around. Of course, you'll want to share it with your champion; its content won't come as a surprise, if you've kept in touch. But don't count on one person to swing the group. Reach out to others on the review committee and solicit their feedback. Ask for their general reaction, their top concerns, and any questions they'd like to see answered in the final product.

These interactions aren't simply pro forma. You'll probably modify your case somewhat based on the input you receive. If you ask for feedback and then disregard it, you may create a worse impression than if you'd asked for nothing at all. If you choose not to incorporate someone's ideas, explain why or create a contingency plan.

The presentation

If you are submitting your proposal for review via a live presentation, prepare by considering your audience. (See chapter 6, "Communicating Effectively," for more information on how to give a good presentation.) But a few tips hold for every situation:

Proofread your presentation materials.

Your materials should be sleek, highlighting only the most important ideas and data, whether presented in a written document or a digital presentation. Limit yourself to one idea at a time, and keep your script for the presentation for reference. Make sure that all the materials you show to decision makers—slides, spreadsheets, a written case—are error-free and follow the basic rules of good writing.

Personalize the conversation.

Don't talk at your stakeholders; talk with them. The more you engage them in the conversation, the more they'll internalize your arguments. "If you're talking about the need, turn to the stakeholder who's feeling the most pain and invite [them] to comment on it," suggest Sheen and Gallo. "This will enroll people in building and supporting your case in front of their peers."

Shine a light on your experts.

This builds your credibility by showing how diligently you've done your homework, and also because, if a particular subject-matter expert is well regarded in the company, their participation in your business case can carry great weight.

Handle the naysayers.

Like all group conversations, this one will probably involve some pushback. If people question whether your plan is realistic, ask your subject-matter experts to speak up. If someone points out a gap or risk they think you haven't addressed, don't try to minimize their point. "Give honest, direct responses," advise Sheen and Gallo. If you really don't think the point is valid, tactfully "ask the rest of the group if they'd like you to do more re-search. If others agree with you, they may step in to say so."

———————

When you're developing a business case, you may feel a tremendous amount of pressure to perform for your superiors. *Your* ideas, *your* creativity, *your* financial acuity—it's all on the line for everyone to judge. But the best busi-ness cases aren't the product of one person's genius but collaboration be-tween colleagues. By involving other people in this process from day one, you create a shared sense of ownership over the final proposal. Everyone whose advice you sought or whose expertise you consulted will see their own ideas reflected in the final product, and they'll want it to succeed.

Recap

- Building a business case relies on both the "soft" and "hard" skills you've learned in this book, from persuasion to financial analysis.

- Understanding your decision makers will help you tailor your presentation and position yourself as compelling and credible to the people whose opin-ions matter.

- The best business cases aren't the product of one person's genius but col-laboration between colleagues.

Action items

To understand what makes a successful business case in your company:

- ❑ Set up a meeting with your boss to understand more about how propos-ing a new business case works in your organization. Put together a list of questions about how the review process works, who's involved, and what their priorities are.

- [ ] Review business cases that have been successful in the past. Talk to the people who ran those projects, if you can, and ask them how they approach the decision-making team.

- [ ] Look at the major communications that have come from your company's leadership in the past year and search for common themes. What challenges, opportunities, and strategies are central to the business right now?

To gather information about your approach:

- [ ] Talk to the people who are directly involved with the problem you want to address or who will implement your solution. Learn how they experience the issue and ask them to help you get some firsthand exposure yourself.

- [ ] Use the information you've gathered from interviews and documents to map the processes you're proposing to change. Form your own judgments about the most important pain points and inefficiencies.

- [ ] Check back in with your stakeholders to find out whether you're on the same page about the scope of a potential solution. If you're not, probe for the source of the misunderstanding and try to negotiate a new, shared agreement.

To perform a cost/benefit analysis:

- [ ] Conduct a cost/benefit analysis for your top option and then adjust your initial calculations to compare with one or two alternatives.

- [ ] Calculate costs by tallying operating and project costs. Calculate benefits by adding revenue (less COGS) to productivity savings.

- [ ] Consult with subject-matter experts and relevant departments to come up with the best estimates for each cost and benefit.

To identify risks:

- [ ] Examine the beliefs that underlie your estimates. Generate a list of possible risks.

- ❏ Create a spreadsheet to track and score potential risks.

- ❏ Ask different members of your team to play around with the numbers in your model. If you're working on the case by yourself, invite a colleague to take a look for you. Other people will spot vulnerabilities or opportunities that you missed.

To write your business case:

- ❏ Decide what format your business case will take: Word document, slide deck, or live presentation.

- ❏ Draft a business case with each of the eight sections.

- ❏ Review your business case to make sure that it compellingly answers key questions that your stakeholders will have. Remember that at the end of the day you'll be sharing this idea with real people who have real motivations. Does your case tell a compelling story about why your idea is great, referencing all the analysis you've done to date?

To get buy-in for your plan:

- ❏ Start building buy-in early. Don't walk into your presentation cold; solicit input from decision makers beforehand, so you can respond to their concerns and prepare for their questions.

- ❏ Don't go it alone. Ask subject-matter experts to back you up, and invite stakeholders in the room to play an active role in the discussion.

- ❏ Anticipate some pushback. One person's skepticism isn't a death knell: engage in good faith with criticisms and questions, and don't fake knowledge that you don't possess.

Epilogue

You began this book with a clear goal: to become a better manager and leader. You're mastering the "how" of leadership, but what about the "why"? Why do you care about the quality of your leadership at all? What's the ultimate purpose—and the ultimate reward—of being a good manager? Why are you investing so much energy and effort in this particular brand of self-improvement?

Some answers to these questions might be obvious to you. You want to be good at your job. You want to advance your career. You want the deep satisfaction that comes from work well done. You're competitive and you want to stand out from the crowd. Perhaps you want to fulfill your potential to be a great leader.

But the point of becoming a great leader isn't simply to *be* a great leader. It's about the impact you have on the world around you, on the people you work with and the things you produce together—those ideas, processes, connections, products, and solutions that spark growth, make the world run a bit more smoothly, or fulfill a deep need.

The extent of your influence over your direct reports may not be apparent to you. A lot of the time, you may feel as if you don't have *enough* influence. But you know from your own experience that bosses have a tremendous effect on their direct reports' lives. You spend upward of two thousand hours a year being led by your managers—talking to them, listening to them, thinking about their moods and motivations. In addition to their effect on your own productivity, output, and career, the relationship also influences who you are as a person. It can change how you relate to your family and friends, and how you think and feel and dream, even when you're not at work. "Management is the most noble of professions if it's practiced well," says Harvard Business School professor Clay Christensen. "No other occupation offers as many ways to help others learn and grow ... [Even d]oing deals doesn't yield the deep rewards that come from building up people."

When you invest in your growth as a leader, you begin to recognize the true power you wield in others' lives. As the months and years go by, you'll measure your success by the innovation and growth you generate for your company, and by the innovations you create that affect your industry at large. You'll find your reward in the whole ecosystem that surrounds your company's success or failure: the economic growth you help create, the customers you serve, the communities you contribute to. But you'll also be able to see the effect of your leadership on the individuals who work for you—in their professional lives, in their personal lives, and in their own successes.

Sources

Chapter 1: The Transition to Leadership

Understanding your role as a manager

Hill, Linda A. "Becoming the Boss." *Harvard Business Review*, January 2007.

"New Manager Transitions." In *Harvard ManageMentor*. Boston: Harvard Business School Publishing, 2016. Electronic.

The difference between management and leadership

Kaplan, Robert Steven. *What You Really Need to Lead: The Power of Thinking and Acting Like an Owner*. Boston: Harvard Business Review Press, 2015.

Kotter, John P. "What Leaders Really Do." *Harvard Business Review*, December 2001.

"New Manager Transitions." In *Harvard ManageMentor*. Boston: Harvard Business School Publishing, 2016. Electronic.

Zaleznik, Abraham. "Managers and Leaders: Are They Different?" *Harvard Business Review*, March–April 1992.

Demystifying leadership

Harvard Business Review. "Becoming a Leader." In *Harvard Business Essentials: Manager's Toolkit*. Boston: Harvard Business Review Press, 2004.

Kaplan, Robert Steven. *What You Really Need to Lead: The Power of Thinking and Acting Like an Owner*. Boston: Harvard Business Review Press, 2015.

Handling the emotional challenges of the transition

Ashkenas, Ron. "First-Time Managers, Don't Do Your "Team's Work for Them." HBR.org, September 21, 2015.

Corkindale, Gill. "How Engaged a Leader Are You?" HBR.org, March 17, 2008.

David, Susan, and Christina Congleton. "Emotional Agility." *Harvard Business Review*, November 2013.

Hill, Linda A. "Becoming the Boss." *Harvard Business Review*, January 2007.

Nadler, David A. "Confessions of a Trusted Counselor." *Harvard Business Review*, September 2005.

"New Manager Transitions." In *Harvard ManageMentor*. Boston: Harvard Business School Publishing, 2016. Electronic.

"Persuading Others." In *Harvard ManageMentor*. Boston: Harvard Business School Publishing, 2016. Electronic.

Walker, Carol A. "Saving Your Rookie Managers from Themselves." *Harvard Business Review*, April 2002.

Chapter 2: Building Trust and Credibility

Gallo, Amy. "How to Manage Your Former Peers." HBR.org, December 19, 2012.

Hill, Linda, and Kent Lineback. "Do Your People Trust You?" HBR.org, March 2, 2012.

Establishing your character

DeSteno, David. "Trustworthy Signals." HBR.org Video, February 12, 2014.

Hill, Linda, and Kent Lineback. "Do Your People Trust You?" HBR.org, March 2, 2012.

———. "For People to Trust You, Reveal Your Intentions." HBR.org, April 20, 2012.

———. "To Build Trust, Competence Is Key." HBR.org, March 22, 2012.

"Persuading Others." In *Harvard ManageMentor*. Boston: Harvard Business School Publishing, 2016. Electronic.

Demonstrating your competence

"Coaching." In *Harvard ManageMentor*. Boston: Harvard Business School Publishing, 2016. Electronic.

Hill, Linda, and Kent Lineback. "To Build Trust, Competence Is Key." HBR.org, March 22, 2012.

Ibarra, Herminia. "Insight: Gaining Credibility in a New Role." HBR.org Video, September 24, 2013.

"Persuading Others." In *Harvard ManageMentor*. Boston: Harvard Business School Publishing, 2016. Electronic.

Watkins, Michael D. "Tip: Establish Credibility in a New Job." HBR.org Video, May 15, 2013.

Cultivating authentic leadership

George, Bill, Peter Sims, Andrew N. McLean, and Diana Mayer. "Discovering Your Authentic Leadership." *Harvard Business Review*, February 2007.

Ibarra, Herminia. "The Authenticity Paradox." *Harvard Business Review*, January–February 2015.

Ethics and integrity

"Ethics at Work." In *Harvard ManageMentor*. Boston: Harvard Business School Publishing, 2016. Electronic.

Nash, Laura. "Ethics Without the Sermon." *Harvard Business Review*, November 1981.

Chapter 3: Emotional Intelligence

Davey, Liane. "Handling Emotional Outbursts on Your Team." HBR.org, April 30, 2015.

Goleman, Daniel, Richard Boyatzis, and Annie McKee. "Primal Leadership: The Hidden Driver of Great Performance." *Harvard Business Review*, December 2001.

What is emotional intelligence?

"Emotional Intelligence." In *Harvard ManageMentor*. Boston: Harvard Business School Publishing, 2016. Electronic.

Goleman, Daniel. "What Makes a Leader." *Harvard Business Review*, January 2004.

Goleman, Daniel, Richard Boyatzis, and Annie McKee. "Primal Leadership: The Hidden Driver of Great Performance." *Harvard Business Review*, December 2001.

Harvard Business Review. "Leading by Feel." *Harvard Business Review*, January 2004.

McKee, Annie. "Quiz Yourself: Do You Lead with Emotional Intelligence?" HBR .org, June 5, 2015.

Ovans, Andrea. "How Emotional Intelligence Became a Key Leadership Skill." HBR.org, April 28, 2015. (The John Mayer passage that opens chapter 3 is quoted in Ovans.)

The power of self-awareness

Coutu, Diane L. "How Resilience Works." *Harvard Business Review*, May 2002.

David, Susan, and Christina Congleton. "Emotional Agility." *Harvard Business Review*, November 2013.

Goleman, Daniel. "What Makes a Leader." *Harvard Business Review*, January 2004.

Jackman, Jay M., and Myra H. Strober. "Fear of Feedback." *Harvard Business Review*, April 2003.

"New Manager Transitions." In *Harvard ManageMentor*. Boston: Harvard Business School Publishing, 2016. Electronic.

Emotional steadiness and self-control

Campbell, Andrew, Jo Whitehead, and Sydney Finkelstein. "Why Good Leaders Make Bad Decisions." *Harvard Business Review*, February 2009.

David, Susan. "Recovering from an Outburst at Work." HBR.org, May 8, 2015.

Lai, Lisa. "Three Ways to Stay Cool—in the Heat of the Moment." *How to Succeed in Business . . . Without Eating Your Soul for Breakfast* (blog), August 2012, http://www.soulforbreakfast.com/2012/08/three-ways-to-stay-cool.html.

Porath, Christine, and Christine Pearson. "The Price of Incivility." *Harvard Business Review*, January–February 2013.

Managing an employee's emotions

Davey, Liane. "Handling Emotional Outbursts on Your Team." HBR.org, April 30, 2015.

Ranieri, Anna. "Why People Cry at Work." HBR.org, May 1, 2015.

Building social awareness on your team

Druskat, Vanessa Urch, and Steven B. Wolff. "Building the Emotional Intelligence of Groups." *Harvard Business Review*, March 2001.

Goleman, Daniel, and Richard Boyatzis. "Social Intelligence and the Biology of Leadership." *Harvard Business Review*, September 2008.

Chapter 4: Positioning Yourself for Success

Goffee, Robert, and Gareth Jones. "Why Should Anyone Be Led by You?" *Harvard Business Review*, September–October 2000.

Redefining success

"New Manager Transitions." In *Harvard ManageMentor*. Boston: Harvard Business School Publishing, 2016. Electronic.

Understanding your organization's strategy

Harvard Business Review. "Setting Goals That Others Will Pursue." In *Harvard Business Essentials: Manager's Toolkit*. Boston: Harvard Business Review Press, 2004.
——. "Strategy." In *Harvard Business Essentials: Manager's Toolkit*. Boston: Harvard Business Review Press, 2004.
"Worksheet for Clarifying Strategic Objectives." In *New Leader Program*. Boston: Harvard Business School Publishing, 2016. Electronic.

Planning for strategic alignment

Harvard Business Review. "Setting Goals That Others Will Pursue." In *Harvard Business Essentials: Manager's Toolkit*. Boston: Harvard Business Review Press, 2004.
Michelman, Paul. "How Will You Better Align with Strategy?" HBR.org, February 27, 2008.

Chapter 5: Becoming a Person of Influence

Positional versus personal power

Conger, Jay A. "The Necessary Art of Persuasion." *Harvard Business Review*, May–June 1998.
Jen Su, Amy. "Signs That You're Being a Pushover." HBR.org, May 15, 2015.
Lai, Lisa. "Positional Power." PowerPoint presentation, unpublished.

Managing up

Harvard Business Review. *HBR Guide to Managing Up and Across*. Boston: Harvard Business Review Press, 2013.
Harvard Business Review. *Managing Up* (20-Minute Manager Series). Boston: Harvard Business Review Press, 2014.

Partnering with your peers

Dillon, Karen. *HBR Guide to Office Politics*. Boston: Harvard Business Review Press, 2015.
Harvard Business Review. *HBR Guide to Managing Up and Across*. Boston: Harvard Business Review Press, 2013.
Hill, Linda A., and Kent Lineback. *Being the Boss: The 3 Imperatives for Becoming a Great Leader*. Boston: Harvard Business Review Press, 2011.

——. "Weave Your Own Web of Influence." In *HBR Guide to Networking*. Boston: Harvard Business Review Press, 2012.

Ibarra, Herminia, and Mark Hunter. "How Leaders Create and Use Networks." *Harvard Business Review*, January 2007.

Silo busting and effectiveness

Charan, Ram. "One Microsoft. Four Ways to Integrate Fiefdoms." HBR.org, July 23, 2013.

Gulati, Ranjay. "Silo Busting: How to Execute on the Promise of Customer Focus." *Harvard Business Review*, May 2007.

Hewlett, Sylvia Ann. "A New Way to Network Inside Your Company." HBR.org, January 8, 2013.

Newton, Rebecca. "Collaborate Across Teams, Silos, and Even Companies." HBR.org, July 25, 2014.

Promoting your ideas to others

Conger, Jay A. "The Necessary Art of Persuasion." *Harvard Business Review*, May–June 1998.

Lai, Lisa. "Focus on Winning Either Hearts or Minds." HBR.org, May 20, 2015.

"Persuading Others." In *Harvard ManageMentor*. Boston: Harvard Business School Publishing, 2016. Electronic.

Chapter 6: Communicating Effectively

Finding your voice as a leader

Antonakis, John, Marika Fenley, and Sue Liechti. "Learning Charisma." *Harvard Business Review*, June 2012.

Mastering the written word

Garner, Bryan A. *HBR Guide to Better Business Writing*. Boston: Harvard Business Review Press, 2014.

Gavett, Gretchen. "The Essential Guide to Crafting a Work Email." HBR.org, July 24, 2015.

Wallraff, Barbara. "Improve Your Writing to Improve Your Credibility." HBR.org, July 29, 2015.

"Writing Skills." In *Harvard ManageMentor*. Boston: Harvard Business School Publishing, 2016. Electronic.

Persuasive presentations

Duarte, Nancy. "Create Slides People Will Remember." HBR.org Video, December 11, 2012.

——. "Finding the Right Metaphor for Your Presentation." HBR.org, November 17, 2015.

——. "Five Presentation Mistakes Everyone Makes." HBR.org, December 12, 2012.

——. *HBR Guide to Persuasive Presentations*. Boston: Harvard Business Review Press, 2012.

——. "Structure Your Presentation Like a Story." HBR.org, October 31, 2012.

Conducting effective meetings

Ferrazzi, Keith. "How to Run a Great Virtual Meeting." HBR.org, March 27, 2015.
Harvard Business Review. *Running Meetings* (20 Minute Manager Series). Boston: Harvard Business Review Press, 2014.

Chapter 7: Personal Productivity

Time management essentials

Harvard Business Review. *Getting Work Done* (20-Minute Manager Series). Boston: Harvard Business Review Press, 2014.
———. "Make Time for Work that Matters." HBR.org, January 14, 2014.
———. *Managing Time* (20-Minute Manager Series). Boston: Harvard Business Review Press, 2014.
———. "Managing Your Time." In *Harvard Business Essentials: Manager's Toolkit*. Boston: Harvard Business Review Press, 2004.

Finding focus

Friedman, Ron. "The Cost of Continuously Checking Email." HBR.org, July 4, 2014.
Griffith, Terri. "Help Your Employees Find Flow." HBR.org, April 17, 2014. (The Csikszentmihalyi passage on finding flow is quoted in Griffith.)
Harvard Business Review. *Getting Work Done* (20-Minute Manager Series). Boston: Harvard Business Review Press, 2014.

Stress management

Frost, Peter J., and Sandra Robinson. "The Toxic Handler: Organizational Hero—And Casualty." *Harvard Business Review*, July–August 1999.
Fryer, Bronwyn. "Are You Working Too Hard? A Conversation with Herbert Benson, MD." In *HBR Guide to Managing Stress at Work*. Boston: Harvard Business Review Press, 2014.
Hallowell, Edward M. "Overloaded Circuits: Why Smart People Underperform." *Harvard Business Review*, January 2005.
Halvorson, Heidi Grant. "Nine Ways Successful People Defeat Stress." HBR.org, December 13, 2012.
Schwartz, Tony, and Catherine McCarthy. "Manage Your Energy, Not Your Time." *Harvard Business Review*, October 2007.
Steinberg, Linda. "Desk Yoga: 6 Poses You Won't Be Embarrassed to Do—Even in an Open Environment." In *HBR Guide to Managing Stress at Work*. Boston: Harvard Business Review Press, 2014.

Work-life balance

Bregman, Peter. "Diversify Your Self." In *HBR Guide to Managing Stress at Work*. Boston: Harvard Business Review Press, 2014.
Friedman, Stewart D. "Be a Better Leader, Have a Richer Life." *Harvard Business Review*, April 2008.
———. "Keep Your Home Life Sane When Your Work Life Gets Crazy." HBR.org, February 23, 2015.

———. "Real Leaders Have Real Lives." *Harvard Business Review*, February 21, 2013.

Knight, Rebecca. "How to Overcome Burnout and Stay Motivated." HBR.org, April 2, 2015.

Saunders, Elizabeth Grace. "How to Plan Your Week to Keep Your Weekend Free." HBR.org, April 27, 2015.

Chapter 8: Self-Development

Career purpose

Christensen, Clayton M. "How Will You Measure Your Life?" *Harvard Business Review*, July–August 2010.

Claman, Priscilla. "There Is No Career Ladder." HBR.org, February 14, 2012.

Craig, Nick. "How to Uncover Your Unique Purpose." HBR.org Video, January 6, 2015.

Craig, Nick, and Scott A. Snook. "From Purpose to Impact." *Harvard Business Review*, May 2014.

Drucker, Peter F. "Managing Oneself." *Harvard Business Review*, January 2005.

Harvard Business Review. "Developing Your Career." In *Harvard Business Essentials: Manager's Toolkit*. Boston: Harvard Business Review Press, 2004.

Schlesinger, Leonard A., Charles F. Kiefer, and Paul B. Brown. "Career Plans Are Dangerous." HBR.org, March 2, 2012.

Look for opportunities within your organization

Batista, Ed. "Help People Help Themselves." In *HBR Guide to Coaching Employees*. Boston: Harvard Business Review Press, 2014.

"Career Development." In *Harvard ManageMentor*. Boston: Harvard Business School Publishing, 2016. Electronic.

Fernández-Aráoz, Claudio. "Position Yourself for a Stretch Assignment." HBR.org, March 27, 2012.

Knight, Rebecca. "How to Get the Most Out of an Informational Interview." HBR.org, February 26, 2016.

Porot, Daniel. *The Pie Method for Career Success: A Unique Way to Find Your Ideal Job*. Indianapolis: JIST Works, 2005.

Feedback from your boss and your team

Batista, Ed. "Make Getting Feedback Less Stressful." HBR.org, August 8, 2014.

Heen, Sheila, and Douglas Stone. "Find the Coaching in Criticism." *Harvard Business Review*, January–February 2014.

Quinn, Robert E., Jane E. Dutton, Gretchen M. Spreitzer, and Laura Morgan Roberts, *Reflected Best Self Exercise*. Ann Arbor: University of Michigan Center for Positive Organizations, 2011. The full exercise can be purchased at http://positiveorgs.bus.umich.edu/cpo-tools/reflected-best-self-exercise-2nd-edition/.

Roberts, Laura Morgan, Gretchen Spreitzer, Jane E. Dutton, Robert E. Quinn, Emily Heaphy, and Brianna Barker. "How to Play to Your Strengths." *Harvard Business Review*, January 2005.

Chapter 9: Delegating with Confidence

Harvard Business Review. "Delegating with Confidence." In *Harvard Business Essentials: Manager's Toolkit*. Boston: Harvard Business Review Press, 2004.
———. *Delegating Work* (20-Minute Manager Series). Boston: Harvard Business Review Press, 2014.

Developing a delegation plan

"Delegating." In *Harvard ManageMentor*. Boston: Harvard Business School Publishing, 2016. Electronic.
Johnson, Whitney, "Three Reasons You Shouldn't Delegate." HBR.org, December 1, 2010.

Chapter 10: Giving Effective Feedback

Giving feedback in real time

Harvard Business Review. *Giving Effective Feedback* (20-Minute Manager Series). Boston: Harvard Business Review Press, 2014.

Giving difficult feedback

Harvard Business Review. *Giving Effective Feedback* (20-Minute Manager Series). Boston: Harvard Business Review Press, 2014.
———. "Handling Problem Employees." In *Harvard Business Essentials: Manager's Toolkit*. Boston: Harvard Business Review Press, 2004.
Manzoni, Jean-François. "A Better Way to Deliver Bad News." *Harvard Business Review*, September 2002.

Coaching and developing employees

Batista, Ed. "Why Coach?" In *HBR Guide to Coaching Employees*. Boston: Harvard Business Review Press, 2015.
Harvard Business Review. "Appraisal and Coaching." In *Harvard Business Essentials: Manager's Toolkit*. Boston: Harvard Business Review Press, 2004.
———. *HBR Guide to Coaching Employees Ebook + Tools*. Boston: Harvard Business Review Press, 2014.
Jen Su, Amy. "Holding a Coaching Session." In *HBR Guide to Coaching Employees*. Boston: Harvard Business Review Press, 2015.

Performance reviews

Harvard Business Review. "Appraisal and Coaching." In *Harvard Business Essentials: Manager's Toolkit*. Boston: Harvard Business Review Press, 2004.
———. *Giving Effective Feedback* (20-Minute Manager Series). Boston: Harvard Business Review Press, 2014.
Knight, Rebecca. "Delivering an Effective Performance Review." HBR.org, November 3, 2011. (The Dick Grote passage on appraisals is quoted in Knight.)

Chapter 11: Developing Talent

Employee development as a priority

"Developing Employees." In *Harvard ManageMentor*. Boston: Harvard Business School Publishing, 2016. Electronic.

Dowling, Daisy Wademan. "Coaching Effectively in Less Time." In *HBR Guide to Coaching Employees*. Boston: Harvard Business Review Press, 2015.

Harvard Business Review. "Developing Your Career." In *Harvard Business Essentials: Manager's Toolkit*. Boston: Harvard Business Review Press, 2004.

Herzberg, Frederick. "One More Time: How Do You Motivate Employees?" *Harvard Business Review*, January 2003.

Creating career strategies with your staff

Hallowell, Edward M. "Set the Stage to Stimulate Growth." In *HBR Guide to Coaching Employees*. Boston: Harvard Business Review Press, 2015.

———. *Shine: Using Brain Science to Get the Best from Your People*. Boston: Harvard Business Review Press, 2011.

Harvard Business Review. "Employee Development." In *Harvard Business Essentials: Performance Management*. Boston: Harvard Business Review Press, 2006.

Developing high-potential talent

Berglas, Steven. "How to Keep A Players Productive." *Harvard Business Review*, September 2006.

"Developing Employees." In *Harvard ManageMentor*. Boston: Harvard Business School Publishing, 2016. Electronic.

Harvard Business Review. *Giving Effective Feedback* (20-Minute Manager Series). Boston: Harvard Business Review Press, 2014.

Stretch assignments

Fernández-Aráoz, Claudio. "Position Yourself for a Stretch Assignment." HBR.org, March 27, 2012.

Chapter 12: Leading Teams

Team culture and dynamics

Hewlett, Sylvia Ann, Melinda Marshall, and Laura Sherbin. "How Diversity Can Drive Innovation." *Harvard Business Review*, December 2013.

Katzenbach, Jon R., and Douglas K. Smith. "The Discipline of Teams." *Harvard Business Review*, July–August 2005.

"New Manager Transitions." In *Harvard ManageMentor*. Boston: Harvard Business School Publishing, 2016. Electronic.

O'Hara, Carolyn. "What New Team Leaders Should Do First." HBR.org, September 11, 2014.

Schwarz, Roger. "What the Research Tells Us about Team Creativity and Innovation." HBR.org, December 15, 2015.

Shapiro, Mary. *HBR Guide to Leading Teams*. Boston: Harvard Business Review Press, 2015.

"Team Audit worksheet." In *New Leader Program*. Boston: Harvard Business School Publishing, 2016. Electronic.

Managing cross-cultural teams

Brett, Jeanne, Kristin Behfar, and Mary C. Kern. "Managing Multicultural Teams." *Harvard Business Review*, November 2006.

Meyer, Erin. "Navigating the Cultural Minefield." *Harvard Business Review*, May 2014.

Managing virtual teams

Harvard Business Review. *Leading Virtual Teams* (20-Minute Manager Series). Boston: Harvard Business Review Press, 2016.

———. *Virtual Collaboration* (20-Minute Manager Series). Boston: Harvard Business Review Press, 2016.

Productive conflict resolution

Gallo, Amy. "Get Your Team to Stop Fighting and Start Working." HBR.org, June 9, 2010.

"Team Management." In *Harvard ManageMentor*. Boston: Harvard Business School Publishing, 2016. Electronic.

Lai, Lisa. Email correspondence with HBR editors, April 9, 2016.

Chapter 13: Fostering Creativity

Plan a creative session

Harvard Business Review. *Innovative Teams* (20-Minute Manager Series). Boston: Harvard Business Review Press, 2015.

Tools for generating ideas

Dyer, Jeff, Hal Gregersen, and Clayton M. Christensen. *The Innovator's DNA: Mastering the Five Skills of Disruptive Innovators*. Boston: Harvard Business Review Press, 2011.

Harvard Business Review. *Innovative Teams* (20-Minute Manager Series). Boston: Harvard Business Review Press, 2015.

"Mind Mapping." Harvard Management Communication Letter, November 2000.

Wedell-Wedellsborg, Thomas. Unpublished interview with HBR editors, June 10, 2016.

Making sure all perspectives are heard

Harvard Business Review. *Running Meetings* (20-Minute Manager Series). Boston: Harvard Business Review Press, 2014.

Dealing with negativity

"Innovation Implementation." In *Harvard ManageMentor*. Boston: Harvard Business School Publishing, 2016. Electronic.

Lai, Lisa. "Dealing with Negativity: Protection from the Storm." *How to Succeed in Business . . . Without Eating Your Soul for Breakfast* (blog), December 2012, http://www.soulforbreakfast.com/2012/12/negativity.html.

Chapter 14: Hiring—and Keeping—the Best

Crafting a role

Harvard Business Review. "Hiring the Best." In *Harvard Business Essentials: Performance Management*. Boston: Harvard Business Review Press, 2006.

Recruiting world-class talent

Bouton, Katie. "Recruiting for Cultural Fit." HBR.org, July 17, 2015.

Fernández-Aráoz, Claudio. "21st-Century Talent Spotting." *Harvard Business Review*, June 2014.

Harvard Business Review. "Hiring the Best." In *Harvard Business Essentials: Performance Management*. Boston: Harvard Business Review Press, 2006.

Menon, Tanya, and Leigh Thompson. "How to Hire Without Getting Fooled by First Impressions." HBR.org, February 15, 2016.

Sullivan, John. "7 Rules for Job Interview Questions That Result in Great Hires." HBR.org, February 10, 2016.

Retaining employees

Fernández-Aráoz, Claudio, Boris Groysberg, and Nitin Nohria. "How to Hang On to Your High Potentials." *Harvard Business Review*, October 2011.

Harvard Business Review. "Keeping the Best." In *Harvard Business Essentials: Performance Management*. Boston: Harvard Business Review Press, 2006.

Motivation and engagement

Amabile, Teresa, and Steven J. Kramer. "The Power of Small Wins." *Harvard Business Review*, May 2011.

Herzberg, Frederick. "One More Time: How Do You Motivate Employees?" *Harvard Business Review*, January 2003.

Chapter 15: Strategy: A Primer

Your role in strategy

Harvard Business Review. "Strategy." In *Harvard Business Essentials: Performance Management*. Boston: Harvard Business Review Press, 2006.

———. *Thinking Strategically* (HBR Pocket Mentor Series). Boston: Harvard Business School Publishing, 2010.

What is strategy?

Harvard Business Review. "Strategy." In *Harvard Business Essentials: Performance Management*. Boston: Harvard Business Review Press, 2006.

Henderson, Bruce D. "The Origin of Strategy." *Harvard Business Review*, November–December 1989.

Porter, Michael E. "What Is Strategy?" *Harvard Business Review*, November–December 1996.

Developing strategy

Christensen, Clayton M. "Making Strategy: Learning by Doing." *Harvard Business Review*, November–December 1997.

Harvard Business Review. "Strategy." In *Harvard Business Essentials: Performance Management*. Boston: Harvard Business Review Press, 2006.

Ovans, Andrea. "What Is Strategy, Again?" HBR.org, May 12, 2015.

Porter, Michael E. "What Is Strategy?" *Harvard Business Review*, November–December 1996.

Leading change and transitions

Beer, Michael. "Leading Change." Class note 9–488-037. Boston: Harvard Business School, 1988; revised 1991.

Bradford, David, and Allen Cohen. *Power Up*. New York: Free Press, 1983.

Harvard Business Review. "Becoming a Leader." In *Harvard Business Essentials: Performance Management*. Boston: Harvard Business Review Press, 2006.

Heifetz, Ronald, and Marty Linksy. "A Survival Guide for Leaders." *Harvard Business Review*, June 2002.

Navigating the schools of strategic thought

Ovans, Andrea. "What Is Strategy, Again?" HBR.org, May 12, 2015.

Blank, Steve. "Why the Lean Start-Up Changes Everything." *Harvard Business Review*, May 2013.

Collis, David and Cynthia Montgomery. "Competing on Resources." *Harvard Business Review*, July–August 2008.

D'Aveni, Richard A. "The Empire Strikes Back: Counterrevolutionary Strategies for Industry Leaders." *Harvard Business Review*, November 2002.

Henderson, Bruce D. "The Origin of Strategy." *Harvard Business Review*, November–December 1989.

Johnson, Mark W., Clayton M. Christensen, and Henning Kagermann. "Reinventing Your Business Model." *Harvard Business Review*, December 2008.

Kim, W. Chan, and Renée Mauborgne. "Blue Ocean Strategy." *Harvard Business Review*, December 2004.

———. "Creating New Market Space." *Harvard Business Review*, January–February 1999.

Luehrman, Timothy A. "Strategy as a Portfolio of Real Options." *Harvard Business Review*, September–October 1998.

MacMillan, Ian, and Rita McGrath. "Discovering New Points of Differentiation." *Harvard Business Review*, July–August 1997.

Mankins, Michael C., and Richard Steele. "Stop Making Plans; Start Making Decisions." *Harvard Business Review*, January 2006.

McGrath, Rita, and Ian MacMillan. "Discovery-Driven Planning." *Harvard Business Review*, July–August 1995.

Peters, Thomas, and Robert Waterman. *In Search of Excellence*. New York: Harper & Row, 1982.

Porter, Michael E. "How Competitive Forces Shape Strategy." *Harvard Business Review*, March 1979.

———. "What Is Strategy?" *Harvard Business Review*, November–December 1996.

Prahalad, C. K., and Gary Hamel. "The Core Competence of the Organization." *Harvard Business Review*, May–June 1990.

Roth, Alvin. "The Art of Designing Markets." *Harvard Business Review*, October 2007.

Stalk, George. "Curveball: Strategies to Fool the Competition." *Harvard Business Review*, September 2006.

Stalk, George, and Rob Lachenauer. "Hardball: Five Killer Strategies for Trouncing the Competition." *Harvard Business Review*, April 2004.

Wessel, Maxwell and Clayton M. Christensen. "Surviving Disruption." *Harvard Business Review*, September 2012.

Yoffie, David, and Michael Cusumano. "Judo Strategy." *Harvard Business Review*, January–February 1999.

Zook, Chris. "Finding Your Next Core Business." *Harvard Business Review*, September 2012.

Zook, Chris, and James Allen. "Growth Outside the Core." *Harvard Business Review*, December 2003.

Chapter 16: Mastering Financial Tools

Likierman, Andrew. "The Five Traps of Performance Measurement." In *HBR Guide to Finance Basics for Managers*. Boston: Harvard Business Review Press, 2012.

The basics of financial performance

Likierman, Andrew. "The Five Traps of Performance Measurement." In *HBR Guide to Finance Basics for Managers*. Boston: Harvard Business Review Press, 2012.

Understanding financial statements

Harvard Business Review. "The Key Financial Statements." In *HBR Guide to Finance Basics for Managers*. Boston: Harvard Business Review Press, 2012.

Budgeting

Harvard Business Review. "Budgeting." In *Harvard Business Essentials: Performance Management*. Boston: Harvard Business Review Press, 2006.

Chapter 17: Developing a Business Case

Sheen, Raymond, and Amy Gallo. *HBR Guide to Building Your Business Case*. Boston: Harvard Business Review Press, 2015.

Index

access-based positioning, 258
accountability, 141
accounting equation, 279
accounts payable, 278
accusations, 160–161
action plans, 166–167
adaptive responses, 42
agency, 131–132
alignment
    communication and, 87
    consistency and, 25
    with organizational strategy, 57–60
    planning for strategic, 60–61
    strategy and, 263
    of your job with your strengths,
        133–134
Allen, James, 273
allies, 265
Amabile, Teresa, 248–249
ambiguity, 13, 122
analogies, 81
animation in speaking, 86
annual reviews, 155
Antonakis, John, 86
apologies, 45, 47
"Art of Designing Markets, The" (Roth),
    272
assets, 279–281
attention
    capturing others', 85
    focusing, 107–111
authenticity
    in communication, 85
    communication and, 87
    cultivating, 29–32

authority
    delegation and, 146
    positional, personal influence vs.,
        8–9
avoidant mindset, 152

balance sheets, 278–284
Batista, Ed, 131–132, 162
BATNA (best alternative to a negotiated
    agreement), 212
Beer, Michael, 267–268
Behfar, Kristin, 203
Being the Boss (Hill & Lineback), 74
benchmarking, 271
Benson, Herbert, 111
best practices, 271
biases, 33, 79, 199–200
Blank, Steve, 273
"Blue Ocean Strategy" (Kim &
    Mauborgne), 272
body language, 26, 86, 159, 170, 226
boundaries, 16, 184–185
Boyatzis, Richard, 38
Bradford, David, 264
brain, response of to stress, 112
brainstorming, 221–222
breaks, taking, 114
Brett, Jeanne, 203, 208
budgets, 205, 289–294
    financial, 291
    master, 290
    operating, 290–293
    See also financial tools
burnout, 115, 184, 218

business case development, 297–312
  cost/benefit analysis in, 302–304
  getting buy-in and, 308–310
  need and value clarification in, 300–
    302
  risk identification and mitigation in,
    305–307
  stakeholder perspectives in, 298–300
  writing, 307–308
buy-in, 264
  for business cases, 308–310
  catchball for gaining, 224, 225
  vision and, 264–266

capabilities, strategy development and,
    260–261
capital expenditures, 303
career development, 121–136
  coaching employees and, 162–167
  finding opportunities for, 124–130
  purpose and, 122–124
cash flow statements, 284–286
catchball, 224, 225
champions, 298–299
change
  buy-in for, 264–266
  cultural, around emotions, 50
  in emotional habits, 42–43
  emotional intelligence and, 38
  leadership in responding to, 10
  leading, 263–268
  personal power and, 69
  strategies for, 261–262
  vision and, 264–266
  waiting to introduce, 24
character
  definition of, 25
  establishing your, 25–27
  trust based on, 23, 25
charisma, 85–86
Christensen, Clayton, 122–123, 224, 259,
    261, 272, 273, 314
clutter, 110
coaching, 162–167
  definition of, 162
  delegation and, 150–151
  feedback in, 156–157
  how to perform, 164–167

to improve employee performance, 171
  on problem solving, 16
  when to provide, 163
Cohen, Allen, 264
collaboration
  across units, 76–78
  conflict resolution and, 208–214
  making time for, 77–78
  with peers for success, 74–76
  skills in, 12
  in teams, 194
Collis, David, 273
comfort, 110
commitment, 196–197
communication, 85–101
  about delegation plans, 145–149
  about your boss's expectations, 72–73
  after informational interviews, 127
  audience for, 88
  audience interaction in, 95
  body language in, 26, 170
  in career strategies, 178–180
  in change efforts, 267–268
  of competence, 28
  in creating alignment, 263
  direct vs. indirect, 201
  editing, 89–92
  employee retention and, 245
  exiting conversations, 109
  finding your voice in, 85–87
  hearing all perspectives in, 225–227
  involving all parties in, 97
  to learn about organizational strategy,
    57–59
  making enemies into allies with,
    75–76
  in meetings, 96–98
  in presentations, 92–96
  questions in, 26
  on transitions to management, 24
  in virtual teams, 204–207
  winning hearts and minds with, 78–82
  written, 87–92
  See also conflict resolution; feedback
compassion, 184–185
compensation, 247–248
competence
  demonstrating, 27–29
  trust and, 23–24

"Competing on Resources" (Collis & Montgomery), 273
competition, 270
competitive strategy, 257
complacency, challenging, 267–268
complexity, 10
compliance
    personal influence vs. positional authority and, 8–9
confidants, 19
confidence, 32
    delegating and, 139–154
conflict
    constructive, 209–210
    in creative sessions, 219–220
    cross-cultural, 199–203
    destructive, 210–214
    finding root causes of, 210–211
    intervention in, 202–203
    overcoming resistance and, 266
    sources of, 201–202
    team norms and, 47, 198–200
    in teams, 199–203
conflict resolution, 47
    productive, 208–214
    in teams, 199–200
consistency, 25
context
    delegation and, 146–147
    financial performance and, 276–277
contrasts, in communication, 86
coping mechanisms, 13, 14, 18–20
"Core Competence of the Organization, The" (Prahalad & Hamel), 271
Corkindale, Gill, 19
cost/benefit analysis, 302–304
cost of goods sold (COGS), 287, 292, 303–304
cover letters, 238–239
Craig, Nick, 123–124
"Creating New Market Space" (Kim & Mauborgne), 272
creativity, 178, 217–231
    brainstorming and, 221–222
    catchball for, 224, 225
    definition of, 217
    mind mapping for, 222–224
    negativity and, 227, 229
    planning sessions for, 217–220

rules of conduct and, 219–220
    setting the scene for, 218–219
    techniques for overcoming resistance and, 228
    tools for, 220–224
credibility
    building, 23–36
    competence and, 28–29
    ethics/integrity and, 32–34
criticism
    asking for and using, 131–132
    constructive, 157
    giving, 158–162
    See also feedback
cross-cultural teams, 198–203. See also diversity
Csikszentmihalyi, Mihaly, 107
curiosity, 237
"Curveball: Strategies to Fool the Competition" (Stalk & Lachenauer), 266–267
customer needs, 61
Cusumano, Michael, 273

data visuals, 81, 94–95
D'Aveni, Richard, 273
deadlines, 116, 144–145
debt-to-equity ratio, 284
decision making
    biases in, 33
    conflict in, 202
    conflict resolution and, 210
    emotional steadiness and, 44–45
    explaining choices in, 28
    identifying decision makers and, 298
    leadership skills in, 12
    letting others shine in, 26
    matrix for, 242–243
    promoting your ideas in, 78–82
    reducing stress of everyday, 113–114
    team guidelines on, 49, 202
    in teams, 198
delegation, 139–154
    benefits of, 140
    choosing the right person for, 144
    coaching and, 150–151
    communicating about with employees, 145–149

delegation (*continued*)
  defining the work in, 142–144
  documenting agreements about, 149
  monitoring progress and, 149–151
  planning for, 141–144
  purpose in, 142
  reverse, avoiding, 151–152
  timelines in, 144–145
  when to avoid, 141–142
deliverables, 143
demands, challenging, 73
depreciation, 281, 288
DeSteno, David, 26
determination, 237
diet, 113
direction, 228
"Discovering New Points of
  Differentiation" (MacMillan &
  McGrath), 272
"Discovering Your Authentic Leadership"
  (George et al.), 31
"Discovery-Driven Planning" (McGrath
  & MacMillan), 271
disruption, 273
distractions, 107–109
divergent thinking, 220, 221–222
diversity, 194–196
  conflict and, 199–200, 214
  in creative sessions, 219–220
  productive conflict resolution and,
    208–214
  recruiting for, 236
documentation, 171, 205
downtime, protecting, 18
Drucker, Peter, 270
Duarte, Nancy, 92–93, 94–95, 223
Druskrat, Vanessa Urch, 48
Dyer, Jeffrey, 224

earnings before interest and taxes
  (EBIT), 288
editing, 89–92
Egon Zehnder, 186, 236–237
email, 149
  organizing, 110–111
  performance check-ins via, 171
  policies for virtual teams, 206

  taking breaks from, 115
  writing tips for, 90–91, 92
emotional intelligence, 37–54
  assessing your own, 52–54
  components of, 39, 40–41
  definition of, 37, 39
  how to build, 38
  self-awareness and, 39–43
  social awareness and, 48–50
  steadiness/self-control in, 43–45
emotions
  avoiding escalation of, 161–162
  coaching and, 162–163
  contagiousness of, 43
  criticism and, 131–132
  delegation and, 148, 152
  giving difficult feedback and, 158–162
  identifying, 46
  labeling, 14
  managing employees', 45–48
  managing hot buttons and, 44–45
  promoting positive, 113
  redirecting, 75
  reframing, 46–47
  regulation of, 25, 40, 43–45
  self-doubt, 13–14
  stress and, 113
  in transitioning to leadership, 13–20
  winning hearts and minds of others
    and, 80–82
empathy, 41, 184–185
  managing up and, 72
"Empire Strikes Back:
  Counterrevolutionary Strategies for
  Industry Leaders, The" (D'Aveni),
  273
employee development, 56
  benefits of, 176–177
  career strategy in, 177–183
  for high performers, 183–185
  interviews, 179–181
  performance reviews and, 167–172
  prioritization of, 176–177
  stretch assignments in, 182, 185–187
  talent development and, 175–189
employees
  delegating to, 139–154
  giving effective feedback to, 155–174

high performers, 183–185
hiring and retention of, 233–252
performance reviews of, 167–172
protecting your time from, 107–109
recruiting, 236–244
retaining, 244–248
reverse delegation by, 151–152
risk factors and, 306
self-appraisal by, 168–169
winning hearts and minds of, 78–82
empowerment, 214
enemies, making allies of, 75–76
engagement, 12
    employee retention and, 248–250
    hiring for, 237
    in virtual teams, 206
escalation, avoiding, 161–162
"Essential Guide to Crafting a Work
    Email, The" (Gavett), 90–91
ethics, 25, 32–35
evaluation, of high performers, 186
executive summaries, 307
exercise, 18–19, 113, 114
expectations, 7–8
    managing up and, 71–73
    for team interactions, 48–50
    for team members, 56
expenses, 287
experience, job interview questions on,
    241
experimentation, 222
extroverts, 11
eye contact, 86

facial expressions, 86
facilitation, 228
failure, learning from, 42
feedback
    after meetings, 227
    champions and, 299
    character and, 26
    coaching/employee development and,
        162–167
    on communication, 92
    corrective, 155
    criticism, 131–132
    emotional intelligence and, 38, 42

giving difficult, 158–162
giving effective, 155–174
for high performers, 185
performance reviews, 167–172
in performance reviews, 167–172
positive, 155
self-awareness and, 30
for self-development, 130–134
in teams, 198, 200
timing of, 156–157
Fenley, Marika, 86
Fernández-Aráoz, Claudio, 186, 236–237,
    247–248
Ferrazzi, Keith, 98
financial budgets, 291
financial leverage, 283
financial statements, 277–290
    balance sheets, 278–284
    in business cases, 307–308
    cash flow, 284–286
    income statements, 286–290
financial structure of firms, 283–284
financial tools, 275–295
    basics of performance and, 276–277
    budgeting, 290–294
    financial statements, 277–290
    literacy with, 275–276
    questioning data with, 277
financing activities, 284
"Finding Your Next Core Business"
    (Zook), 273
flow states, 107
focus, 107–111
    delegation and, 141
fonts, 95
Friedman, Stewart, 117
functional groups, 61
functions, 143
future-focus, 12

Gallo, Amy, 24–25, 213, 214, 298, 301,
    304, 306, 309–310
Garner, Bryan A., 88, 89
Gavett, Gretchen, 90–91
George, Bill, 29–30, 31
"Get Your Team to Stop Fighting and
    Start Working" (Gallo), 213

ghosting, 206
goals
  alignment of with organizational
    strategy, 57–59
  employee retention and, 248–250
  focusing teams on, 213
  for meetings, 97, 99
  in performance plans, 170
  performance reviews and, 168
  setting realistic, 167–168
  strategic alignment with, 60–61
  in teams, 191, 200, 213
  team success based on, 56
  for time management, 105
  in written communication, 90
  See also career development
Goleman, Daniel, 37, 38, 40–41, 43, 52
goodwill, 281
Gregersen, Hal, 224
Grote, Dick, 168
group dynamics, 194–200
group norms, 47, 198–200
  for creative sessions, 219–220
  productive conflict resolution and,
    209
growing in place, 129
"Growth Outside the Core" (Zook &
    Allen), 273
Groysberg, Boris, 247–248

Hallowell, Edward, 112, 179–181
Halvorson, Heidi, 114
Hamel, Gary, 271
happiness, 117–118
"Hardball: Five Killer Strategies for
    Trouncing the Competition" (Stalk &
    Lachenauer), 273
hard sells, 93
HBR Guide to Better Business Writing
    (Garner), 88
HBR Guide to Building Your Business
    Case (Sheen & Gallo), 298, 306
HBR Guide to Leading Teams (Shapiro),
    198–199
HBR Guide to Managing Conflict at
    Work (Gallo), 214
HBR Guide to Persuasive Presentations
    (Duarte), 92–93, 223

health, taking care of, 18–19, 117–118. See
    also stress
hearts and minds, winning, 78–82
Heifetz, Ronald, 265–266
Henderson, Bruce, 256–257
Herzberg, Frederick, 177, 247–248, 249
hierarchy, 201
Hill, Linda, 13, 23–24, 74
hiring and retention, 233–252
  job crafting before, 233–236
  motivation and engagement in, 248–
    250
  for potential, 236–237
historical cost, 281–282
honesty, 17, 28, 38–43
hot buttons, managing, 44–45, 71
"How Competitive Forces Shape
    Strategy" (Porter), 270
"How Engaged a Leader Are You?"
    (Corkindale), 19
"How to Get the Most Out of an
    Informational Interview" (Knight),
    126–127
"How to Manage Your Former Peers"
    (Gallo), 24
"How to Run a Great Virtual Meeting"
    (Ferrazzi), 98
"How Will You Measure Your Life?"
    (Christensen), 122–123
human resources departments, 125, 168,
    181, 236, 238

Ibarra, Herminia, 32
idea-generation tools, 220–224, 261
identity
  as a leader, 11
  of managers, 7
  shaping a new, 32
"if-then" propositions, 114
implementation, 263
imposter syndrome, 17
income statements, 286–290, 304
incremental budgeting, 292
influence, 67–84, 313–314
  definition of, 67
  managing up and, 71–74
  personal, positional authority vs.,
    8–9

positional vs. personal power and, 68–71
promoting your ideas to others and, 78–82
skills in, 12
informational interviews, 125–127
job offers from, 126–127
information gathering, 74–75
"Innovation Implementation," 228
Innovator's DNA, The: Mastering the Five Skills of Disruptive Innovators (Dyer, Gregersen, & Christensen), 224
integrity, 32–34
emotion regulation and, 44–45
personal power and, 71
intellectual traits, 12
interest, demonstrating, 25–27
internships, in-house, 129
interruptions, 107–109
interviews
employee development, 179–181
informational, 125–127, 182
of job candidates, 239–242
introverts, 11
inventory, 282
investing activities, 284
isolation, 14, 16–17, 207
finding confidants and, 19
issue tracking software, 204

job descriptions, 235–236
job enrichment, 249–250
job offers, 243–244
job postings, 238
job proposals, 127–128
job redefinitions, 182
job redesigns, 182
job rotations, 129
job satisfaction, 141
Johnson, Kelley, 213
Johnson, Mark, 272
"Judo Strategy" (Yoffie & Cusumano), 273

Kagermann, Henning, 272
Katzenbach, Jon, 196, 197
Kern, Mary C., 203

key players, identifying, 77
Kim, W. Chan, 272
Knight, Rebecca, 126–127
Kotter, John, 10, 264
Kramer, Steven, 248–249

Lachenauer, Rob, 273
Lai, Lisa, 44–45, 69–71
language differences, 201
lattice, career, 121–122
leaders and leadership
authentic, 29–32
in change and transitions, 263–268
definition of, 10
employee retention and, 245
finding your voice in, 85–87
management vs., 9–10
mindset for, 5–63
of teams, 191–216
traits/skills in, 10–11, 12–13
transition to, 7–21
Leading Change: Why Transformation Efforts Fail (Kotter), 264
learning, human need for, 177
leverage, financial, 283
liabilities, 279–280, 281
Liechti, Sue, 86
Likierman, Andrew, 276–277
Lineback, Kent, 23–24, 74
LinkedIn, 126
Linsky, Marty, 265–267
listening, active, 46, 131–132, 145–146
in coaching, 166
in creative sessions, 219
to high performers, 184–185
in performance reviews, 169–170
listening tours, 57–59
lists, three-part, 87
logical arguments, 81–82
loneliness, 19
Luehrman, Tim, 273

MacMillan, Ian, 271, 272
maladaptive responses, 42–43
management
definition of, 10
delegating in, 139–154

management (*continued*)
emotional challenges in transitions to, 12–20
employee development for, 176–177
of former peers, 24–27
leadership vs., 9–10
of people vs. tasks, 8
of teams, 191–252
vision in, 269
managers
in alignment creation, 263
as communicators, 263
as coordinators, 263
employee retention and, 245–246
expectations of, 7–8
influence of, 67–84, 313–314
managing up by, 71–74
performance anxiety in new, 13–14
personal productivity for, 103–120
responsibilities of, 103
role of, 7–9
self-development for, 121–136
skillsets for, 1
stress management for, 12–20
success for, 1, 55–63
talent development and, 175–189
transition to leadership for, 7–21
trust and credibility of, 23–36
"Managers and Leaders: Are They Different?" (Zaleznik), 9–10
"Managing Multicultural Teams" (Brett, Behfar, & Kern), 203
Mankins, Michael, 273
Manzoni, Jean-François, 158, 160
master budgets, 290
matrixes
for idea generation, 222
for job candidate evaluation, 242–243
Mauborgne, Renée, 272
Mayer, Diana, 31
Mayer, John, 37
McConnell, Matt, 126–127
McGrath, Rita, 271, 272
McKee, Annie, 38, 52–54
McKinsey & Company, 196
McLean, Andrew N., 31
meaningful work, 246
meetings
for coaching, 164–167

conducting effective, 96–99
creative sessions, 217–229
follow-up after, 98
with former peers, 24
giving difficult feedback in, 158–162
hearing all perspectives in, 224–227
norms for, 199
on performance, 171
presentations for, 92–96
sticking to the schedule for, 96
team, 196–197, 199
virtual, 98, 204–207
mentors and mentoring, 172, 176, 181
in self-development, 125
mergers and acquisitions, 281
metaphors, 81
metrics, 61. *See also* financial tools
micromanaging, 149–151
Mind/Body Medical Institute, 111
mind mapping, 222–224
mindsets, 55–56, 78, 152
mission statements, 197
Montgomery, Cynthia, 273
mood contagion, 43
motivation
emotional intelligence and, 40–41
employee retention and, 246, 247–250
engaging preexisting, 9
flow and, 107
giving criticism and, 160
in high performers, 184–185
hiring for, 237
knowing your extrinsic and intrinsic, 30
learning and, 177
success and, 56
understanding across silos, 77
of your managers, 71–72
multitasking, 98
mute buttons, 98

Nash, Laura, 33
need, business case on, 300–302
need-based positioning, 257–258
negativity, 227, 229
negotiation, 228
negotiator's mindset, 78
net income, 287

networks and networking
  job searches and, 130
  personal vs. positional power and, 68
  in self-development, 125
  for success, 74–75
Nohria, Nitin, 247–248
notifications, electronic, 108, 111

offer letters, 243–244
open-mindedness, 202
operating activities/operations, 284
operating budgets, 290–293
operating costs, 303
operating earnings/profit, 288
operating expenses, 287
operating income, 293
opinions, having informed, 69–70
opportunities
  finding self-development, 124–130
  incremental, 129
  reacting opportunistically to
    emerging, 272
  strategy development and, 260
optimism, 49
organization
  of email, 110–111
  for presentations, 92–94
  time management and, 109–110
  for virtual teams, 207
  for written communication, 88, 89
organizational culture
  changing, 50
  creating change-ready, 267–268
  emotional intelligence and, 48–50
  ethics and, 32–34
  hiring for fit with, 234
  job interview questions on, 242
  leadership traits and, 11
  positional power in, 68
  in teams, 194–200
organizational skills, 12–13
organizational structure, 201
origin stories, 30
outlines, 88
outsourcing, 271
Ovans, Andrea, 270–274
overreaching, 28
owners' equity, 279, 281

paraphrasing, 170
participation, 228
passion, 29–31, 176
performance
  delegation and, 141
  feedback on, 156–157
  financial, basics of, 276–277
  financial tools for measuring, 275–295
  finding causes of poor, 169–170
  goals for teams, 197
  high performers and, development of,
    183–185
  monitoring without micromanaging,
    149–151
  personal productivity and, 103–120
  reviews of, 167–172, 234
  risk factors, 306
  stress and, 112
performance anxiety, 13–14
personality, 11
personality conflicts, 208, 210, 211
personal power, 68–71, 78–82
perspective, 19
  giving criticism and, 160–161
  job interview questions on, 241–242
  understanding others', 82
persuasion, 228
planning
  in coaching, 166–167
  creative sessions, 217–220
  for delegation, 141–144
  for difficult feedback, 159
  for performance reviews, 168
  for presentations, 92–93
  risk analysis and, 59–60
  for strategic alignment, 60–61
  for time management, 105
political skills, 13, 75–76
Porot, Daniel, 125–126
Porter, Michael, 257, 259, 262, 270–272
positional power, 68–71
  cross-unit collaboration and, 78
  delegation and, 146
positive reinforcement, 152
power
  cross-unit collaboration and, 78
  delegation and, 146
  demands on, 9
  dynamics of in criticism, 131

power (*continued*)
  positional vs. personal, 68–71
  from strategic alignment, 60–61
  winning hearts and minds of others
    and, 78–82
Prahalad, C. K., 271
praise, 157, 185
  with criticism, 159–160
  See also feedback
preparation
  for meetings, 96–97
  for writing, 88
presentations, 92–96
  of business cases, 309–310
"Primal Leadership: The Hidden Driver
  of Great Performance" (Goleman,
  Boyatzis, & McKee), 38
priorities and prioritization, 18
  employee development and, 176–177
  time management and, 104–107
problem-centric approach, 220–221, 222
problem solving
  coaching and, 164–165
  letting others shine in, 26–27
  personal power and, 69
  quick wins in, 27–28
  stress from, 14, 15–16
processes, 61
  strategy and, 262–263
productivity
  delegation and, 141
  savings from, 304
productivity, personal, 103–120
  focus and, 107–111
  stress management and, 111–114
  work-life balance and, 115–118
profit-and-loss statements (P&L), 287, 289
progress monitoring, 149–151
progress principle, 248–249
project costs, 303
projections, 302–304
project management, 204
project overviews, 307
projects, 143
promises, keeping, 25
proofreading, 91, 309
purpose, 122–124, 176, 196–197
  in delegation, 142
  statements of, 123–124

quality risk factors, 306
questions
  in active listening, 46
  character and, 26
  in clarifying need and value, 301
  in coaching, 166
  for conflict resolution, 212
  disturbing, 81
  to guide job proposals, 128
  for informational interviews, 125–127
  for job interviews, 240–241
  leading, 81
  in listening tours, 57, 58
  rhetorical, 81
  in winning minds of others, 81
question-storming, 223–224
quick wins, 27–28
"Quiz Yourself: Do You Lead with
  Emotional Intelligence?" (McKee),
  52–54

reacting opportunistically to emerging
  opportunities, 272
reciprocating, 76
recognition
  letting others shine and, 26–27
recruiting, 236–237
  for potential, 236–237
  world-class talent, 237–244
"Reflected Best Self" exercise, 132–133
reframing, 46–47, 166
"Reinventing Your Business Model"
  (Johnson, Christensen, &
  Kagermann), 272
relationships
  building in teams, 200
  employee retention and, 245–246
  with peers for success, 74–76
  power based on, 9
  work-life balance and, 116–118
  your boss's, 73
reporting, 198
resistance, techniques for overcoming,
  229, 266–267, 309–310
resources, 7–8
  for creative sessions, 218–219
  delegation and, 141
  employee performance and, 170, 172

silos and, 76–77
strategy development and, 259,
    260–261
respect, 26
    creativity and, 219
    personal power and, 70
    in teams, 198
responsibility, 182–183
    in job descriptions, 234, 235–236
    for tough calls, accepting, 33
résumés, 238–239
retention of employees, 244–250
returns on investment (ROI), 283
revenues, 287, 289
    budgeting and, 291–292
    in cost/benefit analysis, 303–304
reverse delegation, 151–152
risk
    analysis of strategic objectives and,
        59–60
    creativity and, 226, 227
    external, 59
    financial leverage and, 283
    identification and mitigation, 305–307
    internal, 59
    personal, 60
    professional, 59–60
rivals, making peace with, 25
Roberts, Laura Morgan, 132–133
role strain, 14, 15
Roth, Alvin, 272
routines
    in stress management, 112–114

safety, 34, 219, 226
Saunders, Elizabeth Grace, 104
"Saving Your Rookie Managers from
    Themselves" (Walker), 18
saying no, 108–109
scenarios, in budgeting, 293
schedules and scheduling, 104–107
    delegation and, 144–145
    risk factors related to, 306
    sticking to, 96
    work-life balance and, 115–116
scope, 306
second thoughts, 226–227
security issues, 205

self-awareness, 12, 30–31, 38–43
    definition of, 39
    in emotional intelligence, 39–43
    stress responses and, 44–45
self-development, 121–136
    feedback for, 130–134
    knowing your strengths and, 132–134
self-doubt, 13–14, 17, 32
self-image, 11
self-regulation, 40, 43–45
Shapiro, Mary, 199–200
Sheen, Raymond, 298, 301, 304–306,
    309–310
Shine: Using Brain Science to Get the
    Best from Your People (Hallowell),
    179–181
silos, working across, 76–78, 182
Sims, Peter, 31
skills, 1
    delegation based on, 141, 143–144
    developing direct reports', 56
    emotional intelligence, 37–54
    employee development and, 176, 179
    feedback on, 160
    hiring for, 233–236
    job interviews on, 241
    of leadership, 10–11
    social, 41
    strategy development and, 260–261
    in teams, 194–196, 200
sleep, 19, 113
slides, 92–96
Smith, Douglas, 196, 197
Snook, Scott, 123–124
social awareness, 48–50
social capital, 69–71
social life, 25
social skills, 41
socio-emotional traits, 12–13
solution-centric approach, 220–221, 222
Southwest Airlines, 257, 262, 272
stakeholders
    demonstrating concern for, 34
    perspectives of in business cases,
        298–300
Stalk, George, 273
standards, setting high, 268
statistics, 81
status updates, 99

steadiness, 12
Steele, Richard, 273
"Stop Making Plans; Start Making Decisions" (Mankins & Steele), 273
storyboards, 94
storytelling, 80
    patterns in persuasive, 92–93
    in presentations, 92–93
strategy, 255–274
    alignment with, 263
    career, 177–183
    competitive, 257
    definition of, 259–260
    developing, 259–263
    frameworks for, 259–260
    information gathering on, 57–59
    leading change and transitions, 263–268
    manager's role in, 256
    risk analysis and, 59–60
    schools of thought on, 270–274
    understanding your organization's, 57–60
    vision and, 264–266
"Strategy as a Portfolio of Real Options" (Luehrman), 267
strengths, knowing your, 132–134
stress, 12–20
    emotion regulation in, 44–45
    good, 112
    managing, 111–114
    regulation of emotions and, 25
    routines to regulate, 112–114
    sources of, 14, 15–17
    team guidelines on, 48–49
    work-life balance and, 115–118
stretch assignments, 182, 185–187
stretch goals, 32
stretching, 114
success, 1
    helping others with, 70
    high performers and, opportunities for, 186–187
    influence and, 67–68
    learning from, 42
    managing people vs. tasks and, 8
    organization strategy and, 57–60
    partnering with peers for, 74–76

planning for strategic alignment and, 60–61
    positioning yourself for, 55–63
    redefining, 55–56
    risk analysis and, 59–60
    working across units and, 76–78
supplies, 218–219
support, 184
"Surviving Disruption" (Wessel & Christensen), 273

talent development programs, 124–125. See also employee development
Target, 258
tasks, 143
teams
    assembling, 194–196
    auditing, 194, 195
    building social awareness in, 48–50
    conflict resolution in, 208–214
    cross-cultural, 199–203
    cross-functional, 129
    culture and dynamics in, 194–200, 235
    defining success for, 56
    delegation and dynamics of, 144
    diversity in, 194–196
    ensuring ethical behavior in, 34–35
    fostering creativity in, 217–231
    hearing all perspectives in, 224–227
    hiring and retention for, 232–252
    leading, 191–216
    managers' role with, 7–8
    negativity in, 227–228
    norms for, 47, 198–200
    performance goals for, 197
    personal power and, 69
    purpose in, 196–197
    shared goals in, 213
    strategic objectives and, 57–58
    virtual, 99, 203–207
technology
    crisis cards, 206, 207
    as risk factor, 306
    for virtual meetings, 204–207
TED talks, 92
temporary assignments, 125, 182
testimonials, 81

thank-you notes, 127
threat responses, 131
threats, 260
time boxing, 105–107
time management, 18, 103–120
  for collaboration, 77–78
  creative sessions and, 218
  essentials of, 104–107
  focus in, 107–111
  logging current, 104–105
  for meetings, 97, 99
  performance plans and, 170
  team social awareness and, 48–49
Toyota, 257
training, 180–182
traits of leaders, 10–11, 12–13
transition costs, 303
transitions, leading, 263–268
transparency
  ethics and, 34
  self-awareness and, 30
trust, 9
  arranging backup in, 29
  building, 23–36
  definition of, 23–24
  emotion regulation and, 45
  employee retention and, 245
  ethics/integrity and, 32–35
  leadership and, 13
  in teams, 199–200
  working across units and, 76–77
"21st-Century Talent Spotting"
    (Fernández-Aráoz), 236–237

uncommitted, courting the, 265–266
US Department of Labor, 244

value creation, 155, 300–302
values, 25
  authenticity and, 29–31
  communicating, 86
  employee development and, 176,
    180–181
  ethics/integrity and, 31–34
  finding your purpose and, 122
variety-based positioning, 258
video conferencing, 98
virtual teams, 98, 203–207, 225–226
vision, 61, 264–266
visioning, 221–222
visuals, 81, 94–95. *See also* presentations
voice, finding your, 85–87

Walker, Carol, 13, 18
Wallraff, Barbara, 90
Walmart, 258
Watkins, Michael, 27–28
Wedell-Wedellsborg, Thomas, 220
weekends, protecting, 115–116
Wessel, Maxwell, 273
"What Is Strategy, Again?" (Ovans),
    270–274
"What Makes a Leader" (Goleman),
    40–41
white space, 95
"Why the Lean Start-Up Changes
    Everything" (Blank), 273
Wolff, Steven B., 48
working capital, 282
work-life balance, 18, 115–118, 184,
    246–247
work styles, 73–74
writing, 87–92
  business cases, 307–308
  editing, 89–92
  first drafts, 88–89
  presentations, 92–96
  style in, 90–91

Yoffie, David, 273
yoga, 114

Zaleznik, Abraham, 9–10
zero-based budgeting, 292
Zook, Chris, 273

The most important management ideas all in one place.

We hope you enjoyed this book from *Harvard Business Review*. For the best ideas HBR has to offer turn to HBR's 10 Must Reads Boxed Set. From books on leadership and strategy to managing yourself and others, this 6-book collection delivers articles on the most essential business topics to help you succeed.

HBR's 10 Must Reads Series

The definitive collection of ideas and best practices on our most sought-after topics from the best minds in business.

- Change Management
- Collaboration
- Communication
- Emotional Intelligence
- Innovation
- Leadership
- Making Smart Decisions

- Managing Across Cultures
- Managing People
- Managing Yourself
- Strategic Marketing
- Strategy
- Teams
- The Essentials

hbr.org/mustreads

Buy for your team, clients, or event.
Visit hbr.org/bulksales for quantity discount rates.